David Porter Heap

Ancient and modern Light-Houses

David Porter Heap

Ancient and modern Light-Houses

ISBN/EAN: 9783337151799

Printed in Europe, USA, Canada, Australia, Japan

Cover: Foto ©ninafisch / pixelio.de

More available books at **www.hansebooks.com**

ANCIENT AND MODERN LIGHT-HOUSES

BY

MAJOR D. P. HEAP

CORPS OF ENGINEERS, UNITED STATES ARMY

ILLUSTRATED

BOSTON
TICKNOR AND COMPANY
211 Tremont Street
1889

BOSTON
S. J. Parkhill & Co., Printers

PREFACE.

In compiling this work the following authorities were consulted:

European Light-house Establishments. Elliot. Washington, Government Printing Office, 1874.

Extracts from British Light-house Reports. Washington, Government Printing Office, 1871.

Documents relating to Light-houses. Washington, Government Printing Office, 1871.

Smeaton's Narrative of the Eddystone Light-house. London, 1793.

Stevenson's Account of the Bell Rock Light-house. Edinburgh, 1824.

Belidor. Architecture Hydraulique. Paris, 1787–9.

Account of Skerryvore Light-house. By Allan Stevenson. Edinburgh, 1847.

Account of the Holophotal System of Illuminating Lighthouses. By Thomas Stevenson. Edinburgh, 1871.

Light-houses. By David Stevenson. Edinburgh, 1865.

Reports of the Light-house Board of the United States, 1852 to 1887.

Illumination and Beaconage of the Coasts of France. Renaud. 1864.

Electrical Appliances of the Present Day. Heap. New York, 1884.

Engineer Department, U. S. A., at the International Exhibition of 1876. Heap. Washington, Government Printing Office, 1884.

Johnson's Encyclopedia, Encyclopedia Brittanica. Memoir on Minot's Ledge Light-house. B. S. Alexander.

Memoranda concerning Spectacle Reef Light-house. Poe.

The new Eddystone Light-house. Douglass. London, 1883.

More prominence has been given to American Light-houses than to those of other nations, as it was supposed they would be of more interest to American readers.

The sketches of modern Light-houses scattered through the book are in most cases from photographs, and may be relied on as accurate.

D. P. H.

LIST OF CONTENTS.

LIST OF PLATES.

ILLUSTRATIONS IN THE TEXT.

ANCIENT AND MODERN LIGHT-HOUSES.

CHAPTER I.

ANCIENT LIGHT-HOUSES.

Latin Light-house, after a Model in the collection of the Marshal d' Estres.

THOUGH there is incontestable evidence that light-houses did exist in ancient times, the old authors make but meagre reference to them, and of the towers themselves but scanty ruins remain; this is but natural, as they must of necessity have been situated in places not only exposed to wind and storm, but also frequently have formed portion of fortified places, and so subject to all the risks of war. Besides, a tower from its very shape is the least stable of architectural structures, and succumbs to accidents which other buildings successfully resist.

When Hercules put on the shirt of Nessus, he in his agony tore the flesh from his body, and finally unable longer to endure the torture, built and lighted a funeral pyre and threw himself upon it; when the flames commenced to lick his body a cloud descended from the sky, and carried him to Olympus. This legend may perhaps be the reason why the Greeks attribute the first light-houses to him. At Thasos, Smyrna and in Italy he was *σωτηρ* (Saviour), *i. e.*, protector of voyagers, and tithes were vowed to him to be spent in entertainment.

The oldest light-houses known were the towers built by the Sybians and by the Cushites, who dwelt in lower Egypt; in addition to being light-houses they were temples named after some deity; they were held in great veneration by sailors, who enriched them with their offerings; it is supposed that they contained charts showing the coasts and the navigation of the Nile. At first these charts were engraved on the walls; later they were made on papyrus. The priests, who were the light-keepers, taught the pilotage of vessels, hydrography, and how to steer by the use of constellations.

Latin Light-house, after a Medal found at Apamea.

The manner of lighting these towers was very primitive: the fuel was placed in a kind of iron or bronze basket composed of three or four dolphins or other marine animal interlaced together; then the basket was attached to a long pole projecting from the tower towards the sea. The Baron de Zach says, that "the Sybians called these towers *tar* or *tor*, which signifies height; *Is* means fire, hence Tor Is tower of fire; from this comes the Greek *πυῤῥις* and the Latin *turris*, when these signals were situated outside of the villages on rounded eminences they were called *Tith*. Tithon, so celebrated for his longevity, seems to have only been one of these structures dedicated to the sun, and Thetis, former goddess of the ocean, only a light-house near the sea, called *Thit-Is*, fire on an eminence. And the legend of the massacre of the Cyclops killed by the arrows of Apollo is simply the mythological way of expressing the manner in which the signals of the Cyclopian towers on the coasts of Sicily were extinguished by the rays of the rising run." The above, if not true, has certainly the merit of ingenuity.

Lesches, a minor poet, born about 600 B. C., mentions a light-house placed on the promontory of Sigæum in the Troad, near which there was a roadstead. This is the first light-house which appears to have been operated regularly, but though it heads the list, it has not had the glory of giving its name to those succeeding it; this honor was reserved to the tower built on the Isle of Pharos, at Alexandria, which has also served as a model for the most celebrated towers since erected. According to Suetonius, the tower at Ostia, built by Claudius, was copied from the one at Alexandria, and appears to have been the most remarkable of the Latin towers. Italy, however, possessed many fine ones, such as those of Ravenna and Pozzuoli mentioned by Pliny, and the one at Messina, which gave its name to the strait which separates Sicily from Italy, and where the famous rocks of Scylla and Charybdis are found; and finally the light-house on the Island of Capri, which was overthrown by an earthquake a few days before the death of Tiberius.

The shape of these Latin towers is somewhat doubtful. Herodianus says that the catafalques of the emperors resembled light-houses; now the catafalques were square, while the light-houses were not always so. A medal in the collection of the Marshal d'Estres shows a light-house of four stories, circular in plan; another medal found at Apamea, in Bithynia, an ancient country of Asia Minor, also shows the circular form, and finally, the light-house at Boulogne was octagonal.

THE LIGHT-HOUSE OF ALEXANDRIA.

There are several noted ancient light-houses, of whose history and appearance we have more or less authentic accounts. Prominent among all is the famous one at Alexandria, on the Island of Pharos which was regarded as one of the wonders of the world. Opinions differ as to whom to ascribe the honor of building this magnificent structure; by some it has been assigned to Alexander the Great, by others to Cleopatra; but the best evidence is that it was erected by Ptolemy II, Philadelphus, who reigned 283-247 B. C. It is quite certain that Sostratos was the name of the architect. The following rather tricky story is told of him: like many another architect he desired to perpetuate his fame by inscribing his name on the work, a perfectly laudable ambition; to accomplish this he engraved deeply on one of the stones, "Sostratos of Gnidos, son of Dixiphanus, to the Gods protecting those upon the sea." Knowing very well that Ptolemy would not be satisfied with this inscription, he covered it with a thin slab of stone, or coating of cement, which could not long resist the action of the weather, and on this he inscribed Ptolemy's name: as he anticipated, the covering disappeared in some years, and with it the name of the king, thus keeping all the credit to himself. Pliny says that Ptolemy purposely left off his own name so that Sostratos could have all the glory, but this is so directly contrary to the way in which princes ordinarily act, both in ancient and modern history, that such an excess of modesty is hardly probable.

Another disputed point is whether the tower gave the name to the island or the island to the tower; the latter is the more likely; at all events this light-house has given *its* name to its successors, and has become the generic name.

Light-house in Latin is *pharus;* in Spanish and Italian, *faros;* in French, *phare;* and even in English *pharo* was once used, though now obsolete.

The tower was square in plan, of great height, and built in offsets. Edrisi, an Arabian geographer of the thirteenth century, said that in his time it was six hundred feet high, and that the light could be seen one hundred miles; no true American will believe this, for have we not the Washington Monument, five hundred and fifty feet high, the "tallest artificial structure ever erected on the surface of the earth?"

it is more consoling to our vanity to consider that the old Arabian was romancing.

At the top of the tower was the brazier to contain the fuel; it was truly a "pillar of fire by night, of smoke by day," and must have been a welcome sight to the storm-tossed mariner, though the labor of carrying the fuel to the top of that tall tower must have been a wearisome task to the poor light-keepers.

The tower, from all descriptions left us, seems to have been built in a manner similar to the Tower of Babel, which had eight stories, or as Herodotus calls them, towers placed one upon the other. Pliny affirms that its cost amounted to eight hundred talents, or about $946,000.

But to go back to our Egyptian who evidently was an ardent admirer of this structure: "This light-house," says he, "has not its equal in the world for excellence of construction and for strength, for not only is it constructed of a fine quality of stone, called 'kedan,' but the various blocks are so strongly cemented together with melted lead, that the whole is imperishable, although the waves of the sea continually break against its northern face; a staircase of the ordinary width, constructed in the interior, extends as high as the middle of the structure, where there is a gallery; under the staircase are the keeper's apartments; above the gallery the tower becomes smaller and smaller until it can be embraced by the arms of a man. From this same gallery there is a staircase much narrower than the tower, reaching to the summit; it is pierced with many windows to give light within and to show those who ascend where to place their feet. At a distance the light appeared so much like a star near the horizon, that sailors were frequently deceived by it." Arabs and travellers have told wonderful stories about this tower; some say that Sostratos supported this immense mass on four great stone crabs, and even more remarkable, that Alexander the Great placed on the top of the tower a mirror constructed with so much art that by means of it he could see the fleets of his enemies at one hundred leagues distance, and to enter still more into particulars, that a Greek named

Sodorus, after the death of Alexander, broke the mirror, while the garrison of the tower was asleep.

DOVER TOWER.

There are two towers, one at Dover, the other at Boulogne, which for many years lighted the British Channel. But little is known of the history of the former; some believe it to be the same tower that now stands in the middle of Dover Castle; others think that a grand mound of masonry, stones and chalk, near Dover, called the "Devil's

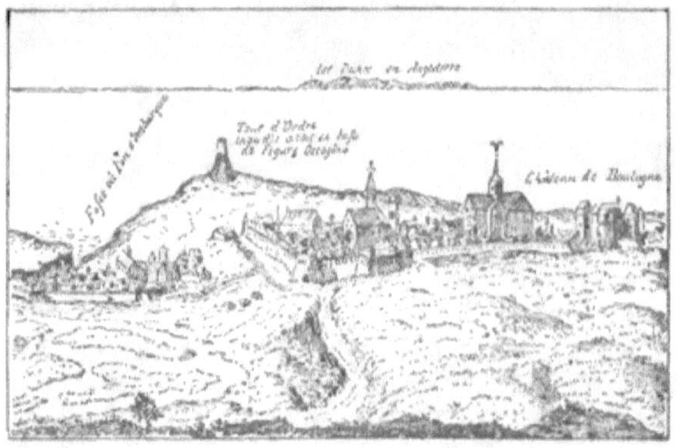

Tour d'Ordre, Bologne, after a drawing by Claude Chatillon.

Drop," are the ruins of the ancient tower. It was built by the Romans, and was probably octagonal in plan, and resembled in other particulars its mate at Boulogne.

Its antiquity no doubt exceeds that of any light-house in Great Britain. It has not been used as such since the Conquest, but before then burned for many centuries those great fires of coal and wood formerly maintained on several towers still standing on those coasts.

LA TOUR D'ORDRE.

Of the tower at Boulogne we have more accurate information. It is well known under the name of the *Tour d'Ordre* or *d'Orde.* Two centuries ago its ruins might still be seen.

The story goes that when the too famous emperor Caligula arrived at the banks of the Rhine, and thought to invade Brittany, chance obtained for him the voluntary surrender of a young Breton prince. To celebrate this piece of unforeseen good luck, he caused to be erected on the cliffs of Gioriacum, now Boulogne, a triumphal monument to perpetuate his renown. The exact date at which this monument was changed to the more useful purpose of a light-house is unknown; but it is certain that a light shone from its summit in 191 A.D., as there is a bronze medal upon which Commodus bears the title of Brittanicus, in remembrance of the victory of one of his lieutenants over the Brittons, and which represents this light-house and the departure of a Roman fleet.

Located at the most convenient place for crossing the British Channel, the tower of Boulogne was kept in careful repair during the occupancy of Gaul by the Romans. It not only served as a light-house, but also as a fortress, and, owing to its position and massive construction, it was well suited for this purpose. In the sixteenth century, during the short and disastrous occupation of Boulogne by the English, the Tour d'Ordre, as it was then called, was surrounded by two ramparts, one of brick and the other of earth, and was armed with pieces of artillery. It was admirably located, either for the defense or the attack of Boulogne, for it commanded the city and both banks of the river.

However, it was not the hazard of war which made this tower lower its haughty front and caused its ruin. All that it suffered was the damage to its lantern, several times repaired. Its final destruction was entirely due to the carelessness of the mayor and aldermen, who took no pains to check the action of the sea at its base, and of subterranean springs which gradually sapped its foundation, so that finally, between 1640 and 1645, tower, fort, and even the cliff itself fell. The Boulognese were rather glad of it, for they had to pay taxes on the land, in virtue of an ancient right to a certain Lord de Bainethun.

They argued that as the land had disappeared they were freed from further obligation to the proprietor. However, Parliament did not take that view of it, but informed Messieurs the Boulognese that as they were responsible for the loss of the tower, they could continue paying a tax of two thousand herrings, delivered at Amiens, Arras, or at other cities at equal distances that the proprietor might designate; or they could replace the tower in its former condition, and relinquish to the Lord of Bainethun, Baron of Ordre, the right of taxing all fishermen entering Havre. They concluded to pay the tax, and continued to do so until the French Revolution.

The accompanying design, after Claude Châtillon, engineer of King Henry IV, is apparently trustworthy. Descriptions of the tower are rather meagre; they give, however, some useful information concerning the situation, dimensions and form of the edifice, and also of the materials employed in its construction. The latter were yellow and gray stone and red bricks. The tower was situated the length of a cross-bow shot from the edge of the cliff; it was octagonal in plan, and one hundred and ninety-two feet in circumference. Like most Roman light-houses, each of its twelve stories was three feet less in diameter than the one immediately beneath it, thus giving the tower a pyramidal shape. It is stated that its height equalled its circumference, or, in round numbers, two hundred feet, which seems to be an unnecessary height for a tower situated on a cliff one hundred feet above the sea level. Each story had an opening in the middle like a door, and there could still be seen, in the beginning of the seventeenth century, three vaulted rooms, one above the other, connected by a stairway, and doubtless intended as dwellings for the keepers. The place where the fire was lighted is conjectural, as the chroniclers of the ninth century state that the summit was repaired so that fires might be lighted on it. It is reasonable to believe that before this repair the fire shone in a room in the upper story.

This ancient light-house is now replaced by modern lights, one a fixed red, visible for four miles, and two fixed white lights,

ANCIENT TOWER OF CORDOUAN.

See page 12.

visible at a distance of nine miles, erected by the French Light-House Board in 1835.

THE COLOSSUS OF RHODES.

The Colossus of Rhodes may or may not have been a light-house The weight of testimony bears toward the latter supposition, and it is also more than doubtful if it stood at the entrance of the port, and that the largest vessels could pass between its legs.

There is no doubt, however, that this colossal statue of Apollo was completed 285 B. C., that it took fifteen years to build, and that, after standing fifty-six years, it was overthrown by an earthquake

The Rhodians received large sums of money from the kings and people of Greece to re-establish the statue and to rebuild their ruined town, but as they probably found it more to their advantage to apply the funds to other than statuary purposes, a convenient oracle informed them that its re-erection would be followed by dire misfortunes, so of course they could not go against the will of the gods.

Chares of Lindus, a pupil of Lysippus was the designer. It is said that he killed himself in despair, because, after he had spent all the money appropriated, the statue was but half finished, and that it was completed by another Lydian named Laches. Such stories are rather doubtful.

The statue was about one hundred and eight feet high, and was made of bronze. After it was overthrown "it was still a marvel," says Pliny. "Few men could put their arms around the thumb; its fingers are larger than many statues. Its disjointed limbs seem vast caverns in which one sees enormous stones by means of which it was weighted. It is said that it cost 500 talents ($590,000), the sum which the Rhodians had taken from the equipages of war abandoned before their city by Demetrius when he raised the siege, fatigued by its length."

The ruins of the Colossus remained for nine hundred years, but in 672 A. D., Mauviah, one of Othman's lieutenants, had it broken to pieces, and sold it to a Jew, who carried it off on a thousand camels, if we can believe the Byzantine chroniclers.

The cuts show what it may have been. The treatment with the rays about the head and the flaming brazier in the hand bears some resemblance to our statue of Liberty enlightening the World.

TOWER OF CORDOUAN.

It is to Monsieur Belidor, Colonel of Infantry, Chevalier of the Military Order of St. Louis, etc., that we are indebted for the best description of the Tower of Cordouan. The following account is taken from his "*Architecture Hydraulique*," published in 1777, "with the approbation and privilege of the King." He says:

"Since the superb light-houses built by the ancients, there has not appeared one more august nor of more importance than the famous Tower of Cordouan, located on a rock in the sea at the mouth of the Gironde, to aid the entrance and exit of vessels in the two rivers, Garonne and Dordogne, whose confluence forms the Gironde. Without this tower many vessels would be wrecked. It serves as a beacon during the day and a light at night, to guide the ships, and to prevent them from running on the reefs, which are numerous in the vicinity. There are but two passes, the one called *le pas des anes*, between Saintonge and the tower of Cordouan, and the other between the same tower and Medoc, named *le pas de grane*, both equally dangerous.

"The tower is about two leagues from Bordeaux, and the rock on which it is built is 500 toises in length from north to south, and 250 toises in width from east to west. The sea, in its vicinity, is filled with sunken reefs, covered with three or four feet of water, against which the waves break with great fury, making the access to the tower extremely difficult.

"This magnificent tower, rising 169 feet above its base, was commenced in 1584, during the reign of Henry II, by Louis de Foix, a celebrated French architect, and finished under Henry IV, in 1610. Sailors deem this light-house the finest in Europe, not knowing any other more magnificent, or as bold in construction. As can be seen by the plan of the tower, there is a platform, surrounded by a circular wall, against which are the various buildings for the residence of the four keepers and for the storage of supplies; the latter contains six months' provisions, and there is a fine cistern for catching an ample supply of water from the tower. In the centre of the platform is the basement floor, containing a large room, two closets, and small room. Underneath are the cellars and the cistern. The first floor, which is called the King's Appartment, comprises a vestibule, closets, and other conveniences. The second story is occupied by a chapel, where mass was said when the weather permitted a priest to land. In this chapel were the busts of Louis XIV, and of Louis XV, placed there in 1735, with a grand Latin inscription containing a condensed history of the tower. There is also a bust of Louis de Foix, over which is the following inscription in a large frame:

"'QVAND IADMIRE RAVI CEST ŒVVRE EN MON COURAGE
MON DE FOIX MON ESPRIT EST EN ESTONNEMENT,
PORTE DANS LES PENSERS DE MON ENTENDEMENT

MODERN TOWER OF CORDOUAN.

See page 14.

LE GENTIL INGENIEVX DE CE SVPERBE OVVRAGE
LA IL DISCOVRT EN LVY ET DVN MVET LANGAGE
TE VA LOVANT SVBTIL EN CE POINT MESMEMENT
QVE TV BRIDES LES FLOTS DV GRONDEVX ELEMENT
ET DV MVTIN NEPTVN LA TEMPESTE ET L'ORAGE
O TROIS QVATRE FOIS BIENHEVREVX TON ESPRIT
DE CE QV'AV FRONTE DRESSE CE PHARE IL ENTREPRIT
POVR SE PERPETVER DANS LHEVREVSE MEMOIRE
TV TES ACQVIS PAR LA UN HONNEVR INFINI
QVI NE FINIRA POINT QVE CE PHARE DE GLOIRE
LE MONDE FINISSANT NE SE RENDE FINY.

A description is unnecessary of the beautiful architecture which forms the interior and exterior decoration, it being easy to judge of it from the section and elevation. I will only add that the arms of France are on the front of the first story, accompanied by two statues, one representing Mars with his ordinary attributes, the other a female figure holding a palm in one hand and a diadem in the other. Lower are two niches: in the right-hand one is the bust of Henry II, and in the other the bust of Henry IV. The portico is opposite the entrance to the platform; on the opposite side is the staircase, partly built in the thickness of the wall, and partly outside.

For more than a century this tower was the admiration of all connoisseurs, but at length, the heat of the fire having injured the walls of the lantern, the Court, in 1717, ordered that it be demolished, to prevent its falling, and that the light be established below it, instead of repairing the damaged parts, and keeping the light at the same height. It was not long before it was seen what a mistake this was, for the lantern had no sooner been taken away than all the sailors complained that the light could not be seen at a distance of two leagues, as was formerly the case.

Things were in this state when, in 1720, the tower passed from the jurisdiction of Rochelle to that of Bordeaux. Then the Count of Toulouse, Admiral of France, and Marshal Asfeld, Director of Fortifications, entrusted the reparation of the tower to Monsieur de Bitre,

Engineer-in-Chief of Bordeaux, who sought the means of reëstablishing the light at its former height by a lantern which should not intercept the light to the same extent as the old one. He accomplished this by building an iron lantern, as shown in the plate. This was successfully placed in 1727. The brazier for burning the fuel held two hundred and twenty-five pounds of coal, which was lighted at sunset, and burned all night. The old brazier was too small. Oak wood was burned in it; the flame was large, but it had to be replenished every three hours. The height of the new lantern was greater than the old one, so that the tower was increased in height to 175 feet from its base to the weather-cock.

This elevation was not sufficient to enable mariners to see the light at a very great distance, so Teulère, Engineer-in-Chief of the district of Bordeaux, performed the difficult task of raising it, at the end of the last century. The height was increased to 197 feet above high tide, giving a great increase to the range, but marring its architectural beauty, as the absence of ornament in the modern part contrasts painfully with the elegance and richness of the work of the Renaissance. The first impression of the tower, however, is still very striking, rising as it does with such majesty and boldness from the bosom of the sea.

About thirty years ago, this light-house was completely renovated, many of the stones, worn by time, were replaced, and the carvings, which had become almost indistinguishable, were recut; it now contains in its lantern, in place of the old oak or coal fire, that nearly faultless piece of apparatus known as the Fresnel lens, by means of which all the light possible is utilized in strengthening the friendly beam.

There is a lofty and ancient tower overlooking the Atlantic Ocean at Corunna, Spain. It is called the Pillar of Hercules, and it is thought that the name Corunna may be a corruption of the word "Columna." By some writers the origin of this tower is attributed to the Carthaginians, by others to Caius Servius Lupus, who dedicated it to Mars. It was restored by Julius Cæsar, and again by Trajan. Its architecture relates to remote antiquity. A tradition states that it was erected by an ancient king of Spain in heroic times; it is now ninety-two feet high. At Ravenna there is a large square tower standing out from the side-walls of the Church of Santa Maria in Porta Fuori, and now used as a campanile or bell-tower: it is supposed to be the pharos of the port constructed by Augustus. In the fifth century this port was so silted up as to be obliterated, and its site was converted into gardens.

The beautiful light-house at Genoa, called Torre del Capo, was originally built on the promontory of San Berrique in 1139, and first lighted in 1326. It was removed in 1512, and re-built by the Republic in 1643. It is a square tower, in two stories, with battlemented terraces, the lower portion nine metres square, the upper seven. Rising from a rock forty-two and one-half metres above the sea, it carries its light at the height of one hundred and eighteen and one-half metres above the water. In 1841 it was fitted with a Fresnel, first-order lens: for beauty and elegance of structure this historic light is one of the finest in existence.

The Pharos of Meloria was built by the Pisans in 1154. It indicated the direction to be taken by ships bound for Porto Pisana, and gave warning of a dangerous sand-bank. This tower was three times destroyed — in 1267 by Charles of Anjou, in 1287 by the Genoese, and in 1290 by the Guelphs. Having determined to abandon Meloria, the Pisans erected, in 1304, the light-house which still exists at Leghorn. It is celebrated by Petrarch. Standing near the entrance of the harbor, to the south of the new mole, it rises forty-seven metres above the level of the sea. It is built of stone, in the form of two battlemented cylinders, surrounded at the base by a polygonal enclosure of thirteen sides.

CHAPTER II.

EDDYSTONE LIGHT-HOUSE.

TO THE KING: —

"I have it not in my power to present YOUR MAJESTY with a fine piece of writing, or of drawing; neither literature, nor the fine arts having been much the objects of my study; but I humbly submit to YOUR MAJESTY, a plain account of the construction of a plain and simple building, that has nevertheless been acknowledged to be, in itself, curious, difficult, and useful; and, as such, I trust, worthy of observation." [1]

Eddystone, the most famous of modern light-houses, built and destroyed so many times, has a history of its own, and though the present structure is not the one built by the famous Smeaton, yet we owe to his genius and strong common sense the design of a tower which has become a type.

Eddystone Rocks, probably so called from the various and conflicting currents running through them, are situated about S. S. W. from the middle of Plymouth Sound, nearly fourteen miles from the town of Plymouth, and ten miles from Ram-Head, the nearest point of land. They are nearly covered at high water, and, being just within the line joining Start and Lizard Points, they must have been very dangerous to vessels coasting up and down the Channel, before they were marked by a light; in fact, many a rich craft, homeward bound from foreign ports, has been lost upon them. From the position of these rocks, near the entrance to the English Channel, they are exposed to the full force of all southwest storms, and what still further augments the force of the waves is the fact that these rocks stretch across the Channel for about six hundred feet, and slope gradually to seaward,

---

[1] Extract from the dedication of John Smeaton's narrative of the building, and description of the construction of the Eddystone Light-house with stone. Second Edition. London, 1793

See page 18.

4

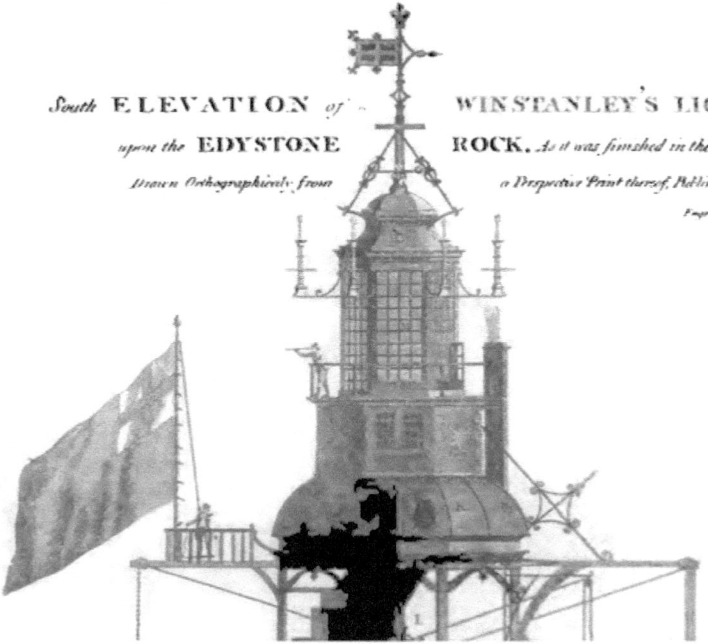

South ELEVATION *of* WINSTANLEY'S LIGHTHOUSE,
upon the EDYSTONE ROCK. *As it was finished in the Year 1699*
Drawn Orthographically from a Perspective Print thereof, Published by himself

Engraved by Hen. Roberts, 1761

so that when the sea is calm elsewhere yet the ground-swell, running up their slope, breaks with great violence; and even when there is only a moderate swell from the southwest, yet, owing to the peculiar shape of the House Rocks, the water flies thirty or forty feet high.

Without going into further detail, it will be seen that the erection of a light-house on this exposed place was an arduous and dangerous undertaking. Yet, in 1696, there having been so many fatal accidents to vessels running on the rocks, there was found a man hardy enough to attempt the task. This was Mr. Henry Winstanley, of Littlebury, in the County of Essex. Mr. Winstanley had a certain turn for mechanics, but his ingenuity ran to the grotesque. At his house in Littlebury there were various amusing and startling contrivances: in one room there was an old slipper carelessly lying on the floor; if you gave it a kick to one side — a most natural thing to do — a ghost would start up before you; if you sat down on a certain conveniently-situated chair — to look at the ghost at your ease, perhaps — you would be immediately clasped by a couple of arms, so strongly and effectually that you would need the assistance of your attendant to release you; should you rest in an arbor in the grounds by the side of a canal to meditate on these marvels, you at once found yourself afloat in the middle of the canal, there to remain until the manager chose to return you to shore.

This bent of Mr. Winstanley's probably accounts for the whimsical structure he erected for light-house purposes. This structure took him four years to erect, the entire work of the first year consisting in drilling twelve holes in the rock and fastening in them twelve large irons. The second year a pillar twelve feet high and fourteen feet in diameter was built. The third year the diameter of the pillar was increased to sixteen feet, and the tower was completed to a height of sixty feet, or to the top of the vane eighty feet, and lighted for the first time the 12th of November, 1698. The fourth year, finding that the sea at times buried the lantern, the thickness of the tower was further increased to twenty-four feet, the tower made solid for a height of twenty feet, the upper part of the building taken down and enlarged, and the height of the tower raised forty feet; yet the sea in storms appeared to fly one hundred feet above the vane, and at times would cover half the side of the house and lantern as if they were under water.

Mr. Winstanley does not state of what material he constructed the base of his tower, but from the appearance of a drawing — said to be made at the rock — it would appear that the material used was stone, and that the joints were protected by iron hoops, to prevent the mortar washing out.

The picture shows the completed tower. With all its whimsicalities and absurdities — its bay-window, derricks, ornamental gim-cracks and mottoes, it was a brave and heroic deed to erect it. Some idea can be formed of the violence of the storms which it withstood, as, after it was finished, it was commonly said that it was possible for a six-oared boat to be lifted up by a wave and driven through the open gallery. Mr. Winstanley believed in its strength, and had the courage of his convictions. In November, 1703, he went to superintend some repairs, and some one expressing fears that the structure was not strong enough, and some day might be overturned, he replied: "I am so very well assured of the strength of my building that I should only wish to be there in the greatest storm that ever blew, that I might see what effect it would have upon the structure."

His wish was gratified. While he was there with his workmen and light-keepers, on the 26th of November, a tremendous storm visited Great Britain, and on the next morning it was found that the light-house had disappeared, with all the people in it. Nothing was ever seen of it except a few of the large irons used for holding it to the rock, and part of an iron chain jammed in a crevice. At the same time that the light-house was destroyed, the model of it, in Mr. Winstanley's house at Littlebury, in Essex, two hundred miles distant, fell down and was broken to pieces. Not long after this accident the *Winchelsea*, a homeward-bound, Virginia man-of-war, was wrecked upon the rocks on which the light-house stood, and most of the crew were drowned.

Though Winstanley proved that it was not impracticable to build a light-house on the Eddystone rocks, and though the light had shown itself to be of great use, yet it was not until the spring of 1706 that an act of Parliament was passed "for the better enabling the Master, Wardens and Assistants of Trinity House at Deptford Strond to re-build the same." The work was commenced the following July. By this act the duties payable by shipping passing the light were vested in the corporation of Trinity House, and they were empowered to contract for its erection. In consequence of these powers, they employed a Capt. Lovel, or Lovet, to build it, giving him in payment the duties for a term of ninety-nine years, commencing from the date the light should first be exhibited and continuing so long as it should be shown.

Captain Lovet engaged Mr. John Rudyerd to be his engineer — an apparently strange choice, as Mr. Rudyerd was a silk mercer, who kept a shop on Ludgate Hill, London.

This choice proved, however, to be a happy one. Mr. Rudyerd avoided the errors of his predecessor; he chose a circle instead of an irregular polygon for the plan of his building, and omitted the unwieldy ornaments, the open gallery, the cranes, and other contrivances.

Rudyerd's light-house was a frustum of a cone, twenty-two feet eight inches in diameter at the base and fourteen feet three inches at the top, sixty-seven feet high to the floor of the lantern; the height of the centre of the light was nine feet above the balcony floor, and the total height of the tower from the lowest part of the base to the ball on top of the lantern was seventy feet.

It was built mainly of wood ballasted with stone; this is probably due to the fact that Mr. Rudyerd's associates in the work were Mr. Smith and Mr. Morcut, shipwrights from the King's yard at Woolwich, and further accounts for the structure being more in the nature of ship-joinery than of ordinary carpenter's work.

To prepare the foundation the surface of the rock was first approximately levelled off in steps, in which holes were drilled to receive heavy iron bolts or branches, as they were called, which were in their turn securely fastened to the timbers.

These holes were made dovetail in shape — two and one-fourth inches wide, seven and one-half broad at top, eight and one-half at bottom and from fifteen to sixteen inches deep, and as they could not all be made alike, each bolt was forged to fit its respective hole; the latter were made four and one-half inches broad at the surface of the rock and six and one-half at the bottom; when placed in the hole a space would thus be left three inches wide at the top and two at the bottom in which a key could be driven.

After all the holes were drilled and the bolts and keys fitted, the holes were cleared of water as far as possible and filled with melted tallow; the bolts and keys were then heated to a blue heat and driven home; thus all the interstices would be filled with the tallow; when this was done coarse pewter was melted in a ladle and run in; it of course displaced the tallow, or a greater part of it. This answered so well that fifty years afterward when these bolts were taken out the tallow still remained fresh and the iron not rusted.

These bolts were not placed very regularly, but the plan in general was to arrange them in two concentric circles, one about a foot inside the other; in addition there were two large bolts fixed near the centre, to which was attached the mast.

The lower part of the tower consisted of a solid oak grillage, carried two courses higher than the top of the rock; on top of this were placed five courses, one foot thick, of stone, laid without cement, but held together with iron cramps, then two courses more of solid timber, surrounded with timbers conforming to the contour of the circle, so that when the outside upright timbers were placed the bolts fastening them would not enter the horizontal timbers with the grain; some courses of the lower grillage were arranged in the same way.

The outside of the tower was then formed of upright timbers,

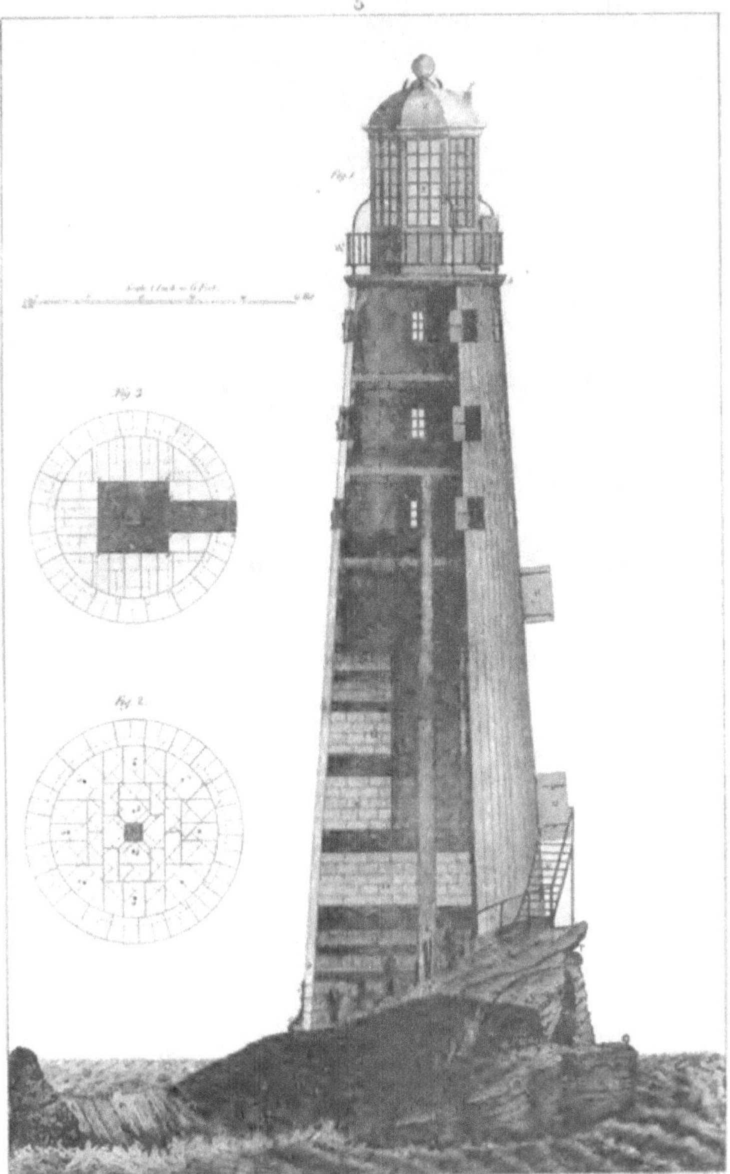

South **ELEVATION** *&* **SECTION** *of* **RUDYERD's LIGHTHOUSE.**

bolted to the grillage courses and to each other, and terminated by a planking three inches thick which formed the floor of the lantern. The seams between these uprights were caulked with oakum and payed with pitch.

The tower was perfectly plain except the cornice at the top and a protection at the bottom; the former served to throw off the sea at the top and prevent it from striking the lantern. The latter was probably an afterthought to protect the bases of the uprights from the shock of the waves.

This structure was a great advance on the first one; it stood for forty-six years and was then destroyed, not by a storm but, by fire.

Three years after it was commenced a light was exhibited from it, and the next year, 1709, it was entirely completed.

Louis the XIV was at war with England during the construction of this light, and once a French privateer captured all the men at work and carried them to France with their tools. The captain quite prided himself on his achievement and expected to be well rewarded, but the king, when he heard of it, clapped the captain and his crew into prison, released the workmen, loaded them with presents and sent them back to their work saying that, though he was at war with England he was not at war with mankind and that the Eddystone light-house was so situated as to be of equal service to all nations navigating the English Channel.

No repairs of any moment were necessary until the year 1723 when it was found that the lower ends of the uprights, especially on the lower side were being eaten by a small worm, possibly the limnoria; they were then thoroughly repaired. In 1744 there was a tremendous storm which tore away thirty of the uprights and made a breach into the store-room, but by great exertion this disaster was repaired before the close of the year.

For many years after the light was established there were but two keepers; this number was ample for its maintenance, but it so happened that one of the men sickened and died, and the other, fearing to throw the body into the sea lest he might be charged with murder, allowed it to remain in the light-house and hoisted a flag, which was the signal that he needed assistance.

The weather was so bad for a whole month that the attending boat could not land, and when they finally succeeded the stench was so noisome that it was with the greatest difficulty that they could dispose of the body by throwing it into the sea, and it was not for long after that the rooms could be rid of the foul odor. After this the proprietors employed three men, to guard against the recurrence of such an accident. This also allowed each one in turn to go on shore for a month during the summer.

The fire which destroyed this light-house, which had withstood the fiercest storms for nigh half a century, took place in December, 1755. The keeper going to snuff the candle at 2 A. M., found the lantern full of smoke, and when he opened the door was driven back by a burst of flame.

The candles were twenty-four in number and weighed two and one-half pounds each; their long continued use must have thoroughly dried the woodwork of the roof of the lantern which besides was probably covered with soot, so that a spark would easily ignite it.

The poor keeper did what he could to put out the fire; he after a while succeeded in awakening the other two keepers and they all tried to throw water on the flames, but as it had to be brought seventy feet high, they soon found their efforts unavailing, and in addition one of the keepers, the one who discovered the fire, was disabled by a curious accident.

While he was looking upwards, endeavoring to see the effect of the water he had thrown, a shower of molten lead fell on his head, neck and shoulders — part of it ran inside his shirt-collar and burned him badly; he also felt an intense burning inside, and supposed that part of the lead had passed down his throat.

The three men gave up the unequal struggle and descended from room to room, as they were driven by the heat and melting metal.

Early in the morning the fire was seen on shore, and a philanthropic gentleman fitted out a fishing boat which arrived at the light-house at 10 A. M. The fire had then been burning eight hours; the light-keepers had been driven from the tower, and to avoid the falling timbers and red-hot bolts, had taken refuge in the hole or cave on the east side of the rocks under the iron ladder, near the landing.

The men were stupefied, and the wind being from the east made a landing extremely hazardous, if not impracticable. They, however, were saved by the crew first anchoring the large boat, then a small boat was rowed toward the rock, paying out a rope which was attached to the large boat; when near enough to the rock a heaving-line was thrown to the men. Each light-keeper in turn fastened the rope around his waist, and jumping into the sea was hauled into the boat.

As the fishing-boat could do nothing to quell the flames it returned to Plymouth to land the keepers; one as soon as he got on shore ran away, it is supposed in a panic; the one burned by the melted lead was sent to his own house for medical attendance; he was ninety-four years old, but remarkably active considering his age. He told the doctor that he had swallowed the molten lead, and that he could not be cured unless it was removed. He lived until the twelfth day, when he suddenly expired—the doctor opened his stomach, and found therein a solid oval piece of lead weighing more than seven ounces. The doctor sent an account of the case to the Royal Society, but that wise body pooh-poohed the whole matter, and doubted the truth of the story. This nettled the good doctor, and to prove that animals might swallow molten lead and still survive, he tried the experiment on dogs and fowls, and found that they did live until he opened them to extract the lead. There is particular mention of one cock, who though dull would eat barley corn, from whose crop was removed a lump of lead weighing three ounces. These experiments seemed to prove the doctor's case pretty effectually, but about all the satisfaction he got was being censured for cruelty to animals.

As soon as the light-house was destroyed, the proprietors set themselves to work to find some one to rebuild it; fortunately their choice fell on John Smeaton, formerly a philosophical instrument maker, but later a mechanical engineer, and Fellow of the Royal Society, and it is to him we owe *the* famous Eddystone Light-House. He went to work methodically, and examined with great care the work of his predecessors, rejecting the weak and retaining the strong points; he then argued the matter out logically. In the first place he concluded that the weight should be as great as possible, and the mass as small, and that the structure must be safe from fire; these conditions he filled by choosing stone as the material from which to build it, and by so shaping the tower as to give it a broad base and slender waist — as he called it — he states that this form was suggested to him from contemplating the trunk of an oak, which had withstood a storm which had prostrated its fellows. He at once saw that the tower would not be secure if built of squared stones, like an ordinary wall, but that the stones must be bonded together so as to form one solid mass; this was in principle, the same as Rudyerd adopted, but as the material used was different, the result had to be accomplished by different means.

A natural solution was to anchor the stones with iron bolts, but this idea was discarded as involving too great time and expense, and instead the original idea was invented of dovetailing the stones to the rock and to each other; in this way the lower courses would be riveted to the rock, and each of the upper ones be equivalent to one solid stone.

In addition, it was considered necessary to fasten the stones of each course more securely to each other so as to prevent all lateral motion among them, and also to fasten each course to the one below it. The first was accomplished by oak wedges; each stone had two grooves, cut from the top to the bottom of the course; these grooves were one inch wide and three broad; when the stone was accurately placed on its mortar-bed, and beaten down with a wooden maul, two wedges were placed in the groove, one point, the other head down; they were then driven home rather gently at first with a rammer; these wedges were three inches wide, one inch thick at the head, and

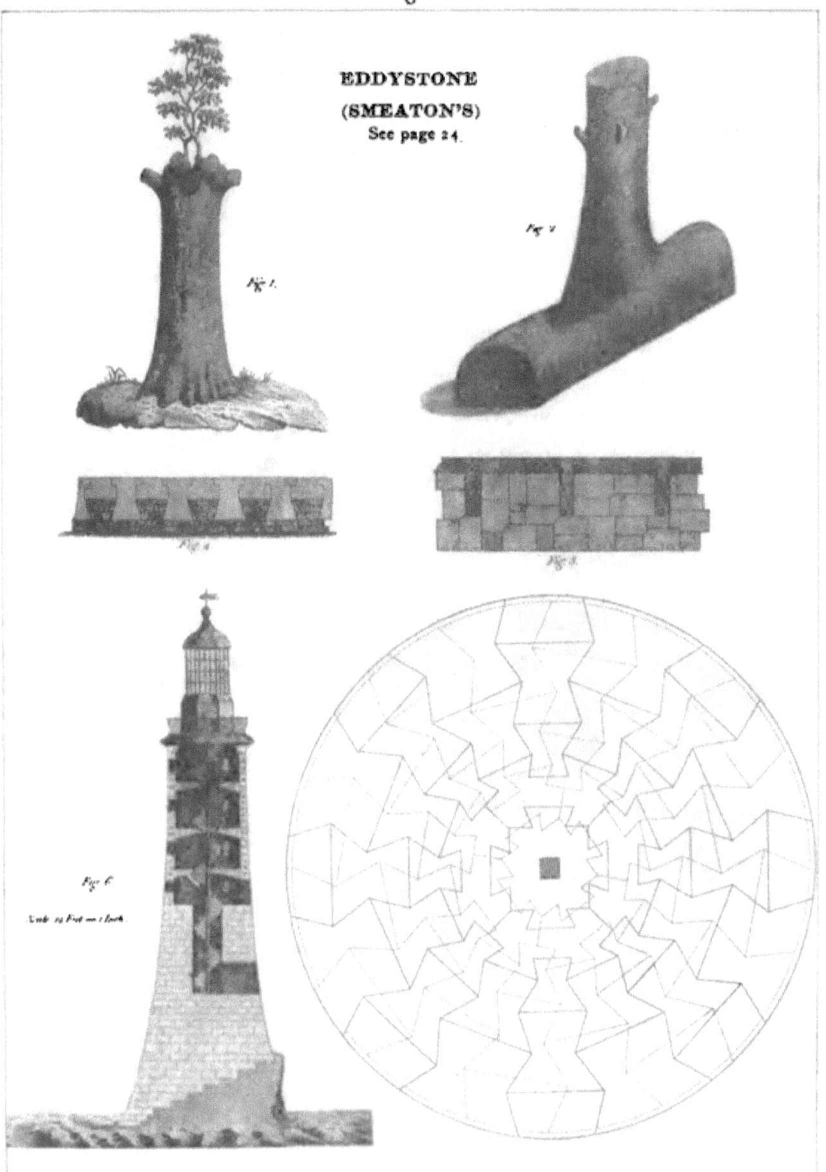

Original **IDEAS, HINTS, & SKETCHES,** *from whence the* FORM *of the* **PRESENT BUILDING** *was taken*

three-eighths inch at the point. As the pressure of these wedges was lateral they solidified the course.

Each course was fastened to the one beneath with oak tree-nails, two one-and-one-fourth-inch holes were bored in the outer end of each stone at the yard; when they were placed and wedged, a hole one-and-one-eighth inch in diameter was bored in the stone beneath, and the tree-nail driven in, to insure its jamming tight in the lower hole, the lower end of the tree-nail was split and a wedge inserted, so that when it reached the bottom the wedge would expand it, and effectually tighten it, the top was then cut off flush with the top of the course, and two wedges at right angles to each other driven into it. All the outside joints were then carefully pointed, and the other joints filled with grout.

I have thus far described the general plan in considerable detail, but it would be tedious to recount all the devices used in bringing this structure to completion; for other information the reader is referred to the accompanying drawings. Every pains was taken that ingenuity could devise to make this tower so strong that the utmost power of the fiercest storm would have no effect upon it.

The light was first shown from the tower on the night of October 16, 1759. On August 5, 1756, the cutting of the rocks to receive the foundation was begun; from the time Rudyerd's light was destroyed by fire till the completion of Smeaton's tower was three years, ten months and sixteen days, the actual working time on the rock itself being one hundred and eleven days and ten hours. Notwithstanding the danger, difficulty and novelty of the undertaking it was completed without the loss of a single life, and scarcely with a serious accident. This was doubtless in a great measure due to the fact that Mr. Smeaton, the designer and builder superintended every part of the work himself, both on shore and at the rock, so that the workmen were never without his intelligent assistance.

When the gilt ball surmounting the lantern was brought from shore, he fastened it in its position with his own hands, standing on a scaffolding consisting of four boards nailed together in the shape of a square, and slipped over the top of the lantern, a workman standing on the opposite side of this precarious platform to balance Mr. Smeaton's weight.

I have been thus particular in the description of this tower, as it is the type of most all that have succeeded it on rocky sites similarly exposed; it was a magnificent conception, and so far as its inherent strength was concerned it might be standing until the present day.

The following inscriptions were engraved upon it. On the first stone of the foundation, 1757, over the entrance, 1758. Round the upper store-room upon the course immediately under the ceiling,

EXCEPT THE LORD BUILD THE HOUSE THEY LABOR IN VAIN THAT BUILD IT. Psalm cxxvii.

Over the south window, 1759; on the outward faces of the basement of the lantern,

✠ . NE. (door) . SE . S. SW . W . NW.

Upon the last stone set, being that over the door of the lantern on the east side,

24th AUG. 1759.
LAUS DEO.

In 1877, Sir James Douglass, member of the Institution of Civil Engineers, explained to the Institution the necessity for substituting a new light-house for Smeaton's famous structure.

There were two reasons — the first was that though the existing structure was "in a fair state of efficiency, yet unfortunately the portion of the gneiss rock on which it is founded had been seriously shaken by the incessant heavy strokes on the tower, and the rock was considerably undermined at its base."

The second reason was that in stormy weather the waves rise considerably above the summit of the lantern, thus frequently eclipsing the light and altering its distinctive character.

The latter defect was of but little importance for a long time after the erection of this light-house, but of late years when the coast lights were so much multiplied, and in addition all vessels carried signal lights, which formerly were not required, it now became a matter of absolute necessity that every coast light should have a reliable distinctive character.

In 1877, the Trinity House (the Light-House Board of England) determined on the erection of a new light-house and directed their Engineer-in-chief to submit a design and estimate of cost including the removal of the upper part of Smeaton's tower, that portion above the solid work; this demolition being necessary for the security of the lower part.

The site selected for the new tower was on the reef S. S. E. from Smeaton's light-house, about one hundred and twenty feet distant.

There was no probability of the rock being undermined here, as there was no surrounding point of attack at a lower level; the main drawback was that the lower courses had to be laid below the lowest tides.

The estimate was $390,000, but as the lowest bid from firms experienced in sea-work was considerably above this sum, it was determined that the Engineer-in-chief should do the work without a contractor.

By reference to the plate it will be seen that the general outline of the tower above the foundation was a curve, but that the face of the foundation was vertical; this change was made because it was found that the tendency of the curvilinear outline was to elevate the centre of force of each wave-stroke on the structure.

Therefore a cylindrical base was adopted and was carried two and one-half feet higher than the highest tides; the difference in height to which heavy seas rise on the two structures is very marked — this cylindrical base has the further advantage of affording a convenient landing platform.

The stones of the various courses are so cut as to interlock into each other, and were also fastened together with bronze bolts; the shapes of the stones differ from Smeaton's, but the principle is the same.

The first landing was made on the 17th July, 1878, when the site was examined and staked off for the workmen.

The first work done was to build a central core of rough granite laid in Portland cement; this core or platform was raised ten feet above low tide, and was of the greatest use.

For a radius of ten feet eight inches from the centre of the core the rock was cut in benches and cleaned, to prepare it to receive the foundation: around this and six inches from where the foundation would come a strong coffer-dam was built of bricks and Roman cement, the rocks were carefully cleared of all sea-weed with picks, and where they projected above the surface of the water strong sulphuric acid was used — every available moment by day and night was utilized in building this dam — it was seven feet thick at the base and its maximum height was also seven feet; three radiating walls were formed in the dam, (1) for strengthening the dam, (2) for reducing to a minimum the quantity of water to be ejected at each tide before commencing work, and (3) for affording, as they frequently did, a lee dam for carrying on the work, when otherwise it would have been impossible to keep the whole area free from water.

While those portions of the dam which were two feet below low water were building, heavy bags of concrete were first deposited along the outside of the dam — occasionally a few courses of brick were carried away, but the dam never suffered any serious injury.

In connection with the work the twin screw-tender *Hercules*, one of the two steam vessels employed in the construction of the Great and Little Basses Rock Light-Houses at Ceylon, was used here; she was fully equipped with all necessary machinery and was moored about thirty fathoms from the rock.

The water was removed from the dam by two three-inch rubber hose, canvas covered and internally wired; they extended from the tender to the rock and the pumps of the tender, together with buckets used by the men, could empty one section of the dam in fifteen minutes.

No blasting was allowed for fear of damaging the rock, so all the

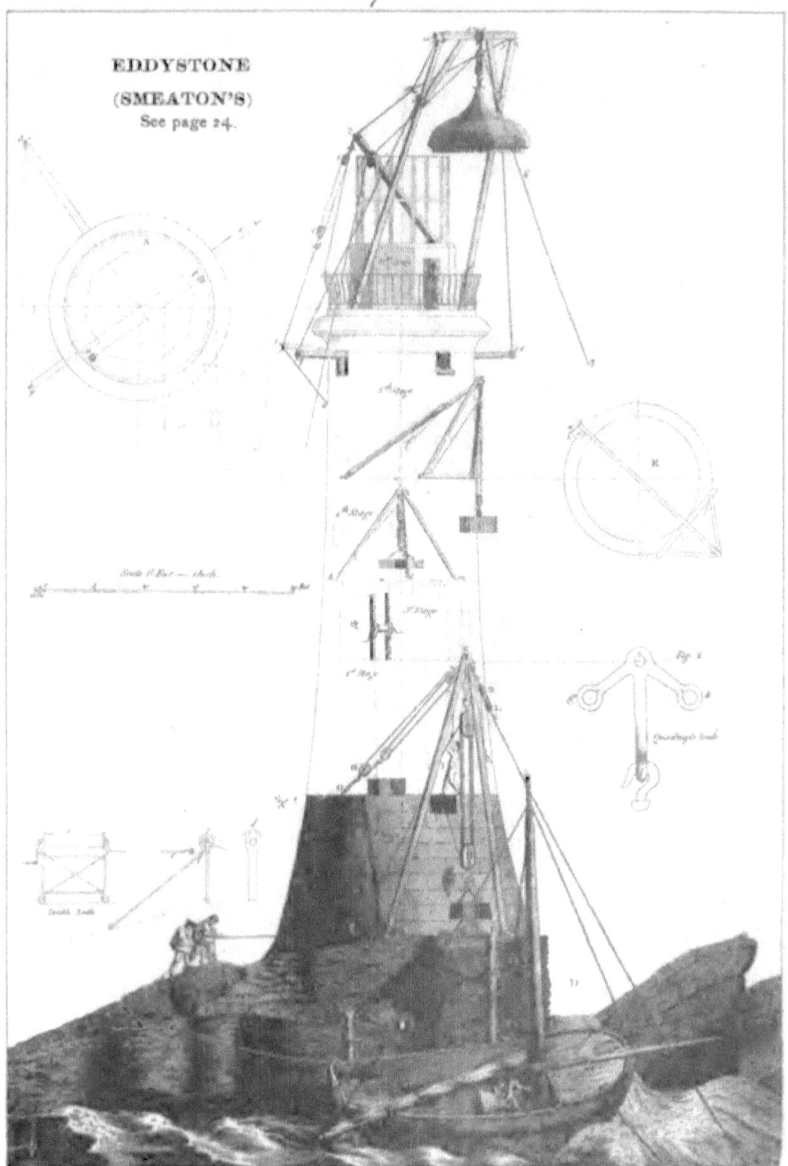

A View of the ROCK *on the* EAST SIDE, *and of the* WORK *advanced to Course* XV *being the first of the* ENTRY COURSES.
Shewing the manner of LANDING *and* HOISTING *the* STONES &c *in every Stage of the* BUILDING.

superfluous rock was removed by drills, jumpers, cleaving tools and picks; this entailed considerable labor as each *face*-stone was sunk one foot below the surrounding rock.

A hollow wrought-iron mast twenty-five feet long and sixteen inches in diameter was firmly fastened in the centre of the work; two jibs were attached to the mast, one for landing the stone from the tender, the other for setting the stone; the drawing shows how these operations were performed.

This is probably the first application of floating steam machinery to the actual erection of a structure at sea.

By June, 1879, the work was sufficiently advanced to lay the stones in the foundation courses and everything was ready for H. R. H., the Duke of Edinburgh, Master, accompanied by H. R. H., the Prince of Wales, Elder brother of the Trinity House, Hon. M. M. Inst. C. E., to lay the foundation stone on the twelfth of the month.

The weather proved so boisterous that the attempt had to be delayed until the nineteenth of August, when the sea being fairly smooth the Royal party landed.

Prior to their arrival the dam had been pumped out and the stone, weighing three and one-fourth tons landed.

A bottle containing a parchment-scroll with full details of the work having been placed in a cavity under the bed of the stone, and the cement bed properly prepared, the stone was lowered and adjusted in position by the Master of the Trinity House, assisted by the Prince of Wales. The stone was then declared "well and truly laid" by his Royal Highness the Master.

Fair progress on the work continued during the working season of 1879–81, so that on the first of June, 1881, the Duke of Edinburgh landed on the rock and placed the last stone of the tower.

The interior fittings were carried to rapid completion, and early in the following year a temporary light was shown. In the meantime the new optical apparatus was installed, and on the eighteenth of May the Duke of Edinburgh completed the work by lighting the lamps and formally opening the light-house.

It takes a good deal of formality to get a light-house fairly under-way in England.

The structure was completed within four years from the time it was commenced, and one year under the time estimated.

To give an idea of the force of the waves, a cannon six feet long and three inches bore, weighing ten cwt. was found at the base of the tower in the winter of 1881. It is supposed that it was one of those carried by the *Winchelsea*, whose wreck has been mentioned.

The Town Council and inhabitants of Plymouth were very desirous that that portion of Smeaton's tower which was to be taken down should be saved and reërected on Plymouth Hoe in place of the sea-mark established by the Trinity House. The Trinity House had no funds available for the purpose, but they delivered to the authorities at Plymouth, at the actual cost for labor, the lantern and four rooms of the tower; these were erected by public subscription on a granite base corresponding to the lower portion of Smeaton's tower, commemorative of one of the most successful, useful and instructive works ever accomplished in civil engineering.

The whole work was accomplished without the loss of life or limb to any person employed. The cost was $296,275, being $93,725, under the estimate.

This completes the history of the four light-houses on the Eddystone Rocks.

CHAPTER III.

BELL ROCK LIGHT-HOUSE.

Bell Rock is a most dangerous sunken reef on the northern side of the entrance of the Firth of Forth, Scotland, and, consequently, a direct danger to all vessels entering the Firth of Tay. The nearest land, at Aberbrothok, is eleven miles distant.

It is uncertain how the rock came to bear its name, possibly on account of its shape, which somewhat resembles a large bell; but the tradition is that an abbot of Aberbrothok caused a bell to be erected on the rock which, by means of a floating apparatus, was rung by the motion of the waves, and that this bell was carried off by pirates. On this legend is founded the ballad of Sir Ralph the Rover, one of Southey's minor poems. It should be mentioned that in old charts this rock was called Inch Cape, or Inch or the Island of the Cape, referring to the Red Head, the highest and most remarkable on that coast.

Southey's ballad is as follows:

No stir in the air, no stir in the sea,
The ship was still as she could be;
Her sails from Heaven received no motion;
Her keel was steady in the ocean.

Without either sign or sound of their shock,
The waves flowed over the Inchcape Rock;
So little they rose, so little they fell,
They did not move the Inchcape Bell.

The Abbot of Aberbrothok
Had placed that Bell on the Inchcape Rock;
On a buoy in the storm it floated and swung,
And over the waves its warning rung.

When the rock was hid by the surge's swell,
The mariners heard the warning Bell;
And then they knew the perilous rock,
And blest the Abbot of Aberbrothok.

The Sun in heaven was shining gay;
All things were joyful on that day;
The sea-birds screamed as they wheeled round,
And there was joyaunce in their sound.

The buoy of the Inchcape Bell was seen,
A darker speck on the ocean green:
Sir Ralph the Rover walked his deck,
And he fixed his eye on the darker speck.

He felt the cheering power of spring;
It made him whistle, it made him sing:
His heart was mirthful to excess,
But the Rover's mirth was wickedness.

His eye was on the Inchcape float;
Quoth he, "My men, put out the boat,
And row me to the Inchcape Rock,
And I'll plague the Abbot of Aberbrothok."

South **ELEVATION** *of the* **STONE LIGHTHOUSE** *completed upon the* **EDYSTONE** *in 1759.*

Shewing the Prospect of the nearest Land, as it appears from the Rocks in a clear calm Day.

See page 25

The boat is lowered, the boatmen row,
And to the Inchcape rock they go;
Sir Ralph bent over from the boat,
And he cut the Bell from the Inchcape Float.

Down sunk the Bell with a gurgling sound;
The bubbles rose and burst around:
Quoth Sir Ralph, "The next who comes to the Rock
Won't bless the Abbot of Aberbrothok."

Sir Ralph the Rover sailed away;
He scoured the seas for many a day;
And now, grown rich with plundered store,
He steers his course for Scotland's shore.

So thick a haze o'erspreads the sky,
They cannot see the Sun on high;
The wind hath blown a gale all day;
At evening it hath died away.

On the deck the Rover takes his stand;
So dark it is they see no land.
Quoth Sir Ralph, "It will be lighter soon,
For there is the dawn of the rising Moon."

"Canst hear," said one, "the breakers roar?
For methinks we should be near the shore."
"Now where we are I cannot tell,
But I wish we could hear the Inchcape Bell."

They hear no sound; the swell is strong;
Though the wind hath fallen they drift along,
Till the vessel strikes with a quivering shock:
"O Christ! it is the Inchcape Rock!"

Sir Ralph the Rover tore his hair,
He curst himself in his despair;
The waves rush in on every side;
The ship is sinking beneath the tide.

But, even in his dying fear,
One dreadful sound could the Rover hear,—
A sound as if, with the Inchcape Bell,
The Devil below was ringing his knell.

At high water of spring tides the southwestern reef is about sixteen feet under the surface of the water, while that part of the rock on which the light-house is built is about twelve feet below. At low water of neap tides hardly any of the rock is visible, but at low water of spring tides the general level of the northeastern end, where the light-house is built, is about four feet above water, and occasional points are six feet above. Owing to the contrary tides the peculiar position of the rock and its dangerous charactèr, ordinarily invisible, the need of a distinguishing mark upon it was early seen, and in 1793 Sir Alexander Cochrane made an official application to the Commissioners of the Northern Light-Houses, and they considered it an object of primary importance that one should be erected whenever funds should become available.

In the mean time public advertisements were inserted in the papers calling for some suitable plan. Several propositions were received. Notably Captain Joseph Brodie prepared a model of a cast-iron light-house supported on four pillars, strongly braced together. The design was not altogether approved by the Light-house Board, but the projectors had so much confidence in their plan that they erected, at different times, two temporary wooden beacons which, unfortunately, were immediately washed away.

The merchants of Leith, pleased by their perseverance, subscribed £150 toward the erection of a stronger temporary beacon, built of four strong spars, well braced and fastened with iron straps. The feet of the spars were let into the rock and also held to it by iron cemented to the rock with lead. This structure was erected with great difficulty in July, 1803. In the following December it entirely disappeared.

Mr. Robert Stevenson, the designer of the Bell Rock light-house, paid the first visit to the rock in August, 1803; as he was favored by both tide and weather he was enabled to land on the rock and remain there long enough to make a good sketch of it, during which time the boatmen devoted themselves to hunting for articles of shipwreck, and to such good purpose that before the tide overflowed they had collected a couple of hundred pounds of old metal of a miscellaneous character, among them being a kedge anchor, a stove, a shoe-buckle, several pieces of money, a ship's marking-iron, etc.

These relics of disaster eloquently spoke the need of a light to mark this spot. The result of this visit was that Mr. Stevenson was convinced that the proper kind of tower to be erected here should be of stone in preference to the pillar form, as there was ample room for a large base, and besides, the tides rose so high that a vessel might come full sail against any erection made there — were the structure pillar-formed it might readily be damaged — but if the building were of solid stone it is not likely that the vessel would have any effect upon it.

The design was, therefore, made the same in principle as the Eddystone, and is shown on the plate.

Various petitions were made to the Light-house Board, setting forth the danger of this rock and the great necessity there was of properly marking it, and though the Board recommended it, it was not until the year 1806 that the act of Parliament passed, authorizing its construction and appropriating a sufficient sum for its erection.

A clause had been introduced into the bill authorizing the collection of light-house duties of one penny half penny per register ton from British vessels, and three pence per ton from foreigners as soon as a ship or vessel was moored or anchored, and a floating or other light exhibited at or near Bell Rock.

In order that shipping might have the benefit of a light while the work was in progress, and also to have the benefit of the duties, a light-ship was fitted out; she was a Prussian fishing-vessel, captured by a British cruiser during the war of 1806, flat bottomed and rounded at both stem and stern; her capacity for rolling and incapacity for steering became proverbial, and later, when she was used as a storeship for the work, occasioned much trouble and uneasiness.

The first work on the rock was to clear it from sea-weed, and to trace the sites of the beacon-house and light-house on the rock; after this was done the first landing for erecting the beacon-house was made, which event was celebrated by three cheers and the regaling of each man with a glass of rum. Little work could be done the first day, but the holes for the holdfasts of the beacon were commenced, and the smith laid out a site for the forge.

The tide only allowed the men to remain two hours on the rock; when they returned on board they were variously employed in fishing, reading, drying their wet clothes, and listening to two or three companions who played the violin and German flute. They were blessed with reasonably good weather, and successfully bored all the dove-tailed holes for the iron holdfasts, and then commenced the cutting of the rock to receive the first course of masonry of the tower.

It was quite a problem as to the best method of landing the large stones for the light-house, and various plans were suggested, such as to attach a córk buoy to each stone and float it to the rock, or to use an air-tank as a float, to load the stones in light-draught, flat-bottomed vessels which could sail over the rock at high tide and drop the stones overboard; to build so much of the light-house ashore in a sort of coffer-dam as would raise the building to the level of the highest tide, and, having prepared the foundation to receive it, to tow the coffer-dam to its site and lower it to its place.

The method decided upon was to bring the vessels loaded with stone conveniently near the rock and to moor them, and then to transfer the stones to smaller deck boats, called praams, and to tow the latter to the rock at low tide, while the artificers were at work and ready to lay the stones in their proper positions. This method succeeded admirably; and when the first stone was landed all hands collected to welcome it and greet it with three cheers, and a glass of rum was served to each man. This formality accompanied every important step of the work. The next day after the first stone was

9

EDDYSTONE (SMEATON'S) IN A STORM.

landed, there occurred what might have been a most serious disaster. Soon after the workmen landed in the morning, the tender's boat and crew put off from the rock to examine the tender's moorings. The boat had no sooner reached the tender than the latter went adrift carrying the boat with her; as it was blowing hard it was with great difficulty that the crew could set the sails, and by the time this was done she had drifted some three miles to leeward, rendering it impossible for her to return to the rock until long after it would be overflowed.

The situation was indeed critical; there were thirty-two men on the rock, and only two boats which could carry in pleasant weather twenty-four men. For a long time the disaster was noticed only by Mr. Stevenson and the landing-master, as the men were busily employed at their respective tasks. When, however, the tide rose and the work of necessity stopped, the men went toward their respective boats, and to their astonishment found but two instead of three; no one uttered a word, the men looked at each other and at Mr. Stevenson; each man fully aware of the gravity of the occasion, and apparently calculating the chance of escape.

Mr. Stevenson had been considering various schemes by which to save the men, and attempted to address them; but his mouth was so parched that he could not utter a word; he stooped to get a little sea-water to moisten his throat, and as he rose he heard the cry of "a boat! a boat!" and on looking round saw through the haze a large boat coming toward the rock. This proved to be the pilot-boat from Abroath with letters; half the men were put on board of her, the other half took the two boats and after a hard row, for the wind had increased to a gale, arrived on board worn out and drenched to the skin.

The next morning but eight of the twenty-six workmen reported for duty, the rest had not got over their scare. When the eight returned from the rock, they saw the other eighteen on deck; but as the boat approached they went below; ashamed of their conduct. This was the only instance when the men refused to work, except the case of four Scotchmen, who would not work on Sundays.

After various untoward accidents, and a narrow escape from shipwreck of the whole party during a most violent storm the wooden temporary beacon was finally successfully erected; this was a most important proceeding, for the workmen could now safely remain at the rock all day; and the blacksmith could have his forge and bellows on a platform above the reach of the tide. When the beacon was finished, a small flag was displayed from its top "by which its perspective effect was greatly improved." The event was celebrated by three hearty cheers, and the custom of serving a dram of rum to each man was not forgotten. This closed the first season's work, and the workmen returned to Abroath. During the first season the actual working time was but thirteen-and-a-half days.

During the following winter the stones were cut to shape, and as may be seen by the plan, were dovetailed together; the outside shell was to be of granite to a height of thirty feet on the solid part of the structure; the rest of the building was of sandstone.

Various experiments were made as to the kind of mortar to be used, and it was found that a mixture of pozzolano and lime in a state of dry, impalpable powder, and clean sharp sand in equal proportions by measure, mixed with sea-water, formed a mortar equally good in all respects as when no sand was added.

Ordinarily it would have been difficult to obtain a sufficient number of good men to go on with the work, but as the men were exempt from the danger of being impressed on men-of-war, Great Britain being at war with France at the time, the work became very popular. The men were furnished with a ticket descriptive of their persons, to which was attached a silver medal having on one side a figure of Bell Rock Light-House, and on the other the word "medal." The Impress officers generally respected this.

On the 25th May, 1808, the workmen again embarked for the rock and landed; on the next day, the light-house colors were hoisted on the beacon.

The first course for the foundation of the light-house was finished at the stone-yard on the 4th June, the birthday of King George III.

Work was carried on briskly at the rock, and by the 9th of June the foundation pit was completed and the first stone landed. At 11 A. M. the next day the stone, on which had been chiseled "1808," was securely placed, and Mr. Stevenson pronounced the following benediction: "May the Great Architect of the universe complete and bless this building," on which three hearty cheers were given, and success to the future operations drunk with the greatest enthusiasm.

By the 26th of July, the eighteen detached pieces of stone forming the foundation-course had been laid, and the whole surface brought to uniform level.

As the other courses when laid would be under water at high tide, their weight was not alone relied upon to retain them in place, but they were also held by oaken treenails, as described in the construction of the Eddystone tower.

By the end of the season the base of the tower had been built to a level with the highest part of the foundation pit, or about five feet six inches above the lower end of the foundation stone. The men were at work during low water two hundred and sixty-five hours, only eighty of which were employed in building. During the storms of the following winter but slight accidents happened to the beacon, and these admitted of easy repair.

The first thing done the next season wrs to fit up the wooden beacon as a temporary residence. Work was commenced laying the stones, and by the 8th July the work was so far advanced that the high tide for the first time did not overflow the building, and the usual cheering and rum were indulged in.

On August 25 the last stone of the solid part of the building was laid, and the work on the tower closed for the season; this event also was observed with the usual ceremonies. The tower was now thirty-one feet six inches above the foundation course and seventeen feet above high water. In the next year the last stone was laid on July 30. During the year there had been various accidents and several narrow escapes, but fortunately no loss of life.

It is sufficient to show how high the waves would run up this tower, when it is stated that the men were occasionally driven from their work, even when the tower had reached the height of eighty feet. When the stonework had been completed, the tower was one hundred and two feet six inches high, and had reached the lintel of the door of the lantern. The lantern was built and glazed by the 25th of October. This closed the season's work.

Two light-keepers were left in the tower in October; the following November, when an additional supply of water and provisions were taken out to them, they were asked as to their experience. One of them stated that in storms when particular seas struck the light-house would tremble, and reminded him of the effect produced when a round log was hit sharply with a mallet, and though he had every confidence in the stability of the building, yet it "made a man look back upon his former life."

The lamps and reflecting apparatus were safely placed in the tower in December, 1810, and on the 17th of the month notice was given that on the night of February 1, 1811, the light would first be exhibited.

On the 30th July, 1814, Sir Walter Scott, Mr. Stevenson and several other gentlemen visited the light-house. They took breakfast in the library, and at the earnest entreaty of the party, Sir Walter, after inscribing his name in the album or visitor's book, wrote the following verse:—

Pharos loquitur.—
Far in the bosom of the deep,
O'er these wild shelves my watch I keep,
A ruddy gem of changeful light,
Bound on the dusky brow of Night,
The seaman bids my lustre hail,
And scorns to strike his timorous sail.

In conclusion, it may be of interest to state that this important structure contains 28,530 cubic feet of material, and weighs 2,076 tons.

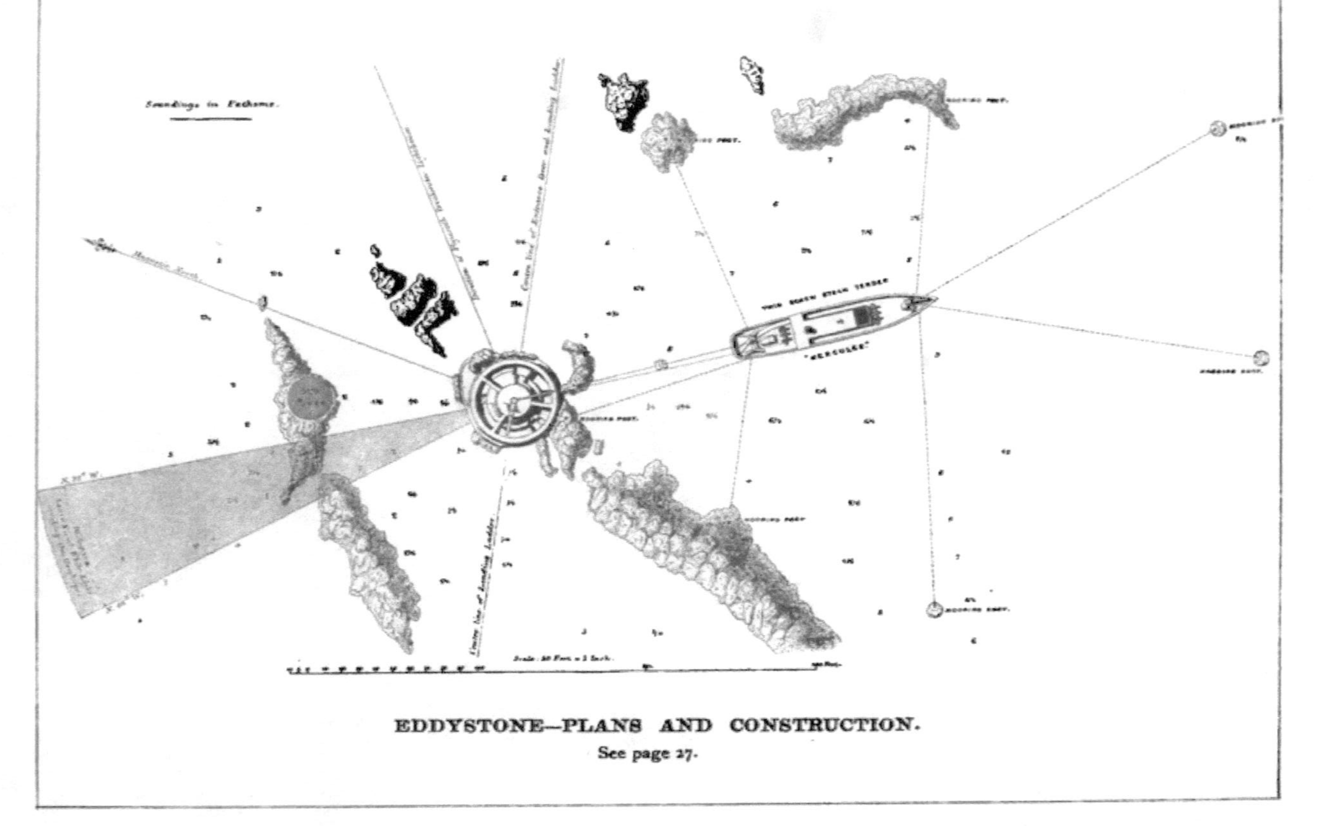

EDDYSTONE—PLANS AND CONSTRUCTION.

See page 27.

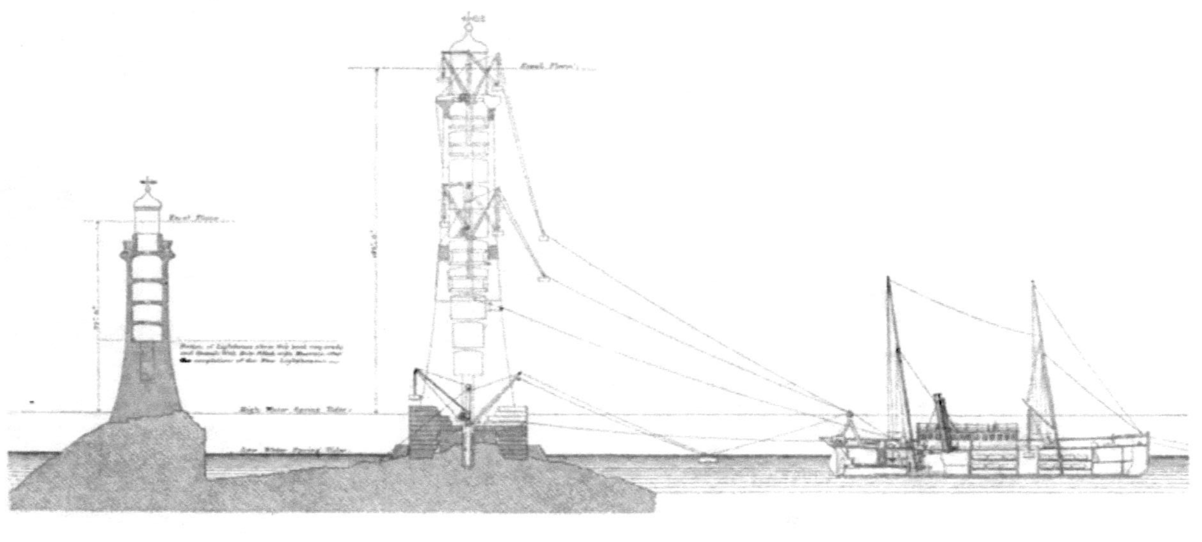

PLAN AND SECTION AT LOW WATER SPRING TIDES, SHOWING LANDING AND SETTING ARRANGEMENTS.

CHAPTER IV.

SKERRYVORE LIGHT-HOUSE.

PORTLAND HEAD LIGHT, MAINE

The light-house at Skerryvore is another of those remarkable structures, of which Eddystone was the type, which we owe to the genius of the Stevenson family.

The cluster of rocks opposite the west coast of Scotland, the largest of which is known as the Skerryvore, has long been a standing menace to the mariner, and, from the great difficulty of access to it, exposed as it is to the full fury of the Atlantic and surrounded by almost perpetual surf, the erection of a light-house upon it has always been regarded as a most formidable undertaking.

The success of Stevenson, the elder, at Bell Rock and the valuable experience gained there warranted the attempt to erect a similar structure at this place, as its importance as a light-station was too evident to require argument.

A long list of disasters, comprising the total loss of many vessels and of most of their crews, is a melancholy proof of the dangerous character of the reef and of the need of a light which would convert it from a source of danger to one of safety.

As the plate shows, the Skerryvore reef is a tract of foul ground, consisting of a number of small rocks, many below the level of high water: the surface of the principal rock on which the light-house is placed measures, at the lowest tides, about two hundred and eighty feet square. It is extremely irregular and is intersected by many gullies of considerable breadth and of unlooked-for depth, which leave it solid only to the extent of one hundred and sixty by seventy feet. One of these gullies, at the southeast corner of the rock, formed the landing-creek after clearing it by blasting under water; its sides and bottom were left comparatively smooth, and a landing could be effected here when the rocks were elsewhere inaccessible.

Another gully, immediately to the southeast of the light-house, was quite a natural curiosity; it was found to undermine the rocks for eight or ten feet and to terminate in a hollow submarine chamber which threw up a jet of water about twenty feet high accompanied by a loud noise like the snorting of some sea monster. Notwithstanding the beauties of this jet, it was a source of considerable discomfort and inconvenience, as it drenched any one whose work carried them near it. One calm day, at a very low tide, Mr. Alan Stevenson explored its interior by means of ropes and a ladder: he found the cavern to terminate in a polished spherical room, about seven feet in diameter, its floors strewn with boulders whose incessant motion had hollowed it out of the veined rock and rendered its interior beautifully smooth and glassy. As the cavern penetrated too far toward the place which Mr. Stevenson had selected for the site of the tower he changed somewhat the location of the foundation, and he also filled the cavern to prevent the discomfort of being drenched by the column of water which spouted from it even during calm weather.

Another peculiarity of the rock, in addition to its shattered and disjointed appearance was the glassy smoothness of its surface, which proved throughout the whole duration of the work, but especially at its commencement, a serious obstacle and hindrance to the operations. At first sight this peculiarity may seem to be of little moment, but, as landings had often to be made in very bad weather, there was considerable danger in springing from a boat in a heavy surf upon an irregular mass of rocks as smooth and slippery as ice, and many awkward accidents occurred. The foreman of the masons said it was "like climbing up the side of a bottle."

During the progress of the work the rise and fall of the tides was measured — at high spring tides the rise was from twelve to thirteen feet, and three feet at dead low neap tides. The velocity of spring tides is between four and five miles, and of neap tides between two and three miles an hour. Although an act of Parliament in 1814 provided for the erection of this light, yet the undertaking appeared so formidable it was not until 1834 that the Light-house Board of Scotland took any measures to carry the provisions of the act into effect.

The first thing done was to make a careful survey of the site, an operation attended with much labor, as in connection with the work it was particularly desirable to have exact details of the depths, rocks and shallows of the surrounding sea with the nature of the bottom accurately laid down. This information afterward proved extremely useful during the progress of the work, as some of the vessels lying near the rock were frequently driven, by change of wind, to seek shelter among the neighboring islands.

Up to this time seamen knew but little of the extent of the reef. On one occasion a vessel was boarded within three-fourths of a mile of Skerryvore, between it and a rock known as Bo-rhua, or red rock. So little did the captain know of his proximity to these dangerous reefs that he was found lying at ease on the companionway, smoking a pipe, with his wife sitting beside him knitting stockings.

During the survey Hynish, a creek twelve miles from Skerryvore, was selected as a site for the work-yard and harbor for the vessels. The Duke of Argyle gave free permission to quarry materials for the purpose of a light-house on any part of the Argyle estates, and during the summer of 1836–7 about 3,800 feet of gneiss rock were quarried and a rip-rap wharf or pier was commenced to improve the harbor at Hynish. In 1838 a steam-tender was ordered and a contract let for building a temporary barrack on the rock.

Mr. Alan Stevenson chose an outline for the Skerryvore tower different from either the Eddystone or the Bell Rock, as the accompanying sketch shows.

The outline of the Skerryvore approaches more nearly to a conic frustum than either of the other two. This shape was chosen so that the thickness of the walls at the top might be increased — besides, the more nearly the walls approach a perpendicular the greater pressure is exerted on the stones near the base, and operates to prevent them from being drawn from the wall as well, if not better than by any system of *dovetailing* or *joggling*, devices chiefly useful in the early stages of the work when it is exposed to storms and before the tower is raised to such a height as to prevent the seas from breaking over it. Consequently, the other important differences in this work from the others was the absence of dovetailing and joggles between the courses. During the early progress of the work the stones were retained in their places chiefly by common diamond joggles, and the courses were temporarily held together with wooden treenails, like those used at Eddystone and Bell Rock. Ribbon joggles were used in the higher part of the tower, where the walls begin to get thin, both to prevent any tendency of the stones to spread outwards, and also to make a better joint against the intrusion of water. The walls were also tied together at various points by means of the floor-stones which were connected by dovetails let into large circular stones, forming the centres of the floors.

The first season's operations consisted solely of fixing in place the beams forming the pyramidal support for the temporary barrack; this was accomplished with great difficulty and danger, and the disgust of Mr. Stevenson can well be imagined when he was informed of its total destruction the following winter.

The next year, 1839, a stronger framework was put up, the bar-

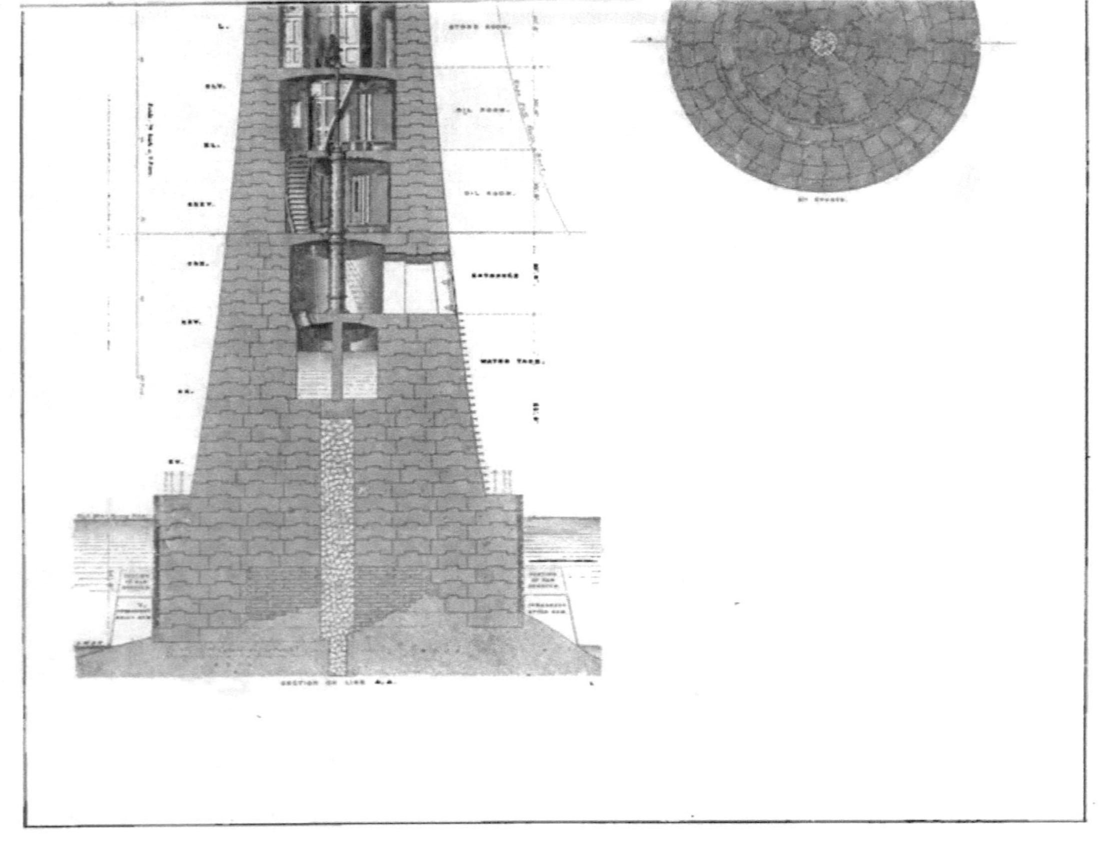
STORE ROOM.
OIL ROOM.
OIL ROOM.
ENTRANCE.
WATER TANK.
SECTION ON LINE A.B.

THE NEW EDDYSTONE LIGHTHOUSE.

See page 29.

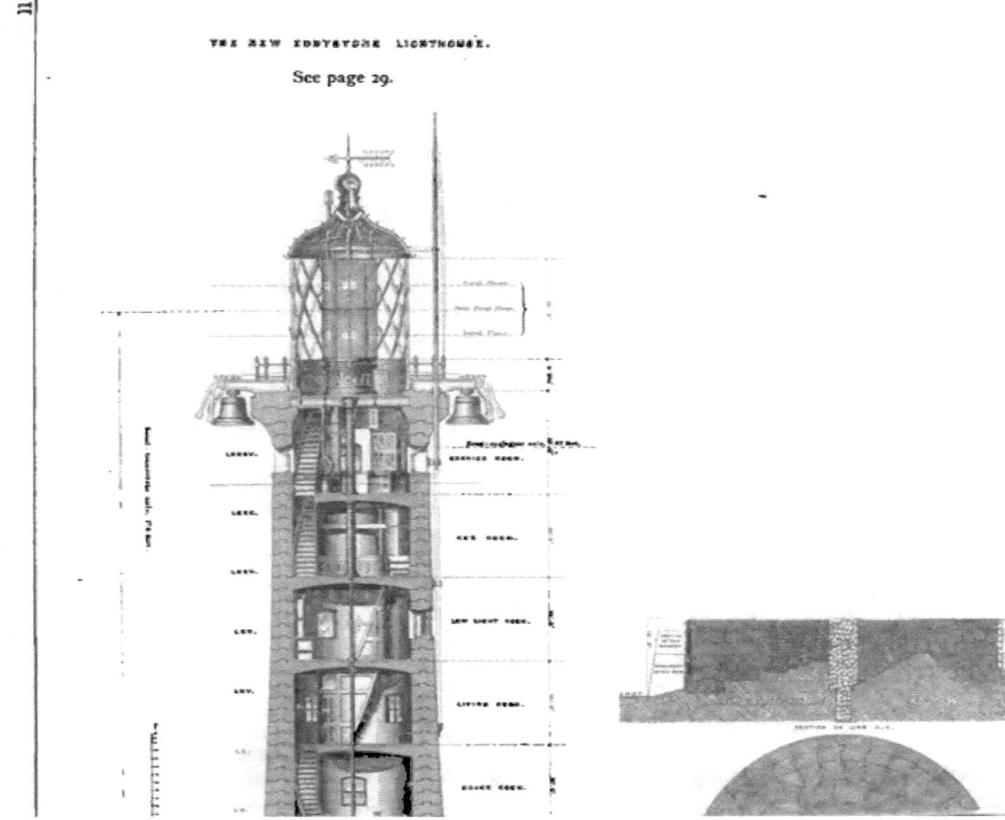

rack-house built upon it and the levelling of the rock to receive the foundation of the tower began. The cutting of the rock to a level surface was mainly done by blasting; injury to the men, who were of necessity in close proximity to the blasts, was avoided by covering the mines with mats made of old rope. It is of some interest to note

Eddystone. Skerryvore. Bell Rock.

that Mr. Stevenson made use of a galvanic battery to fire the mines though its use was mainly restricted to blasts under water, or when several blasts were to be fired simultaneously. After the year's work was closed a report was received that the temporary barrack had again been destroyed; this, fortunately, proved untrue, the damage being confined to the loss of all the timbers and other material which had been left lashed to the rock, and of the moorings of the tender.

The next year found the barrack all secure, and the stock of provisions left in it for the use of any seamen who might be wrecked on the rock was in sufficiently good condition to be used by the workmen who, with Mr. Stevenson, took up their abode in the barrack, — a comfortless residence in stormy weather, when, for days together, it was impossible to descend to the rock, and it was impossible to keep warm except by remaining in bed.

The plate shows the nature of their singular dwelling; immediately under the tower was a wooden gallery for the storage of coal, tool-chests, beef and beer casks, and other materials which could not be safely left on the rock itself. The floor of this gallery was removed at the end of each season so as to leave free passage for the waves during the winter storms. Next came a kitchen and store-room, which, curtailed as it was by the seven beams passing through it, contained a caboose capable of cooking for forty men, and various cupboards and lockers lined with tin for holding the provisions.

The room above was divided into two apartments, one for the superintendent of the landing-gang and the foreman of the masons, the other for Mr. Stevenson.

The highest apartment, surmounted by a ventilator, was lined round the sides with four tiers of berths or bunks, capable of accommodating thirty people. The closeness of the room was most intolerable, especially during the heat of summer. These were, indeed, cramped quarters for so many people when it is considered that this odd, twelve-sided house, perched up like a bird-box on a pole, was only twelve feet in diameter.

The following was the daily routine when weather permitted: the men were roused at half-past three in the morning; at four the work commenced, breakfast at eight, for which half an hour was allowed, work until two, when there was another half hour for dinner, when the work was again resumed and carried on till seven, eight, and even nine o'clock, when anything urgent was on hand; supper was then eaten in the cool of the evening. These protracted hours produced continual drowsiness, and any one who sat down generally fell asleep.

The ceremony of laying the foundation-stone was performed on the 7th July, 1840, by His Grace, the Duke of Argyll, who was accompanied by the Duchess of Argyle, the Marquis of Lorne, Lady Emma Campbell, and a party of friends; he left a donation of £10 to be divided among the workmen.

During the year the tower was carried to the height of eight feet two inches, and contained a mass equal to 10,780 cubic feet, not much less than the whole mass of Smeaton's Eddystone tower. From this time forward the building of the tower made comparatively rapid progress, and finally, on the 21st July, 1842, the last stone was successfully laid.

The masonry of the tower is one hundred and thirty-seven feet high and contains 58,580 cubic feet, weighing about 4,380 tons.

The lantern was placed the same year, and the work for the season was closed on the 14th September. In 1843 the interior fittings of the tower were completed and the light was exhibited to the mariner on the night of the 1st February, 1844. In the course of the summer of 1844 a marble tablet, bearing an inscription in letters of gold was, by order of the commissioners, placed over one of the windows in the visiting officer's room.

LIGHT-HOUSE OF HEAUX DE BRÉHAT.

On the coasts of France, light-houses were needed, as in England, on difficult sites, and it is interesting to compare the different manners in which similar problems were solved in the two countries. I have selected the Light-house of Heaux de Bréhat as one comparative type; it is situated about three miles from the most northerly end of the Peninsular of Brittany, on the plateau of Heaux de Bréhat, which consists of a porphyritic rock about five hundred and sixty yards in diameter at low tide, and entirely submerged at high tide except a few scattered projections.

Here the currents are very strong, at times running as high as eight knots an hour, and the sea in gales attaining an extraordinary violence.

The tower instead of being placed on the highest part of the rock, was situated at a place near which landings could most conveniently be made in order to reduce as much as possible the cost and delay of landing the materials used in its construction.

At the Isle of Bréhat near by, a natural harbor was improved; and the storehouses and work-shops were built. All the stones were cut here, and in order to insure accuracy each course was laid out on a platform; the stones were then shipped on barges of about forty tons burden, each stone carrying its number, its sling, and surrounded with straw mats to prevent its edges being chipped. The stones were unloaded, and placed by means of a series of derricks, which passed the stones to each other. A flying scaffold was also used for the convenience of the workmen, and was carried up as the work progressed. It consisted of a series of small fir trestles clasped against the tower by means of two chain bands which were tightened by jack-screws. When the scaffold was to be raised, the men stood on the masonry; the screws were loosened, each man seized a trestle, and at the word of command all lifted together. The chain bands were then retightened; the entire operation did not take more than half an hour.

The accompanying drawing, taken at low tide, shows how the work was carried on when the tower had reached the height of about one hundred and thirty-five feet above the rock. It was important that the men should live on the rock, so that they could be usefully employed, even during bad weather.

No matter how well and carefully the stones might be prepared, they had to be finished on the spot; and notwithstanding that arrangements had been perfected to assure rapidity in the landing of material, it was at times impossible to lay all of the stones of a cargo during one low tide.

Two adjacent slender peaks, near the centre of the plateau with their summits almost twenty feet above the highest tides, offered a good site for the erection of the necessary buildings. The space between them was filled with loose stone retained in place on one side by a vertical wall, and on the other by an inclined plane, both built of heavy blocks of stone laid in cement. A nearly square platform was thus made about thirty feet on the side, on which was erected a stout frame building, well anchored to the rock, and containing store-rooms, a small forge, and rooms for the engineer, foremen and workmen. The building was surmounted by a small tower, from

Drawn by Miss Stevenson

Engraved by J. Horsburgh

See page 31.

Pharos loquitur

Far in the bosom of the deep
O'er these wild shelves my watch I keep
A ruddy gem of changeful light
Bound on the dusky brow of Night
The seaman bids my lustre hail
And scorns to strike his timorous sail

which was shown a temporary light. In this building were accommodated sixty men, who worked on the rock as soon as it was uncovered by the falling tide, and who found it their only refuge when the tide again rose.

In the light-houses at Eddystone and Bell rock, the lower courses were bonded together in a complicated manner by means of dovetails, and were held to each other by numerous iron or wooden dowels; at Skerryvore there was a departure from this system, which in addition to the expense it entails, materially retards the work at its critical stage. At the light-house of Bréhat there was a still farther departure from precedent, and it was decided not to fasten each stone separately; but to limit the quantity of masonry to that which could be put in solidly during one low tide.

Each course was divided into a certain number of sections or keys, each of which was connected by means of four small granite blocks; fitted in each course, and placed in the angles of the sections. The angular stones belonging to the exterior facing, being thus kept in place, form tie pieces, supporting the facing stone which come between them, and are attached to those which compose the sides of the key by means of dovetails let in their whole thickness. Finally, the interior face, maintained upon the preceding course by two stones, is also held by the stone belonging to the course above, which being placed across the joint allows the tie pieces on that side to be suppressed. The perimeter thus being made firm, artifices of construction were not required for the interior; and in the lower courses where it was necessary to finish rapidly, and where there was considerable surface, it was completed in rubble masonry. This method was entirely successful; in no case was any damage sustained when an entire course could be finished before the return of the tide, which was generally accomplished; it was the same even when the work had to be discontinued, without having to place any other stones than those of the facing, from which the work was always commenced; occasionally they were not prepared in time, and some stones were raised and moved a short distance out of place.

These were readily reset, and the method was found advantageous both as to economy and rapidity of execution.

The porphyritic rock on which the light-house is built is of extreme hardness, and rapidly wears out the best tools; but in many places it is fissured, and the sea breaks off small fragments. This prevented the establishment of the foundation on the same level throughout, and it was found necessary to divide it into several parts so as to avoid any chance of its being swept away, and also to diminish the cost of excavation.

In the centre a circular space fourteen feet in diameter, corresponding to the interior hollow of the tower, was left untouched; outside this an annular space thirty-nine feet in exterior diameter was levelled off six inches below the lowest portion of this part of the plateau; then at the circumference there was hollowed out a trench forty inches wide, of a depth varying with the condition of the rock so that no part of the base should be protected by less than sixteen inches in height of compact porphyry.

The light-house consists of a tower with an interior cylindrical opening fourteen feet in diameter, and one hundred and fifty-eight feet high from its base to the lantern floor. It consists of two principal parts, the lower trumpet-shaped and solid to three feet four inches above the highest tides, the upper, considered as standing on an immovable base has a degree of lightness about the same as that usually given to towers of the same height built on shore; the thickness of the walls is four feet four inches at the bottom and decreases to two feet ten inches at the top under the cornice.

The interior is divided as follows: the two lower stories are store-rooms, the four above are the kitchen and keeper's quarters; the seventh, fitted up rather better than the rest is a room for the engineer; the eighth is a watch-room, and above that is the lantern-room.

The casing of the stairway is built in the tower wall on one side, and forms on the other a projection, upon the cylindrical opening of the tower, the recesses on each side of which are utilized as closets. The entire work is built of granite of fine, close grain, and of a bluish tint. The arches are built of brick, made according to pattern, except the one supporting the floor of the service-chamber which is of concrete, the brick not arriving in time.

The cost of this structure was $106,365 exclusive of the lantern and illuminating apparatus.

LIGHT-HOUSE OF AR-MEN.

More difficult than the preceding was the building of the foundation of the light-house of Ar-men, France. The island of Sein is situated on the western extremity of the department of Finisterre, in the northwest part of France, and extends in a westerly direction by a succession of reefs to a distance of nearly eight miles from the island. The tops of some are elevated above the highest tides; others are alternately above and below the surface of the water, while the greater number are always submerged. They constitute a sort of dam, whose direction is nearly perpendicular to that of the tidal currents, and the sea constantly breaks over them with great violence.

In April, 1860, the Light-house Board of France determined that the subject should be thoroughly investigated, in order to know if it would be possible to erect a first-order light-house on one of the rocks not covered by the sea and as near as possible to the end of the reef. Next June this action was approved, and a commission of engineers and officers of the navy were charged with the duty of making surveys of the locality.

In July this Commission had made a careful examination of the local conditions, and ascertained that there were three rocks at the extremity which projected above the water, even in strong tides. Of these rocks, which are called Madion, Schomeor and Ar-men, the two first are nearly covered, while the third rises to about five feet above the lowest ebb-tides.

The state of the sea had not permitted the Commission to land, or even to go alongside Ar-men, but from the view that could be obtained its dimensions appeared insufficient for the construction of a great light-house, and landings seemed impossible, even in the most favorable weather.

The Commission, therefore, unanimously recommended the selection of the Rock Neuerlach as a site, about five miles inward from the end of the reef. This recommendation was not approved by the Board, as it did not tend to ameliorate the existing state of things sufficiently for the needs of navigation, and the Ministry of Marine was requested to order a thorough hydrographic survey of the end of the reef.

Various circumstances retarded the execution of this work. In 1866, M. Ploix, engineer and hydrographer, was sent to the spot, and though he was not able to gather all the necessary information, still, his investigation was sufficient to enable the Board to decide upon a plan — his conclusion was that Ar-men was the proper site. In true French style he said, "It is a work exceedingly difficult, almost impossible, but considering the paramount importance of lighting the reef, we must try the impossible."

The currents passing over the reef are most violent; in high tides their speed exceeds eight knots, and in the calmest weather they cause a strong chopping sea as soon as a breeze meets them. It is only possible to go alongside the rock during very gentle winds between the north and east.

The impossibility of anchoring a floating light was recognized as much on account of the great depth of water as of the fact that the bottom was thickly studded with rocks, about which the anchor-chain would be fouled.

Owing to the great difficulty of construction the project of establishing an iron structure resting directly on the reef was not entertained, the Board finally deciding that a solid masonry foundation must be established of such dimensions as would be suitable for the construction of a light-house.

The size of the rock, which was of tolerably hard gneiss, was about twenty-five by forty-five feet at low tide; the surface was

13

GENERAL VIEW OF THE BELL ROCK WORKS.

See page 38.

very unequal and divided by deep fissures, and, while almost perpendicular on the eastern side, there was a gradual slope on the western.

The following mode of construction was decided upon: To bore holes a foot deep, and three feet four inches apart, all over the site of the intended structure, with other holes outside this limit, for ring-bolts necessary to hold boats coming alongside. The first set of holes was to receive wrought-iron gudgeons, to fix the masonry to the rock and to make the construction itself serve to bind together the various parts and the fissures, and thus consolidate a base whose precarious nature gave rise to some misgivings. Other additional gudgeons were to be used as became necessary, and strong iron chains were to be introduced into the masonry as it progressed, so as to prevent any possible disjunction.

For the work of boring the holes the services of the fishermen of the Seine were called into requisition, as they were familiar with all the rocks of the reef, and were in a position to take advantage of every favorable moment. After many difficulties, they accepted a contract, the Government agreeing to furnish tools and life-belts.

In 1867 work was vigorously begun and every possible chance was seized. Two men from each boat landed on the rock, and, provided with their life-belts, lay down upon it. Holding on with one hand, they held the jumper or the hammer in the other, working with feverish activity, the waves constantly breaking over them.

One was carried off the rock, and the violence of the current bore him a long distance from the reef, against which he would have been dashed to pieces, but his life-belt kept him afloat and a boat went to fetch him back to work. There is no record as to whether he was docked for lost time.

During the building of Minot's Ledge light-house, near Boston, a similar accident happened, and though the man was saved he lost his tools. To prevent a recurrence of this disaster, he fastened the tools to his wrists with long cords. Another heavy wave washed him off, and he floated away as before, with the exception that this time his feet instead of his head appeared above water; however, he was rescued in time, but not in a condition to do any further work that day. It is unnecessary to add that he tied himself to his tools no more.

At the close of the season's work at Ar-men, seven landings had been made and eight hours' work accomplished, during which time fifteen holes had been bored in the higher parts of the rock.

The following year more difficulties were encountered, as it was necessary to commence on the part hardly above water; but the experience gained was valuable, and the fishermen were stimulated by higher wages. The season proved favorable. Sixteen landings were effected, giving eighteen hours of work, during which forty new holes were bored, and they even succeeded in partially levelling and preparing the rock for the first course of masonry.

The actual building of the masonry was not commenced until 1869. The galvanized wrought-iron gudgeons, forty inches long and two and four-tenths inches square, were fixed in the holes, and the masonry of small undressed stone was laid in Parker-Medina cement. A cement of the most rapidly hardening character was essential, for the work was carried on in the midst of waves breaking over the rock, and which sometimes wrenched from the hand of the workman the stone he was about to set. An experienced sailor, holding on to one of the iron stanchions, was always on the watch to give warning of such waves as were likely to sweep the rock, when the men would hold on, head to the sea, while the water washed over them. On the other hand, when he announced a probable calm, the work went on with great rapidity.

All the workmen were supplied with life-belts, as the fishermen had been, as well as with spike-soled shoes to prevent slipping. The foreman, also, and the engineer, who by their presence always encouraged the men, were similarly furnished.

When a landing was practicable, the stone and small bags of cement were landed by hand, and care was taken to dress the surface of the masonry before commencing a new course. The cement was used pure, and of necessity mixed with sea water. Since 1871,

Portland cement was substituted for Parker, the resistance of the former to the action of the water having been found superior to the latter, and the stonework at the foot of the tower was preserved by refilling the interstices with this material.

As the tower grew in height, the work naturally proceeded more rapidly, but it was not until 1881 that the structure was finally completed, and the light shown.

The light is of the first order, fixed white, with its focal plane ninety-six feet above the level of the sea. This limit might have been exceeded so as to make it of the usual height of a first-order tower, had it not been for the insufficiency of the base. The stability of the structure was necessarily of paramount importance. There are eight stories, one of which contains the fog signal. The various dimensions are shown in the drawing. It will be noticed that a similar arrangement of the staircase is used here as in the light-house of Heaux de Bréhat.

The work was conceived and planned by M. Léonce Reynaud, director of the light-house service. It was carried on under the greatest of difficulties, and too much praise cannot be given to the brave sailors and Breton workmen who insured the success of an enterprise bolder and more rash than any preceding undertaking of a similar nature.

CHAPTER V.

OTHER LIGHT-HOUSES WITH SUBMARINE FOUNDATIONS.

Another method for constructing a foundation under water was successfully practised during the building of the light-house at Haut Banc du Nord. This is a limestone plateau about two miles off the northeastern extremity of the Isle of Ré. It is nearly horizontal and about fifteen hundred feet long by five hundred broad. It is cut up by numerous channels of various depths, and is only uncovered at low spring tides, when the wind happens at the same time to be off shore. The rocky shoals surrounding it permit only crafts of small tonnage to approach, and at low tide the winding channels render this approach difficult even for the smallest boats. It was therefore necessary to anchor the transports at some distance from the rock, and to convey the material to it in barges — a difficult and risky business, even in a moderately rough sea.

To establish the foundation there was first constructed a large iron bottomless caisson, in the form of a twelve-sided prism, which was suitably braced on the inside. It was nearly forty-seven feet in diameter, four feet high, and weighed about five tons. Sustained by means of floats, it was towed into place at high tide by a small steamer and then grounded on the rock. After the tide had fallen sufficiently, and while it was not too rough, a movable flooring was placed on the upper frame of the interior bracing, and on it the workmen made the concrete for filling the caisson.

The lower part of the foundation was made of concrete poured through copper tubes one foot in diameter, and funnel-shaped at top.

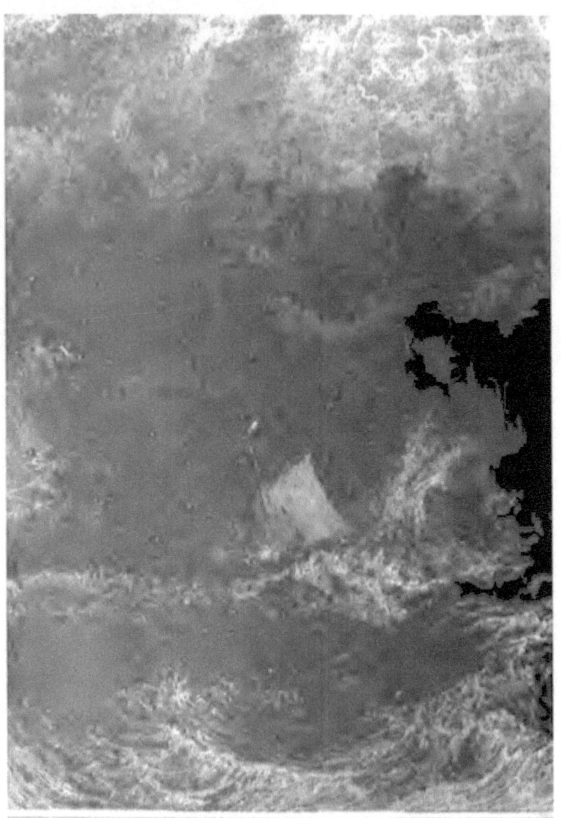

As soon as the water had fallen sufficiently to uncover the concrete, the remainder of the foundation was built of rubble masonry, which could be laid much more rapidly. The solid masonry then built was protected by a band of cut stone, which was placed after the tower was completed.

This work was commenced in 1849 and completed in 1853. The cut-stone protection, however, was not placed until some years later. Its cost was about $66,000.

It is a third-order light-house. The base is a solid mass of masonry. Above are the rooms communicating with each other and with the lantern by means of a series of small stairs. The size of the tower did not admit of a separate staircase, as in the preceding instances.

As reference has been made in the preceding pages to lights of various orders, it is proper to state, for the benefit of the lay reader, that light-houses are divided into various orders, from the first to the sixth, according to the lens apparatus for which they are designed; the first order being the most powerful and also necessitating the highest towers, so that the curvature of the earth will not cut off the light too soon; these are placed on outlying capes, rocks and headlands, to give warning of approach to the coast line. The range assigned to first-order lights varies from eighteen to twenty-seven nautical miles, according to their character.

Second and third order lights are employed to mark the secondary capes, islands, rocks, reefs and sand-bars embraced between the more prominent headlands, while lights of inferior order designate the entrances to harbors and channels, and vary in intensity according to the distance at which they should be seen. These are general principles, but geographical reasons prevent them from being applied rigorously.

LONGSHIPS AND WOLF ROCK.

In 1795 a light-house on Longships Rock and beacons on the Wolf and Rundlestone were erected in order to mark the dangers of the coast near Land's End, England. In 1841 a light-ship was moored in forty fathoms of water off the Sevenstones Rocks, midway between the Land's End and Scilly. These were all works of considerable difficulty.

The Longships' light-house is a granite structure, but as the light is only seventy-nine feet above high water of spring tides, the lantern, owing to the terrific seas, was so much under water during stormy weather, that it was difficult to determine the character of the light.

As it was not considered safe to raise the tower to a sufficient height to render the lantern safe from the heaviest seas, it was determined to replace it by a granite column one hundred and ten feet above the water. The work was commenced in 1869 and was completed, with the exception of setting the lens, in 1873.

There is an arrangement for marking the dangers of the Rundlestone Rocks to the southward and the Brissons Rocks to the northward, by sections of red light. As these rocks are well out from land they were great dangers to navigators.

The Rundlestone lies about four miles to the southeastward of Longships, and is three-quarters of a mile from shore. It measures about seventeen feet nine inches by eight feet nine inches at low water of spring tides, but the only available portion for a beacon is a place about four feet in diameter at a level of seven feet above low water of spring tides. The rock, composed of hard gray granite, forms part of a dangerous group of shoals, and is the only portion visible at low water.

The beacons mentioned as having been placed on the Rundlestone and Wolf rocks were wrought-iron poles about four inches in diameter, sunk into the rocks and held in their places with melted lead. That on the Wolf was twenty feet high and supported by six wrought-iron stays; the one on Rundlestone was shorter, as there was not room for the stays. Both were surmounted by spherical iron cages to make them distinguishable. Both were soon carried away by the sea.

Another beacon was placed on the Rundlestone with great difficulty and danger during the years 1841–43: it was twice carried away, and finally a bell-buoy of peculiar construction, designed by Sir James N. Douglas, was substituted.

Wolf Rock is composed of hard feldspathic porphyry; its highest part is seventeen feet above low water of spring tides, high tides rise two feet above it. The water is twenty fathoms deep on all sides, except on the southeast, where a shoal extends for a considerable distance.

It took from 1836 to 1840 to erect a beacon on this rock. During these five years the men were only able to work three hundred and eight hours, and the cost of the work was over $55,000. The mast, which was of selected English oak, one foot in diameter, was carried away as early as November of the last-mentioned year. It was decided to replace it with a wrought-iron one seven and five-eighths inches in diameter, but no opportunity occurred until August, 1842. The succeeding winter it was bent three feet from the perpendicular, and in 1844 was broken off. The next July a nine-inch mast was placed, and the globe reduced to a diameter of four feet. This stood until 1848. In 1850 another nine-inch mast was put in, the globe reduced to three feet, and an iron cone filled with concrete was built round it; this stood for thirty years, until taken down during the construction of the light-house.

From the preceding statements some idea can be obtained of the tremendous seas to which this rock is exposed.

The first survey for the purpose of determining the exact position of the proposed tower was made by James N. Douglas in 1861. He landed upon the rock and made the best use possible of the short time he could stay; but the sea, getting up meanwhile, put a stop to his work, and as a boat could not with safety approach the rock owing to the increased swell, he was hauled on board through the surf by a line fastened around his waist. This mode of taking the workmen from the rock, when caught by a sudden change of weather and increase of surf was frequently employed afterwards under similar circumstances.

In March, 1862, the working party was landed and commenced

work on the foundation pit. The insecurity of the foothold, and the constant breaking of the surf over the rock, rendered great precautions necessary for the safety of the men. Heavy iron stanchions were sunk into the rock around the site for the foundation, to which were attached safety-ropes within easy reach of the men. An experienced man was stationed on the summit to look out for the seas, and would give warning of such waves as would be likely to sweep the rock, when the men would hold on, head to the sea, while it washed over them. Picks, hammers, and jumpers, some exceeding twenty pounds in weight, were frequently carried away.

During the first year, 1862, only twenty-two landings had been effected and eighty-three hours of work obtained during the season, although not a single opportunity had been lost to work, even if only for half an hour. The work was confined to blasting and cutting out the foundation pit for the tower, and in the erection of the landing-platform.

By the end of the season of 1864, thirty-seven stones of the first entire course or second course of the tower were set, the landing-platform was nearly completed, and the landing-derrick or crane erected on the end of it.

This landing-platform was constructed on account of the great difficulty of landing upon the Wolf, which can only be effected on the northeast side, and even there the surface is rugged and without any vertical face for a boat to approach. As the material for this platform could only be landed from boats, small granite ashlar set in cement, similar to old English bond, was adopted, with the exception of some larger ashlar used for the steps and coping, and some rubble filling obtained from the foundation pit. The stones were each 24″ x 12″ x 6″ rough pick dressed and laid in fresh Medina Roman cement. Frequently tides which were not low enough to allow work on the foundation pit allowed the men to work at this platform, which greatly facilitated the erection of the light-house and proved of permanent value, from the convenience it affords for landing and embarking at times when it would be impossible without it.

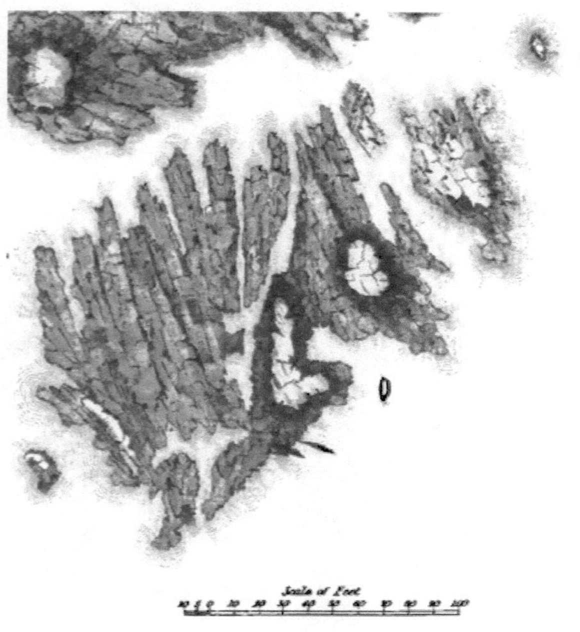
Scale of Feet
10 5 0 10 20 30 40 50 60 70 80 90 100

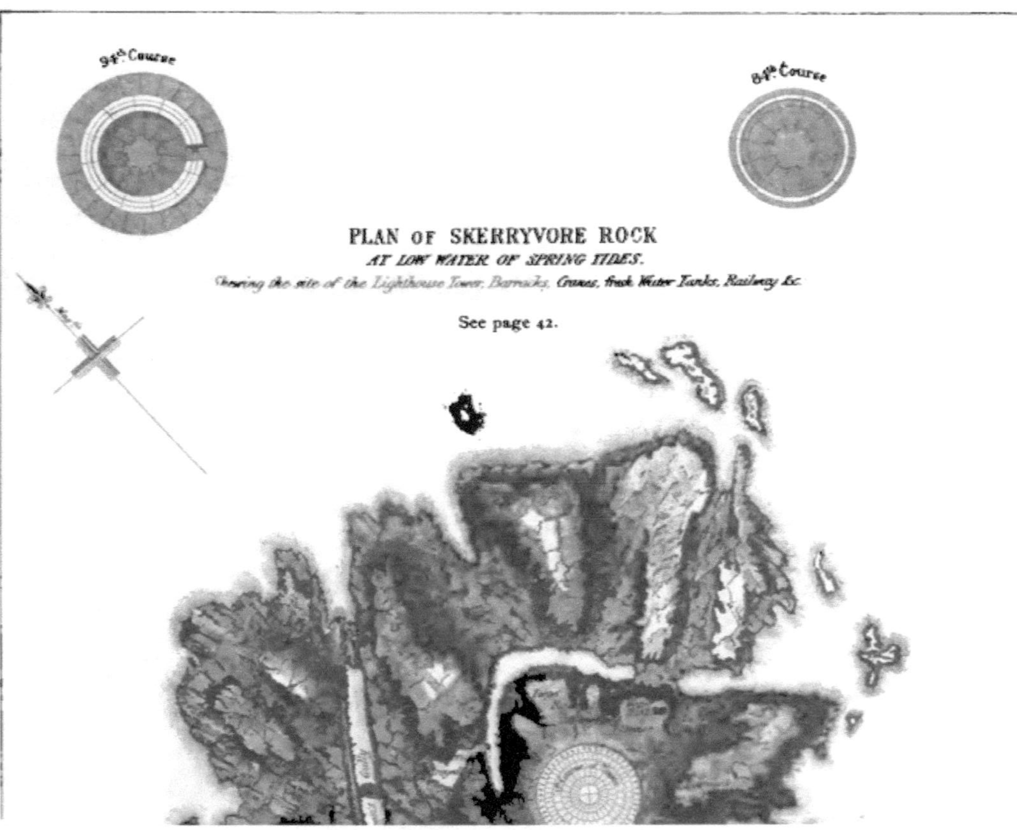
94th Course
84th Course
PLAN OF SKERRYVORE ROCK
AT LOW WATER OF SPRING TIDES.
Shewing the site of the Lighthouse Tower, Barracks, Cranes, fresh Water Tanks, Railway &c.

See page 42.

The accompanying plate shows the amount of work accomplished each working season up to 1868. The last stone was successfully laid in 1869. The general internal arrangements are shown on the section of the tower. The same plate shows the methods of dovetailing adopted.

The step-ladders for ascending from floor to floor, and the partitions between the rooms and staircases are of cast-iron, and the use of wood for fittings has been avoided as much as possible as a precaution against fire. The doors, windows and storm-shutters are constructed of gun-metal. The windows of the service-room are specially arranged for the air-supply of the lantern by means of valves which admit the air above the heads of the keepers, and upwards through an iron grating in the lantern floor.

The relative position of the mooring buoys, barges and landing-boat, when at work, are shown on the plan. S S are the stone barges, L the landing-barge, and M M the mooring buoys.

Each barge, when at the landing-crane, was moored, stem and stern, with ten-inch coir-hawsers, and the stern hawsers, which were the shorter, were frequently parted, notwithstanding their large size.

The barrack schooner, containing the resident engineer, his assistants, and the working party, was moored east-northeast from the rock, at a distance of three-fourths of a mile, and remained there as long as there was any opportunity of doing any work.

The landing-boat was built diagonally, of two five-eighths inch thicknesses of elm plank, without timbers or floors, and was provided with a landing-deck and mast forward. This deck and the gunwale were covered with rough rope matting, to afford a good foothold in jumping from or into the boat. Each workman was provided with a life-belt, which he was required to wear while landing on or embarking from the rock, and it was frequently necessary for the safety of the men that they should wear them while at work.

A similar landing-boat is still used. It is warped in by means of a line made fast to a buoy astern and two lines from the bow, the latter being managed by men on the rock. The person who is to land stands on the landing-deck forward, holding fast to the stout mast or stake, and when he is warned by the coxswain that the proper instant has arrived, he seizes the rope lowered from the derrick-boom on the landing-platform, places his foot in a loop at the end, and is quickly hauled up by the men at the winch on the rock.

When the keepers are relieved it is sometimes impracticable to drop them into the boat; in such cases they are hauled to it through the surf.

This light-house contains, exclusive of the platform, 44,506 cubic feet of granite, weighs 3,296 tons, and cost a little over $300,000. It is one of the most striking examples of light-house engineering of which the Eddystone furnishes the type. It was lighted for the first time on January 1, 1870.

The actual time snatched from the sea which the men could work is shown in the following table: —

Year.	No. of landings.	Hours of work.
1862	22	83
1863	30	206¼
1864	42	267
1865	41	256
1866	31	224
1867	40	313¼
1868	30	276¼
1869	21	194¼
Total	266	$1814\frac{1}{12}$

MAPLIN SAND LIGHT-HOUSE.

Mr. Alexander Mitchell, of England, invented the screw-pile for submerged sand-banks; it is described by him as a "project for obtaining a much greater holding power than was possessed by any pile or mooring then in use; the former being nothing more than a pointed stake of considerable size, easily either depressed in or extracted from the ground. . . . The plan which appeared best adapted for obtaining a firm hold of soft ground or sand was to insert, to a considerable distance beneath the surface, a bar of iron having at its lower extremity a broad plate or a disk of metal in a spiral or a helical form, on the principle of the screw, in order that it should enter into the ground with facility; thrusting aside any obstacles to its descent, without materially disturbing the texture of the strata it passed through, and that it should at the

same time offer an extended base, either for resisting downward pressure or an upward strain."

In 1838, the inventor and his son built for the corporation of the Trinity House the foundation of the light-house on Maplin Sand, at the mouth of the Thames. This was the first screw-pile light-house, so far as the foundation was concerned, although the one at Fleetwood was actually completed before the Maplin.

It is an hexagonal structure, with one central and eight exterior piles. The piles were driven vertically; but above the water-line they bend toward the centre, and incline in a pyramidal form to the lantern floor. The screws are four feet in diameter; the piles five inches, and they support cast-iron columns twelve inches in diameter, which are strongly braced.

The principle of the screw-pile has been very largely used in light-house construction in the United States: it is specially applicable to inland waters, not exposed to very heavy seas, where the bottom is such that a screw-pile can be forced through it. In places where there is much running ice, it has been found advisable to protect these structures against the impact of the ice, either by a wall of rip-rap, or by ice-breakers detached from the foundation.

TEMPORARY BARRACK.

SKERRYVORE LIGHT-HOUSE.

See page 45.

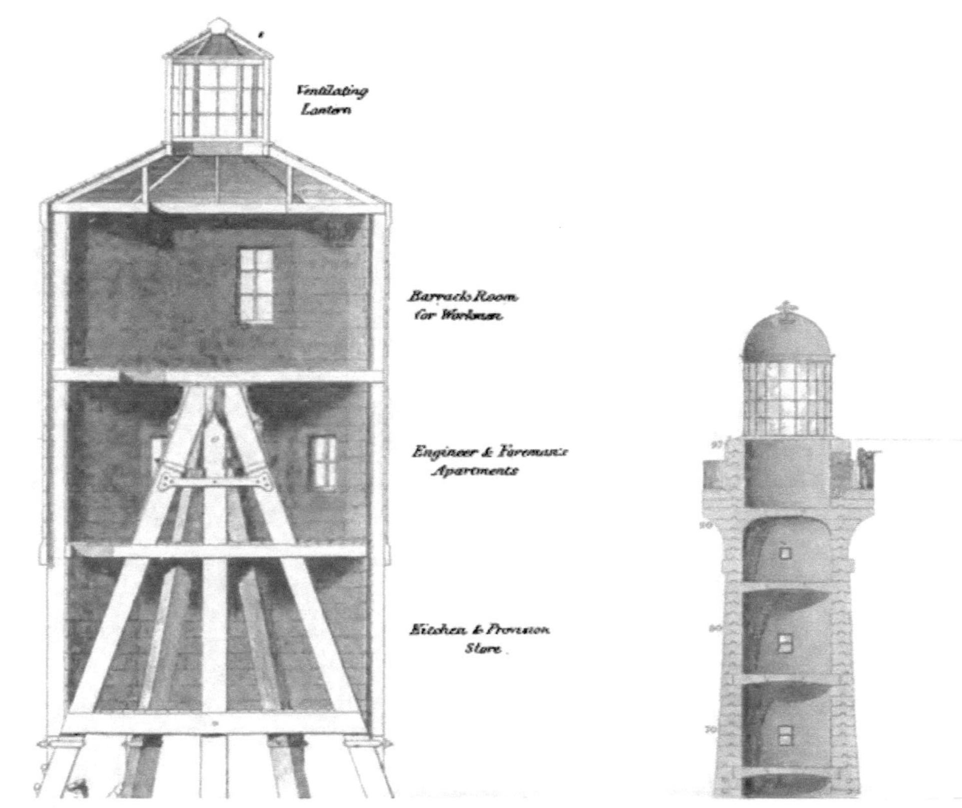
Ventilating Lantern
Barrack Room for Workmen
Engineer & Foreman's Apartments
Kitchen & Provision Store

CHAPTER VI.

MINOT'S LEDGE LIGHT-HOUSE.

Capt. W. H. Swift, U. S. Engineer's, strongly impressed by the successful application of Mitchell's mooring-screws to the forcing of iron posts into the sand as a framework to iron-skeleton light-houses, built the first work of the kind in the United States: an iron beacon at the entrance of Black Rock Harbor, Conn. He then designed and erected a more important structure. The following account is taken from his official report (November, 1848).

"Minot's Rocks — or as they are more generally called 'The Minots,' — lie off the south-eastern chop of Boston Bay. These rocks or ledges, with others in their immediate vicinity, are also known as the 'Cohasset Rocks,' and have been the terror of mariners for a long period of years; they have been, probably, the cause of a greater number of wrecks than any other ledges or reefs upon the coast, lying as they do at the very entrance to the second city of the United States in point of tonnage, and consequently where vessels are constantly passing and repassing. The Minots are bare only at three-quarters ebb, and vessels bound in with the wind heavy at north-east, are liable, if they fall to the leeward of Boston light, to be driven upon these reefs. The rock selected for the site of the light-house is called the 'Outer Minot,' and is the most seaward of the group. At extreme low water an area of about thirty feet in diameter is exposed, and the highest point in the rock is about three feet and a half above the line of low water. It is very rarely, however, that a surface greater than twenty-five feet in diameter is left bare by the sea. The rock is granite, with vertical seams of trap rising through it. The form of the light-house is an octagon, twenty-five feet in diameter at the base. The structure is supported on

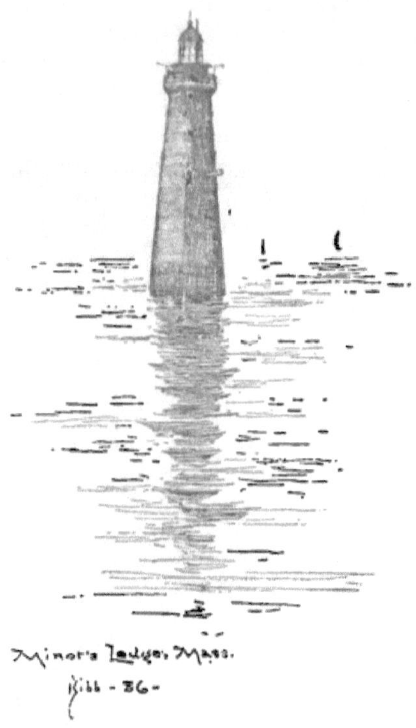

nine heavy wrought-iron piles, one at each corner of the octagon, and one at the centre; holes twelve inches in diameter, and five feet deep were drilled in the rock to receive these piles; the outer holes at such an inclination that at an elevation of sixty feet above the base of the middle pile, the pile-heads would be brought within the periphery of a circle fourteen feet in diameter. The centre pile was eight inches in diameter at the bottom, and six inches at top; the other piles have the same diameter, eight inches, at the bottom, and four-and-a-half inches at the top; at their upper ends they are securely keyed and bolted to the arms of a heavy casting or cap. It is understood that the foundation piles do not extend the whole sixty feet; but that there are in all three series of piles joined to each other by very stout cast-iron sockets and strongly braced."

In that exposed situation, where the sea was so constantly breaking over the rock, the drilling of holes of the required size could only be done by machinery raised above the reach of the sea. This operation consumed the greater part of two seasons. The erection of the tower was less difficult. The work commenced in 1847, was finished in November, 1848. Next year, in order to stiffen the piles, and to prevent in as great a degree as possible the tendency to vibration, there was introduced a series of wrought-iron vertical tie-rods between the first and second series of braces. It was intended to place another series of these ties between the foot of the piles at the rocks, and the first or lower series of horizontal braces. This structure was carried away in April, 1851. Captain Swift reported as follows: "On Monday night, April 14th, the wind, which had been easterly for several days, gradually increased. On Tuesday it had become a severe gale from the northeast. It continued to blow with the utmost violence through Tuesday night, Wednesday, Thursday, and even Friday; but the height of the storm was on Wednesday, the 16th, and at that time it was a perfect hurricane.

"The light on the Minot was last seen from Cohasset, on Wednesday night at 10 o'clock; at 1 o'clock, Thursday morning the 17th, the light-house bell was heard on shore, one-and-one-half miles distant; and this being the hour of high water, or rather the turn of the tide, when from the opposition of the wind and the tide it is supposed that the sea was at its very highest mark; and it was at that hour, it is generally believed, that the light-house was destroyed; at daylight nothing of it was visible from shore, and hence it is most probable it was overthrown at or about the hour named."

The appearance of the site when it was visited on April 22d, is

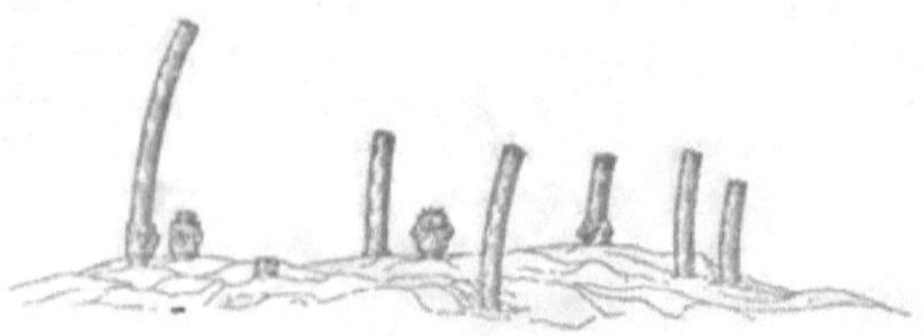

shown in the sketch. A portion of the wreck of the structure was found one hundred feet from the site.

The second series of horizontal braces was thirty-eight-and-a-half feet above the rock. Captain Swift says: "Upon these braces the keeper had improperly built a sort of deck or platform, upon which were placed heavy articles such as fuel, water-barrels, etc., which should have been in the store-room designed for their reception. The

deck, in addition to the weight placed upon it, was fastened together and secured to the piles and braces, thus offering a large surface, against which the sea could strike. In addition to this, the keeper had attached a five-and-a-half-inch hawser to the lantern deck, and anchored the other end to a granite block, weighing, according to his account, seven tons, placed upon the bottom at a distance of some fifty fathoms from the base of the tower. The object of this was to provide means for running a box or landing-chair up and down; but it is very clear that so much surface exposed to the moving sea had the same effect upon the light-house as would have been produced by a number of men pulling at a rope attached to the highest part of the structure, with the *design* of pulling it down. . . . At 4 o'clock on Wednesday afternoon, the 16th, or ten hours before the light fell, the platform above mentioned came ashore at Cohasset. As this was

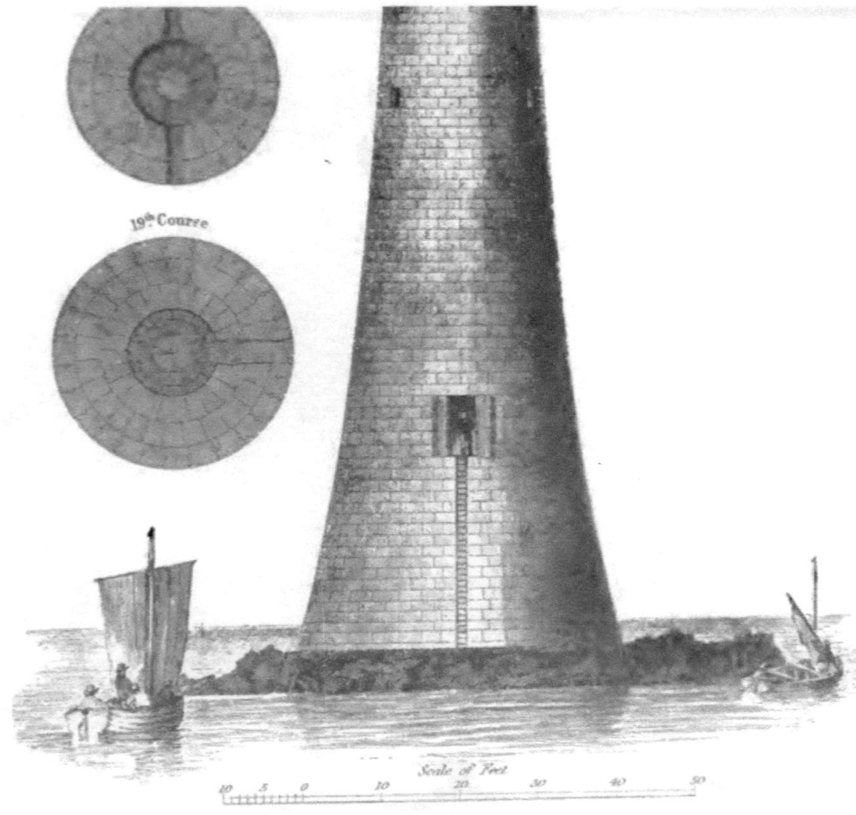

SKERRYVORE LIGHT. See page 47.

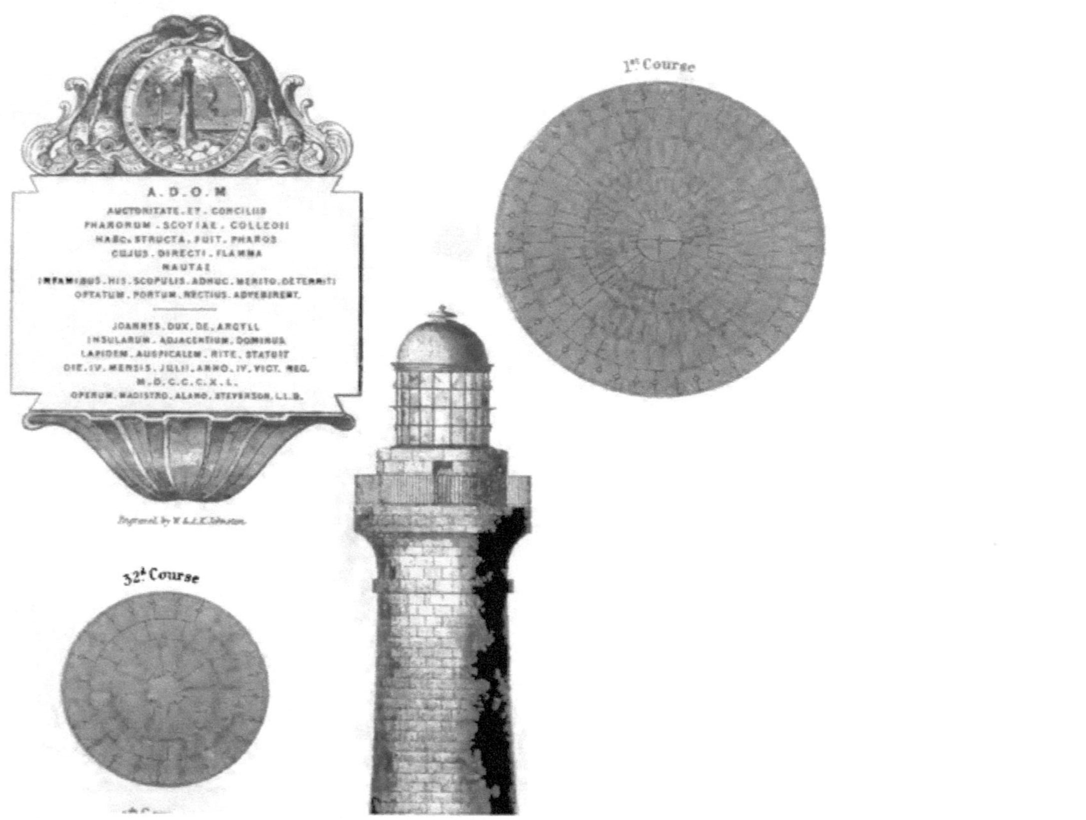

Engraved by W. & A. K. Johnston.

forty-three feet above the line of low water, and twenty-eight feet above high water, spring tides, the sea had at that time reached within seven feet of the base of the store-room of the light-house. Without undertaking to speculate upon the probable shock that the structure must have received from the effect of the sea upon a platform fastened to the piles forty feet above the rock, it is enough to know that the sea had reached within seven feet of the body or solid part of the structure. Still increasing, it required but a slight increase in the height of the wave, after having reached the deck, to bring it in contact with the main body of the structure. When this took place it is plain to perceive that such a sea, acting upon the surface of the building at the end of a lever fifty or sixty feet long, must be well nigh irresistible, and I doubt not that the light-house was thus destroyed."

Two light-keepers were at the tower, and were involved in its destruction. So far as I know their bodies were never recovered.

General J. G. Barnard, Corps of Engineers, in his comments on the destruction of this tower says: "In this isolated case of the destruction by wave-violence of a completed structure, there can be little doubt that the engineer's conclusions are correct. The 'main body' (*i. e.* the keeper's dwelling and store-rooms) should never be attainable by waves; all appurtenances, such as scaffoldings (which keepers are so apt to make) and attached hawsers, should be prohibited. A further remark should be made, for in judging of this work it must be borne in mind that it was built at a time when the large grants of money necessary for great engineering works of light-house construction were with difficulty attainable from Congress,[1] at a date, too, when the newly-invented method of skeleton-iron construction for light-houses was still in its infancy.

"The real defect of the Minot iron tower was want of magnitude. It should have had at least a forty-foot base, and a height of one hundred feet. The keeper's dwelling and storerooms could then

[1] The Minot's light-house cost less than $40,000.

have been placed beyond the reach of storm waves, the enlarged base affording requisite stability for the increased height. The limited sum at the disposal of the engineer forbade such dimensions. The difficulties of drilling the shaft-holes were, as we have seen, very great, even where the most available parts of the rock were chosen. The enlarged tower, which we *now* know to be necessary, would have cost three times the sum at the command of the engineer."

The importance and necessity to commerce and to life of a light at this point were so apparent that Congress promptly made an appropriation for the purposes of relighting the Minot's Ledge rocks, stipulating, however, that the tower should be erected on the outer Minot and charging the Topographical Bureau with its construction. This Bureau, after advertising for proposals, finally recommended, in view of the great difficulties in the way, and bearing in mind the awful fate of its predecessor, that one of the inner rocks should be selected as the site. While the matter was pending, the present Light-House Board was created (in 1852), and the whole subject was turned over to it.

General G. J. Totten, Chief of Engineers, then a member of the Board, devised the project for the new structure; he advocated and designed a light-house to be erected on the original site. The plans were drawn under his directions and he selected for its execution Captain (afterwards General) Barton S. Alexander, Corps of Engineers, an officer whose experience, skill, boldness and self-reliance eminently fitted him for this arduous task. Alexander thus described the difficulties of the work.

"It was a more difficult work of construction than either the Eddystone, the Bell Rock, or the Skerryvore, for the Eddystone was founded all above low water, part of its foundation being up to high-water level. The foundation of Bell Rock was about three feet above low water, while the Skerryvore had its foundation above high-water level; whereas a good part of the Minot's light was below low water. There had to be a combination of favorable circumstances to enable us to land on the Minot rock at the boginning of that work: *a perfectly smooth sea, a dead calm, and low spring tides.* This could only happen about six times during any one lunation; three at full moon and three at the change. Frequently, one or the other of the necessary conditions would fail; and there were at times months, even in summer, when we could not land there at all. Our working season was from April 1 to September 15. Work was prosecuted with all possible diligence for more than three years before a single stone could be laid. The difficulty was to cut the foundation rock into the proper shape, and then to lay these stones."

Major Ogden, under the orders of the Board, made a careful topographical survey of the rock, with the horizontal curves only three inches apart. The survey showed a plan of the rock at low water, with the curves where horizontal planes, passed three inches from each other vertically both above and below that level, would intersect the rock, these curves being projected on the rock. This survey showed that the highest point of the rock was three feet six inches above low water, and also that it would not be possible to obtain a tower of greater diameter than twenty-two feet without going outside the low-water limit, but by going outside this limit in five places, a diameter of thirty feet could be obtained.

On the first of May, 1855, Captain Alexander first visited Minot's Ledge; he found the stumps of the broken iron piles on the rock, and the wreck of the old light-house was visible under the water. It was difficult to stand on the rock, covered as it was with mussels and sea-weed; but he succeeded in remaining on it for about an hour, and in remeasuring it at dead low water, with the hope that he could get a few inches more than the thirty feet for the foundation; but in this he was disappointed.

Captain Alexander arrived at the following facts and conclusions: Landings, even in summer, could not be made for weeks at a time; parts of the ledge were always under water, and the remainder was only bare for three or four hours; the space was contracted, and during easterly weather the sea broke with such violence that no coffer-dam was possible. The cutting of the rock into shape would evidently be a long, tedious, troublesome and expensive operation, requiring incessant vigilance and the employment of a large party of skilled workmen with all the necessary tools and implements. To have engaged such a party and placed them on board vessels near the rock with instructions to work at every favorable opportunity would have been an easy matter; but the men would have been idle nine-tenths of the time. Their discipline would become lax; when wanted they would not be at their posts, and even if they had they could not have worked like men inured to daily labor. Their hands and muscles would soon have become soft, and they would shortly have been disqualified for the hard labor and exposure in store for them.

A better plan was, therefore, to combine the operation of cutting down the rock with that of preparing the stone for the tower, and to have both done by the same party of workmen, who would thus have constant employment and full wages. To do this an establishment on shore was necessary, with wharf accommodations, store-rooms, work-shops and a stone-yard. In addition there were required the necessary vessels and boats; a gang of stone-cutters could then work on the ledge when sea, weather and tide would permit, and when these would not they would find full employment on shore cutting stone for the tower. A permanent scaffold on the ledge, not a beacon-house, was considered essential. This was to be a structure of iron, to which the workmen could be secured to prevent their being washed from the rock, and would afford temporary security in case of accident to boats or vessels. It would also answer the purpose of a derrick for laying the lower courses of masonry in the tower, and its legs, being enclosed in the masonry, would be so many huge bolts to secure it to the rock. These ideas were embodied in a report to the Board dated May 31, 1855, and were approved.

On the 20th of June a few men were employed to loosen the wedges around the stumps of the old iron piles, and to remove the mussels from the ledge, which was accomplished in a few days.

The first landing for cutting down the rock was made at daylight

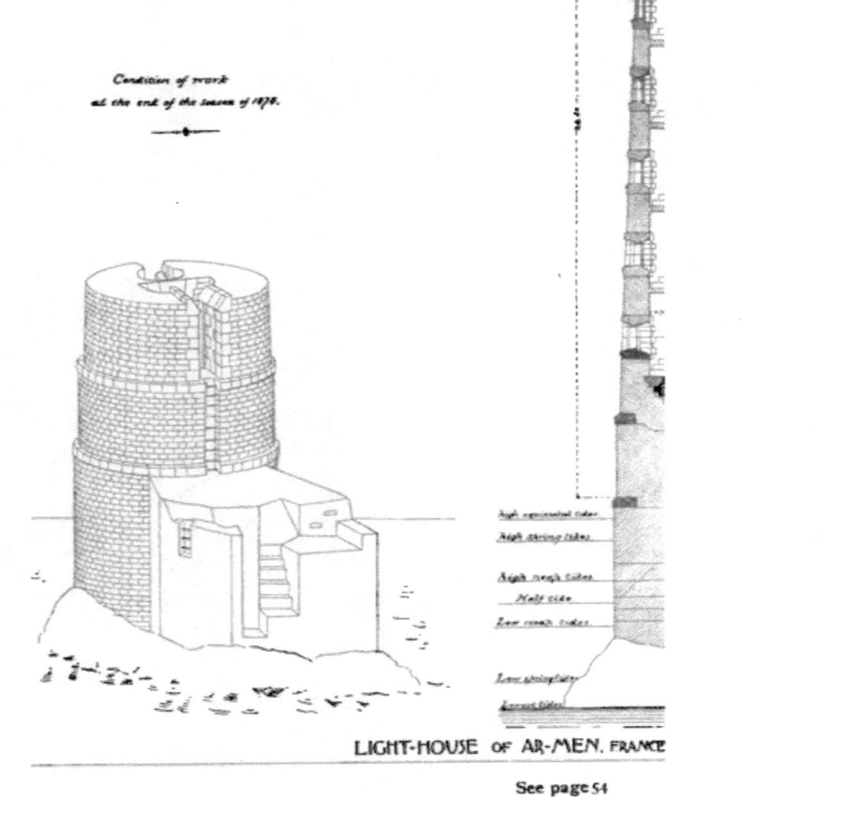

LIGHT-HOUSE OF AR-MEN, FRANCE

See page 54

LIGHT-HOUSE OF HEAUX DE BRÉHAT, FRANCE.

See page 49

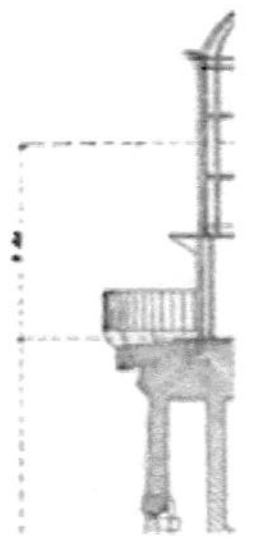

on Sunday, July 1, 1855. But a small party of men were employed, and the first season's work was confined to marking points of the various levels which were to be cut away, to cutting level spaces around the rock upon which the workmen could stand and upon which tools could be placed in comparative safety, and in general to laying out work for a larger party the next year.

During the year 1855 there were one hundred and thirty hours' work on the rock. During the season of 1856 the iron scaffold previously mentioned was erected. It consisted of nine wrought-iron shafts inserted into the holes of the old iron light-house, and rising to a height of twenty feet above low water, the whole bound together at the top by a strong wrought-iron frame; these shafts were ten inches in diameter at the bottom and seven inches at the top. It gave great confidence to new hands. By stretching lines between the posts across the rock in various directions, and about two or three feet above it, every workman had something within easy reach to lay hold of when a wave broke over the rock.

This year and nearly the whole of the next was consumed in cutting the rock to receive the masonry: the foundation pit was nearly completed, and in 1857 four stones of the foundation were laid. On the nineteenth of January, 1857, the bark "*New Empire*," loaded with cotton, was thrown against the scaffold and swept it from the rock, breaking off the iron posts very much as those of the iron light-house had broken when it was carried away, and shattering the top of the rock in some places so that a portion of the work of the preceding year had to be done over again; in 1856 and '57 the work on the rock was one hundred and fifty-seven and one hundred and thirty hours respectively.

Although a permanent coffer-dam about this rock was impracticable, temporary coffer-dams around small portions of the rock were of great use, both in completing the foundation-pit and in laying the lower stones of the structure. These coffer-dams were made of sand-bags similar to those used in building sand-bag batteries. The bags were about half filled with sand and, being made of heavy cotton duck, were practically water-tight. They were easily handled. Two or three hundred of these bags built up, at low water, around the small portion of the foundation-pit which it was desired to finish, or where a stone was to be laid in mortar, would keep out the water for fully half an hour if the sea was very smooth; the water in the little pits thus made was then bailed out and by means of large sponges was kept nearly dry. These dams required but a few moments in construction, and, as they were easily removed, they were inexpensive. They enabled the engineers to see that the work was properly done, that the foundation was properly completed, that the wooden patterns for the lower stones were correct, and that the lower stones were laid in a bed of mortar properly spread on its foundation.

Nearly all the stones were thus laid. The lowest stone, laid July 11, 1858, and some others, had to be laid in water. The method for securing a bed of mortar under these stones was as follows: A large piece of thin muslin was spread on the platform and a layer of mortar of the required thickness was then spread over it; the stone was then laid on this bed of mortar, the vertical joints of the stone were then plastered with mortar and the cloth was folded up and laid smooth against these vertical joints, cutting away its superfluous parts. After remaining five or ten minutes the mortar would begin to set so that it and the cloth would adhere to the stone. The stone was then laid in its envelope which protected the mortar from the dissolving action of the water, while it was being lowered into position.

Previous experiments on shore on stone cemented together in this way under water, showed that the mortar would ooze through the cloth and make a good bond to the stone below.

All the lower courses of stone were laid from an iron mast which was set up in the central hole of the former light-house. The machinery and rigging which completed the derrick had to be put on and taken off every day that landings were made for laying masonry. It was of simple construction and so arranged as to float in the water, so that all that had to be done in "stripping the derrick" after a tide's work was over, was to cast the machinery loose from the mast and throw it, with the attached rigging, overboard; it could then be towed to the tender.

The mortar used throughout the work was the best quality of pure Portland cement; no lime nor sand was used.

The sketches show how the stone was landed on the rock at different stages of the work.

During 1858 the foundation-pit was finished and the masonry carried up to the sixth course inclusive; this took two hundred and

eight working-hours. In 1859 the tower was finished to the top of the thirty-second course, sixty-two feet above low water, in three hundred and seventy-seven working-hours; and in 1860 the tower was completed, the last stone being laid on the twenty-ninth of June, just five years, lacking one day, from the time the workmen landed on the ledge.

No life was lost nor was any one seriously injured during the building of the light-house.

The following were the principal regulations for the safety of the workmen while cutting-down the ledge and laying the masonry of the foundation :

1. No person should be employed on the work who could not swim, or who could not pull an oar and manage a small boat.

2. No landing should be attempted on the rock from one boat; there must always be, at least, two boats.

3. While the workmen were on the ledge, a small boat, with at least three men in it, should be stationed immediately alongside the

rock, on its lee side, to pick up the men who were occasionally washed from the rock.

After the destruction of the scaffold which had been erected on the ledge, a new one was prepared similar to the first, but it was never erected as a scaffold. The eight outer posts, however, were inserted in the eight outer holes of the former light-house, after the masonry of the tower had been carried up to the tenth course, the spaces around the posts being filled with a grout of Portland cement. They are supposed to give additional strength to the tower, holding it more securely to its rock foundation.

The light was exhibited for the first time at sunset, November 15, 1860. The cost of the light-house and of the keeper's dwellings on shore, was $300,000.

The structure is solid, around a central well up to the level of the entrance door. Above that there is a hollow cylindrical space, fourteen feet in diameter, arched over at the level of the cornice; this space is divided into five stories by four iron floors; these five compartments and a sixth immediately under the lantern constitute the keeper's rooms, store-rooms, etc.

The shaft is purely conical, the limited bottom area forbidding the expansion required for the tree-like spread to the base, usual in European sea-rock light-houses, which is now believed to be a useless expense and founded on a false analogy.

The following tables may be useful for reference:

Year.	Working-hours.
1855. Excavating foundation-pit,	130
1856. " " "	157
1857. " " " and laying 4 stones,	130.21 m.
1858. " " " and laying 6 courses,	208
1859. Laying 26 courses,	377

Number of tons rough stone,	3514
" hammered stone,	2367
Number of stones in light-house,	1079

Height from bottom of lowest stone to top of pinnacle,	114 ft. 1 in.
Height of focal plane above lowest point,	96 ft. 1 in.
" " " " mean high water,	84 ft. 7 in.
Diameter of third, or first full course,	30 ft.
" top of 22d course (solid part),	23 ft. 6 in.

(See Appendix A.)

CHAPTER VII.

SPECTACLE REEF LIGHT-HOUSE.

There is but one other light-house in the United States of the same type as Minot's. This one is situated on Spectacle Reef, Lake Huron, and is not properly a *sea*-rock light-house, as the destructive agencies to which it is exposed are not sea-waves, but chiefly ice-packs.

It stands on a reef at the northern end of Lake Huron, off the eastern end of the Straits of Mackinac. There are two shoals of limestone rock *in situ*, covered with boulders so situated with respect to each other as to resemble a pair of spectacles. The light-house stands on the southerly end of the most northerly shoal.

In 1868 the Light-house Board recommended an appropriation to erect this light, estimating the cost to be about $300,000. The wreck of two vessels at one time, the preceding fall, gave emphasis to its necessity, as these wrecks involved the loss of a sum greater than that necessary to mark this danger. An appropriation of $100,000 was granted to commence the work, and next year an additional sum of $100,000 was appropriated.

An examination of the site showed that the least depth of water on the shoals was about seven feet, and at the locality selected for the light-house, rock was found at a depth of eleven feet.

The nearest land is Bois Blanc Island, about eleven miles distant. A depot for this work was established at Scammon's Harbor, in Les Cheneaux, sixteen miles from the site.

The greatest exposure to waves is from the southeast, the sea having a fetch of about one hundred and seventy miles. Their force, however, is not so great as to require any great precautions to insure stability. But at times currents are developed here having a velocity of from two to three miles per hour, and during the winter season serve to move to and fro ice-fields two feet thick and thousands of acres in extent. This ice, formed in fresh water, is of extreme solidity, and when in motion has a living force which is almost irresistible. The object was, therefore, to oppose to it a structure against which the ice would first be crushed, and then its motion so impeded as to cause it to ground upon the shoal itself, thus forming a barrier against subsequent action.

To give some idea of the necessity for this, it may be mentioned that in the spring of 1875, when the keepers returned to the station, the light being discontinued during the winter months, they found the ice piled up against the light-house, seven feet above the sill of the door-way, which is twenty-three feet above the lake, and they were only able to obtain entrance to the house by cutting their way through the ice.

The plan contemplated building first a crib-work or "protection pier," with a large central opening, in which was to be placed a coffer-dam. The water was then to be pumped from the coffer-dam, the rock levelled, to prepare it for the foundation of the light-house, and then the light-house was to be built of stone, carefully cut and strongly fastened together.

The protection pier was built at Scammon's Harbor during 1870–71. In the former year a careful survey was again made at the site, when it was discovered that the hull of the schooner *Nightingale*, wrecked the preceding fall, covered, with her cargo of iron ore, a good portion of the bed of rock on which the tower was to stand. As there was no other place on the reef where bare bed-rock could be found, except in eighteen feet of water, it was necessary to remove that portion of the wreck covering the area required for the coffer-dam.

It was intended to build the light-house of granite, but the contractor utterly failed to furnish this stone. Limestone from Marblehead, Ohio, was therefore purchased in sufficient quantity to continue the work. The coffer-dam was framed at Detroit, Mich., during the winter, and was taken to Scammon's Harbor on the opening of navigation of 1871, to be in readiness for use as soon as the crib should be placed in position.

The original intention was to put this crib in position in four sections, but upon further consideration it was decided to attempt placing it as a whole upon the reef. This was successfully accomplished as follows: four temporary cribs, each fifteen by twenty-five feet, of round timber, were placed in from eight to ten feet of water, in a line corresponding with the proposed eastern face of the pier of protection, and filled to the level of the water with ballast-stone. They were then connected together and decked over. On this deck were placed about seventy cords of ballast-stone, ready at the proper time to be thrown into the pier of protection. The two lower courses of this pier, fastened together with screw-bolts, forming a raft, were towed to the site and moored directly over the position to be occupied by the finished pier. Its position was marked upon the temporary pier mentioned above, and soundings taken at intervals of two feet along each timber in the raft, thus obtaining accurate contours of the surface of the reef within the limit of those timbers. The raft was then towed back to the harbor, hauled out upon ways, and by means of wedges of timber the bottom was made to conform to the surface of the reef. The raft, now become the bottom of the pier of protection, was then launched and additional courses of timber added, until its draught of water was just sufficient to permit its being floated into position on the reef.

Meanwhile five barges at the harbor had been loaded with ballast-stone, making, with that at the temporary pier, 290 cords (about 1800 tons) at command, with which to load the pier of protection and secure it to the reef, as soon as it should be placed in position.

This crib was ninety-two feet square, and between eleven and twelve feet high, with a central opening forty-eight feet square. It thus occupied a space nearly a quarter of an acre in extent.

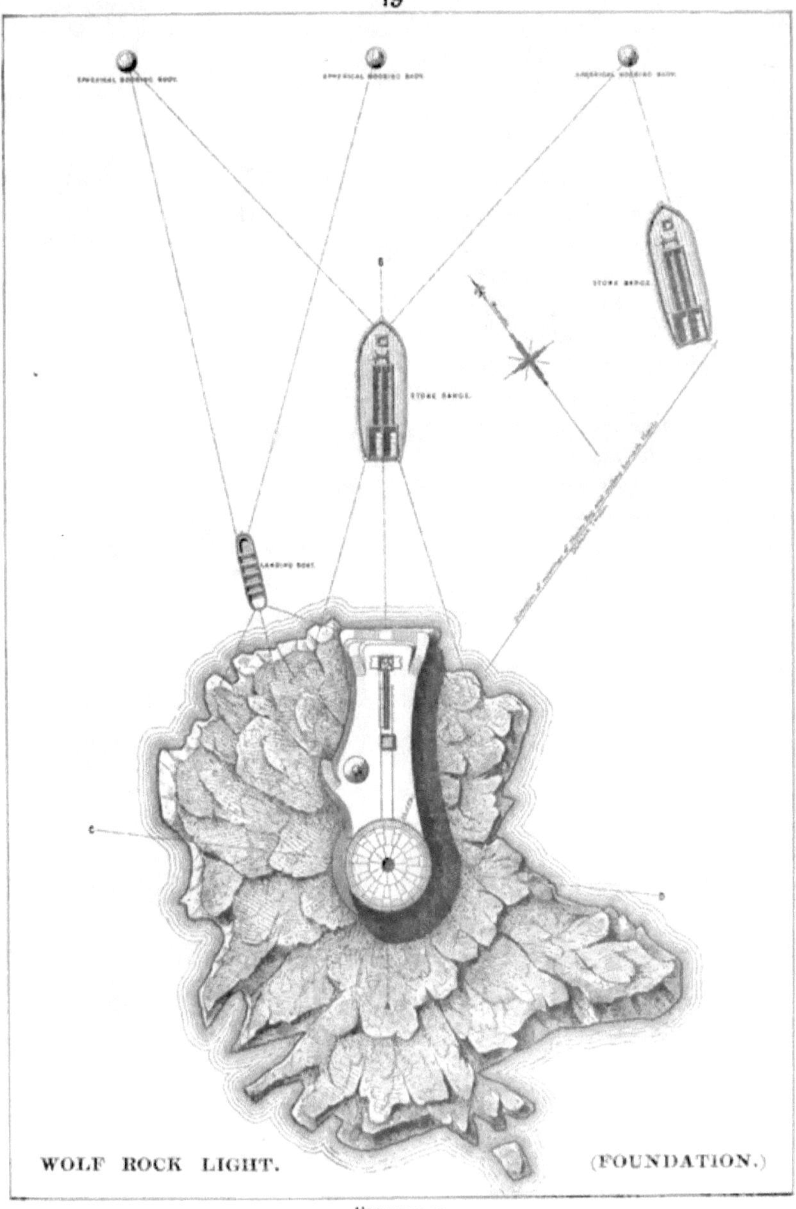

WOLF ROCK LIGHT. (FOUNDATION.)

See page 59

On the evening of the 18th July, 1871, everything being in readiness, and the wind, which had previously been blowing freshly from the north-west for three days, having somewhat moderated, at 8 P. M. two tugs took hold of the immense crib, and started to tow it to the reef, fifteen miles distant, followed by the fleet of stone barges. The construction-scow, with tools, etc., on board, was towed with the crib. At 2 A. M., next day, the fleet hove-to off the reef, awaiting daylight, and the abatement of the wind, which had again freshened up. At half-past six, it having moderated, the pier was placed in position, with considerable difficulty, and after being secured to the temporary pier, and to moorings previously set for it, all hands went to work, and by 4 P. M. had succeeded in throwing 1200 tons of stone into the compartments.

By this time the wind had so increased that the rising sea made it necessary to stop work, but early next morning the rest of the reserve stone was put into the compartments.

After the pier was in position, a schooner was moored on the reef, to serve as temporary quarters for the workmen, who proceeded at once to build up the pier to the required height, twelve feet above water. More stone was brought, and by the 12th of September the pier reached its full height, and, by the 20th, quarters for the workmen were built upon it, when the schooner was discharged. A diver was then employed to clear off the bed-rock within the opening of the pier, and the coffer-dam was commenced.

This coffer-dam consisted of a hollow cylinder, forty-one feet in diameter, composed of wooden staves, each four by six inches, and fifteen feet long; it was braced and trussed internally, and hooped with iron externally to give it the requisite strength. It was put together at the surface of the water, and, when complete, was lowered to its position by means of iron screws.

As soon as it rested on the rock, whose contour was quite irregular, each stave was driven down to fit as closely as possible, and a diver then filled with Portland cement all the openings between its lower end and the rock. A loosely-twisted rope of oakum was then pressed closely down outside the lower end of the coffer-dam, and outside this a larger rope made of hay.

The pumping-machinery having been got ready in the meanwhile, the coffer-dam was pumped dry, and on the same day, October 14, a force of stone-cutters descended to the bottom and commenced the work of levelling-off the bed-rock so as to prepare it for the first course of masonry.

The rock sloped from the west to the east, and, in order to make a level bed, it was necessary to cut down about two feet on the highest side, involving a large amount of hard labor, and rendered still more difficult by the water forcing its way up through the seams in the rock. This work was finally accomplished, as much care being taken to cut and level the bed as with any of the masonry courses. The first course of masonry was set and completed October 27. The water forcing its way through the seams gave much trouble as it disturbed the mortar; for this reason water was let into the dam every evening and pumped out in the morning, to give the mortar time to harden during the night. The mortar was composed of equal parts of Portland cement and screened silicious sand, and became as hard, or harder, than the bed-rock or the stone of which the tower was built.

As the weather now became boisterous, frequent snow-squalls interfering with the work, it was determined to close operations for the season, so everything was put in safety for the winter, and by the end of October all the men had left the rock except two, who were left to tend the fog-signal and the fourth-order light, which had been erected on the men's quarters; they were taken off at the close of navigation.

The degree of success of this model coffer-dam may be inferred from the fact that, though provided with pumps having an aggregate capacity of 5,000 gallons per minute, not more than a capacity of 700 gallons was used, except when emptying the coffer-dam, and then only to expedite the work; once emptied, a small proportion of this capacity was ample to keep the coffer-dam free from water, and this at a depth of twelve feet of water, on rock, at a distance of eleven miles from the nearest land. Every one connected with this work may well feel a just pride in its success.

The following season opened a month later, so work was not resumed at the harbor until the 3d of May, 1872, and upon the reef on the 20th of the same month. On May 13 the ice was a compact mass of some feet in thickness, and masses of ice lay on top of the pier itself. As soon as possible the ice was cleared away, and the work of setting the additional courses began.

By the close of the season the work had been carried to the seventeenth course inclusive, completing the solid portion of the tower. In September there was a violent storm, and the following account will give some idea of its violence and the damage done:

"The sea burst in the doors and windows of the workmen's quarters, tore up the floors and all the bunks on the side nearest the edge of the pier and the platform between the quarters and the pier. Everything in the quarters was completely demolished except the kitchen, which remained serviceable. The lens, located on top of the quarters was found intact, but out of level. Several timbers on the east side of the crib were driven in some four inches, and the temporary cribs were completely swept away. The north side was so completely filled up that the steamer can no longer lie there. A stone weighing thirty pounds was thrown across the pier; but the greatest feat accomplished by the gale was the moving of the revolving derrick from the northeast to the southwest corner. At three o'clock in the morning the men were obliged to run for their lives, and the only shelter they found was on the west side of the tower. The sea finally moderated sufficiently to allow them to seek refuge in the small cement shanty standing near the southeast corner of the crib. Many lost their clothing."

During the following winter the workmen's quarters, from which the light had been exhibited, was carried away by the ice, and together with the lantern was totally destroyed. This was not unexpected, and in view of the probable result, the lens had been re moved and stored in a place of safety. The fog-signal was uninjured and was sounded whenever required. Work was continued during the working-seasons of 1873-4, and the light was exhibited for the first time on the night of June 1, 1874.

The exterior of the tower is a frustum of a cone, thirty-two feet in diameter at the base and eighteen feet at the spring of the cornice, eighty feet above the base. The cornice is six feet high and the parapet seven feet. The focal plane is four feet three inches above the parapet. Hence the entire height of the masonry above the base is ninety-three feet, and of the focal plane ninety-seven feet three inches.

The tower is solid to a height of thirty-four feet; above this it is hollow, and divided into five stories, each fourteen feet in diameter. The walls of the hollow portion start with a thickness of five feet six and three-tenths inches, and are eighteen inches thick at the spring of the cornice. The whole interior is lined with a brick wall four inches thick, separated from the outer wall by an air-space of two inches. All stones below the cornice have a uniform thickness of two feet. All sashes, shutters, and doors are made to open outward, which admits of such an arrangement of the rabbets as to effectually prevent the entrance of water at the window and door openings.

The stones in the solid portion are cut to form, in the simplest manner, a most complete lock upon each other in each course, and the several courses are bolted to each other with wrought-iron bolts two and one-half inches in diameter and two feet long. The lower course is bolted to the rock with bolts three feet in length, which penetrate the rock to a depth of twenty-one inches. All the bolts are wedged at each end with conical wedges, and all bolt-holes are filled solidly with pure Portland-cement mortar.

Above the solid portion no bolts are used except in the first course, but on the build of each course a ribbon has been cut, fitting into a corresponding recess in the course above.

The reader will notice the similiarity of the "bond" in this tower to that used at Minot's Ledge.

Deducting the time while work was suspended for the winter, and that consumed in giving notice to mariners, the aggregate working-time was twenty-four months, but as at least two week's time was lost at the beginning and end of each season getting ready for and in securing the work, the actual available time did not exceed twenty months.

The total cost, including the steamer and appliances of every kind was, in round numbers $375,000.

The crib and coffer-dam were designed by Col. and Bvt. Brig.-Genl. W. F. Raynolds, and the tower by Lt. Col. and Bvt. Brig.-Genl. O. M. Poe, both of the Corps of Engineers of the United States Army. The latter officer had charge of the difficult part of the work until the foundation was brought above water. The tower was completed by Maj. and Bvt.-Brig.-Gen. Godfrey Weitzel, Corps of Engineers, since deceased. Any account of Spectacle Reef Light-House should give much credit to Mr. Anthony L. Ederle who was the Superintendent of Construction from the beginning until the completion of all work of any difficulty.

The construction-pier, which has been repaired from time to time, is still standing, and is most useful as a landing-place and a site for the steam fog-whistles.

Of late years, however, it has become much deteriorated and is beyond economical repair; next summer the Light-house Board will probably build an iron caisson filled with concrete adjacent to the tower, to form a foundation for the fog-signal apparatus, after which it will be a matter of little moment whether the construction-pier is destroyed or not.

The sea-rock light-houses of the world are few in number; the following is a list of all, including those already described: Eddystone; Bell Rock; Bishop Rock (1853), off the Scilly Islands; the Small's Rocks, entrance to the British Channel; Hanois Rocks (1862), Island of Alderney; Bargus d'Olonne (1861), west coast of France; Wolf Rock (1869), off Land's End, England; Alguada

Reef (1865), Bay of Bengal; Great and Little Basses Light, off the coast of Ceylon; Minot's Ledge, Boston, and Spectacle Reef, Lake Huron.

The examples selected show sufficiently well the various difficulties and dangers attending this class of work, and how they were over-

come in each case; so it is not considered necessary to give detailed descriptions of every work of this kind.

Though the above are all the sea-rock light-houses properly so called, there are many light-houses in this and other countries which are built upon isolated rocks in the sea, yet these rocks are sufficiently above the surface of the sea, to afford a moderately safe base of operations when a landing has once been effected upon them. Among these latter may be mentioned John of Unst's House, or "North Unst." The erection of this tower, finished in 1854, though not offering difficulties comparable to those at the sea-rock light-houses described, yet was a work of much interest. As shown in the sketch it is rooted upon an isolated rock, near the Shetland Islands, called Muckle Flagga; the tower is sixty-four feet high, and the light is two hundred and thirty feet above high water, and can be seen twenty-one miles away.

The north face which is perpendicular, is exposed to the full fury of the ocean; while the south face, though less abrupt, is extremely difficult of ascent; the summit is just large enough for the foundations of the tower which contains the lantern-room, bed-room, kitchen and office. At its base is the store-room for oil, coal and water.

Landings are only possible in fine weather. There are four keepers, those not on duty live on the Island of Unst, about four miles from the light.

CHAPTER VIII.

TILLAMOOK ROCK.

On June 20, 1878, Congress appropriated $50,000 for building a light-house on Tillamook Head, and on June 16, 1880, appropriated $5,000 more for continuing the work. On March 3, 1881, there was appropriated $25,000 for completing the work *on the rock of Tillamook.* There were many reasons for this change: the Head is inaccessible by sea, so that a road about twenty miles long would have to be built and maintained through an unknown and difficult country; the crest is too high above the sea for a light to be visible during foggy weather; and there is no natural bench or lower level where the light could be placed, which would not be endangered by land-slides.

Maj. G. L. Gillespie, Corps of Engineers, U. S. A., Brevet Lieut. Col., was then in charge of this work, and in June, 1879, he made an inspection of the rock from the deck of a light-house tender, the sea being too rough to permit a landing; he reported as follows to the Light-House Board:

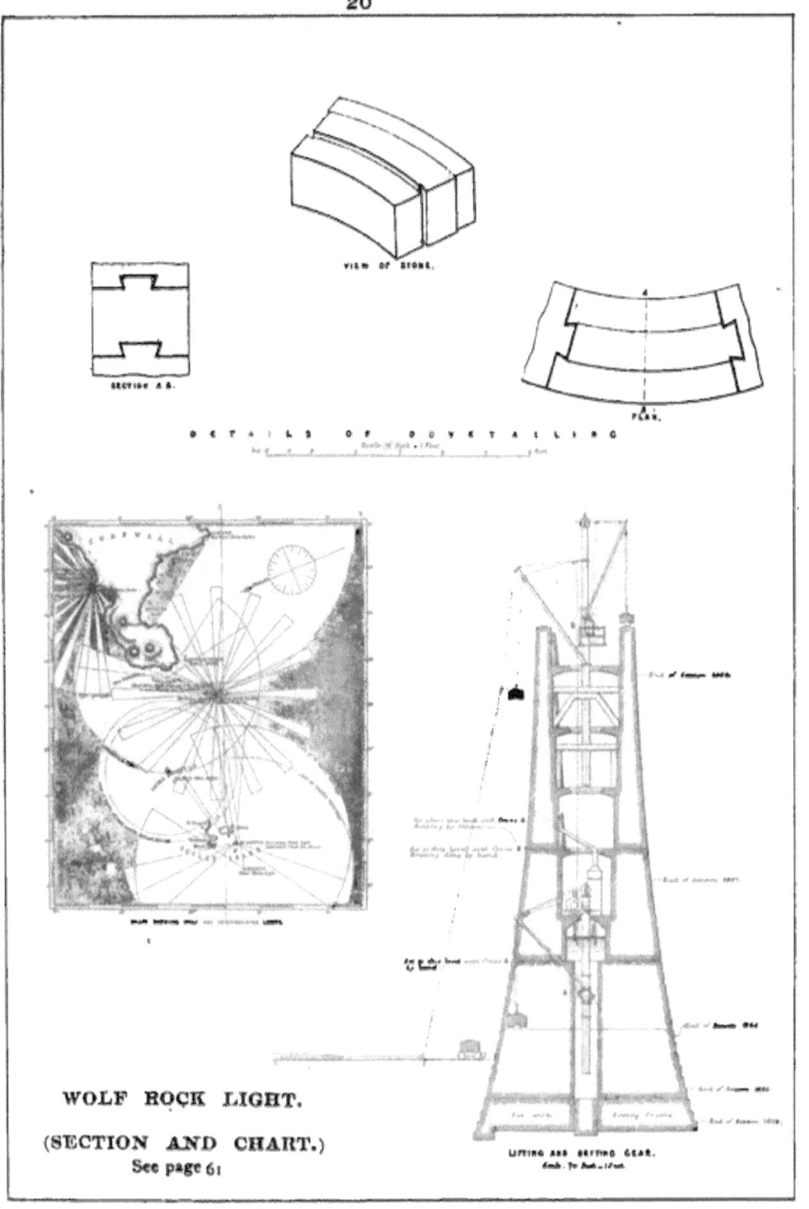

WOLF ROCK LIGHT.

(SECTION AND CHART.)

See page 61

"I was enabled, however, to approach sufficiently near to become convinced that the rock is large enough, and the only suitable place for the light. To be efficient, the light should be exhibited as low as it is safe to have it; the headland is entirely too high, even on the lowest bench, and if located ashore, a costly road must be built. Though I could not make a landing, I am of the opinion that it is practicable to use the rock for a light station, and am desirous of being allowed to make the attempt."

As will be seen farther on, the great difficulty was in effecting a landing on this rock, around which the sea is almost constantly boiling and surging even in moderate weather.

In June, 1879, Mr. H. S. Wheeler, superintendent of construction, went to the rock, and succeeded in landing two men, but they were unable to do anything, as the sea commenced to rise, so fearing that they would be separated from their companions, they jumped into the sea, and were rescued by life-lines. On the 25th of the same month, Mr. Wheeler made another attempt which was more successful, as he succeeded in landing in person, and by means of a tape-line, taking measurements of the most important dimensions.

The plan for the buildings and the course to be pursued in adapting them to the rock was, in general, the occupancy of the rock by a small working force, well supplied with provisions and tools for a stay of four or five months, with instructions to first prepare quarters for themselves, and then to reduce the summit of the rock by blasting until a level was reached, above the destructive action of the sea, sufficiently large to contain all the necessary buildings.

While this work was going on, it was proposed that all the various appliances, such as derricks, engines, etc., should be got ready and sent to the rock as rapidly as possible, and that all the stone should be quarried, dressed to dimension, and shipped to Astoria ready for use, together with all other needed material, such as cement, sand, brick, etc.

Before any work was definitely ordered to be begun, it was necessary that the rock should be carefully surveyed by a competent person, so that the proper places for the quarters, derricks and engines could be selected, the size of the force be determined, and other useful data collected.

Mr. John R. Trewavas, a master-mason of Portland, Oregon, was selected for this work. He had at one time been employed upon the construction of Wolf Rock, England, and was a most capable man. He attempted to land on the 18th of September, and he, with a sailor named Cherry, had succeeded in reaching the eastern slope of the rock; as Trewavas stepped on the wet slope he slipped and fell and was almost instantly swept off by a receding wave. The sailor jumped into the sea and made a gallant attempt to rescue him, and the boat's crew, with life-lines, rowed quickly to the spot where he was struggling, but the poor fellow was drawn under by the undertow and his body was never recovered. This unfortunate accident prejudiced the public against the work, and it became necessary to act with vigor before the public mind became so saturated with the idea of danger that it would be impossible to obtain labor. In this emergency Mr. A. Ballantyne was appointed superintendent, with orders to organize a party of eight or nine skilled quarrymen, to make a lodgment on the rock, to prepare comfortable quarters, and to proceed at once to reduce the crest to the level previously adopted.

On the 21st of October four men were successfully landed, with their tools, provisions, supplies, and an abundant supply of canvas to form temporary shelter. Five days later the rest of the men, additional supplies, and a small derrick were placed on the rock, and this may be considered the date of the commencement of the work.

The building of this light was dependent upon the occupancy of the rock and the erection of appliances for making the landings with safety and despatch, it is proper, therefore, to note the successive steps which led to the successful completion of the plans and to properly understand the various operations, it is necessary to give a description of the rock and its surroundings, and also of the manner in which the landings were effected.

Tillamook Rock is a bold, basaltic rock, standing isolated in the Pacific Ocean, about a mile off Tillamook Head, and twenty miles south of the mouth of the Columbia River, Oregon. The water on the west, north and east sides is from one hundred and fifty to two hundred and forty feet deep, but shoals to ninety-six and one hundred and four feet on the south side, over a limited area. Midway between it and the Head is a small rock, awash at low water, upon which the sea breaks heavily during storms. As it rises from the sea the face of the rock is somewhat precipitous on the west side for the first fifteen feet and then breaks back under a gentle but very irregular slope for a short distance, forming a narrow bench on part of the south face, and all of the west and north faces. As it springs from this bench it takes a remarkable form; it rises to a height of eighty feet, terminates in a rounded knob, resembling the burl of a tree, and overhangs the sea. The south side is bounded by a deep fissure dividing the rock into two unequal parts. This fissure is about twenty-five feet wide, and, starting on the sea-face, near the water-level, rises on an incline to thirty feet above the sea, where it is abruptly closed by a natural wall forming part of the east slope; into this fissure the waves break violently during storms, throwing their spray to the very top of the rock, and at times leaping over the resisting wall, sweep down the opposite slope.

The detached portion of the rock on the south side of the fissure is a narrow spine, whose surface is rendered very irregular and rugged by scales of rock resting against its sides, and by sharply-pointed needles projecting above its surface. Before the crest of the principal portion of the rock was disturbed it was exceedingly irregular in shape and measured only about one hundred square feet. Little needles projected everywhere, forming narrow and deep crevices, in and through which, extending some distance down the east slope, was a mass of various-sized cubical blocks, from three to twelve inches on a side, cemented together with a tough and unyielding matrix, the original columnar formation having been destroyed and these being the remains.

The earliest records show that this rock has been a favorite resort for thousands of sea lions — a large species of seal, valuable only for oil — which, before the work commenced, completely covered the slopes and even the summit of the rock. At first they were quite hostile and disposed to discuss with the workmen the ownership of the rock, but eventually retired to rocky resorts farther to the southward.

As has been shown, it was both difficult and dangerous to land on the rock; it was equally so to leave it in a small boat, as there is no harbor within twenty miles where a landing could be made with safety; no light-keeper would ever attempt to row ashore unless he were a skilled boatman and was driven by an urgent necessity.

The first landing was, of necessity, from a boat, but this involved so many dangers to life that a plan of procedure was adopted which would restrict the dangers encountered to the smallest number of men practicable. When the four men landed, on the 21st October, the revenue cutter, which brought them, moored to the spar buoy — previously placed about three hundred feet from the rock. The surf-boat, which had landed the men, returned to the cutter and received the end of a four-and-one-half-inch rope which had previously been made fast to the mast of the vessel, and carried it to the rock. The outer end was then run up the slope and wound round a projecting ledge eighty-five feet above the sea, and drawn taut from the vessel. This main line, which is called the "cable" was rigged with a large single block, called the "traveller," which moved freely along it and carried a large projecting hook underneath, and two fixed blocks, one at the vessel the other at the rock. The traveller was designed to be hauled back and forth along the cable, from the deck of the vessel, by an endless line made fast to the hook of the traveller, one branch going direct to the vessel from the hook, and the other returning after passing through the block at the rock. The object of the traveller was to furnish means for transferring men and supplies from the vessel to the rock with facility and security, if not with comfort; the articles subject to injury from water were enclosed in tight casks slung from the hook attached to the traveller; by hauling on the lower and easing off on the upper line the traveller could be drawn from the vessel to the rock; by reversing the process the traveller would return. The men were transported by an arrangement known as the "breeches-buoy" consisting of an ordinary circular life-preserver, slung from the traveller, to which were securely lashed a pair of stout breeches cut off at the knees; the latter would support the man right side up while in the air, and the former would keep him afloat should he fall in the water. After the buoy was attached to the traveller the man would take his position in it facing the rock, and be hauled out in the usual way. The plate shows the details of the operation. It was never possible to keep the cable taut as the vessel was in constant motion, sometimes very violent; for this reason the traveller ran, at times, very close to the surface of the sea, and it was not unusual to have the passenger or the package dip under several times while making this very unattractive "rapid transit."

As soon as the necessary men, tools, etc., were landed, the vigorous prosecution of the work depended upon fair weather alone. The first fifteen days were devoted to providing shelter for themselves and supplies. There were no caves nor recesses in which they could take refuge, so the only shelter which could be obtained against the driving rains was by cutting up the canvas into A-tents, which were held down by rope-lashings made fast into ring-bolts in the rock. In a short while a bench was levelled in a retired spot on the south side near the ninety-foot level on which it was intended to place a frame house for sleeping-quarters; but the attempt had to be abandoned as it was soon found that the site selected was subject to be deluged by the waves which broke in the fissure; so the quarters were located on the north side. As soon as they were completed a site for the main derrick was levelled near by. A rude pathway was excavated from the landing at the thirty-foot level to the quarters, and a bench was commenced at the ninety-foot level, to be carried around the rock. This was necessary as the crest was so irregular and narrow that but few men could work on it in concert, and was, moreover, so wind-swept that it was dangerous to remain on it during a gale.

The outer surface of the rock was covered with thin scales, and could be readily removed with moderate charges of black powder. The nucleus was very firm and tough; black powder made but little impression on it; but by opening the mass with giant-cartridges and then using large charges of black powder the rock was blasted with better success.

The hardy little party of quarrymen, notwithstanding their constant exposure to danger and the discomforts of their rude quarters, worked diligently all winter without complaint, and by May 1 the rock had been reduced in height about thirty feet by the removal of four thousand six hundred and thirty cubic yards of solid rock.

Early in January, 1880, this coast was visited by a terrific tornado which caused the waves, after rebounding from the face of the rock and filling the fissure, to be thrown by the winds entirely over the rock at every point continuously and uninterruptedly for many days, carrying away by their impetuous descent down the opposite slope the supply-house on the thirty-foot level, endangering even the quarters of the men. The storm reached its maximum during the night of the ninth, when the men were in their bunks. To the courage and presence of mind of Mr. Ballantyne the party owed its safety; his determined action arrested a panic and prevented the men from deserting their little house for an apparently safer refuge on a higher level, an attempt which could only have been followed by their destruction so dark was the night and so violent the wind. The supply-house was a slight structure, and, for want of a better locality, had been established temporarily at the thirty-foot level. Fortunately the superintendent had stored in the quarters plenty of hard-bread, coffee, and bacon, to last, with economy, for several months.

It was not until the 25th of January that the storm subsided sufficiently to allow a vessel to cross the bar at the mouth of the Columbia River, to render assistance to the force, or to ascertain the truth of the reports adverse to their safety, which had been so freely circulated, and which had had their origin in the wrecks washed upon the beach north of Tillamook Head. She found all safe and well, though in want of fresh provisions.

On the same night that the safety of the workmen was so endangered, the English Iron bark "*Lupata,*" of ten hundred and thirty-nine tons' burden, was dashed to pieces on the main shore, not a mile from the light-house, with the loss of every one of the twenty persons on board. She came so near the rock that the creaking of the blocks and the voices of the officers giving orders could be distinctly heard, but the night was so dark that nothing could be seen except her lights. The superintendent had a bonfire built on the rock as soon as possible, but the vessel was probably lost before the light could be seen.

By the 30th of May, all of the rock was removed to the required plane, without accident of any importance. During the work an attempt was made to fill the fissure with the débris, but without success, the waves promptly removing every fragment thrown in, though many of them were of large size. As soon as the rock had been levelled, the work of landing the material for and of erecting the tower, dwelling, fog-signal, etc., was at once commenced, and was much expedited by the use of the boom-derrick and of the large derrick shown on the drawings, which also give the general appearance of the buildings.

The dwelling is a one-story stone structure forty-five by forty-eight feet, with an extension for the fog-horns twenty-eight feet six inches by thirty-two feet, under the same roof on the west side.

The light, which is of the first order, showing a white flash every five seconds, is exhibited from a stone tower sixteen feet square, rising from the centre of the main dwelling.

There are four keepers at the station, and there is ample storage-room for six months' supplies.

The corner-stone of the dwelling was laid on the 22d of June, 1880, and the station was completed on the 11th of February, 1881, though the light had been exhibited about three weeks before.

The total cost of the work was $123,492.82. Since the station has been built, the landing-stage has occasionally been destroyed.

There is no doubt that this light station is one of the most exposed in the world. Every year it is visited by severe storms. As an example of the height to which the waves can reach, and of their power, I quote the following, from an official report:—

"On December 16 and 17, 1886, the seas from the southwest broke over the rock, throwing large quantities of water above and on the building. The roof on the south and west sides of the fog-signal room, and on the west side of the building, were crushed in. . . . The concrete covering of the top of the rock around the building was broken, and a brick parapet and concrete filling in a low place outside the fence, at the south-east corner, were carried away. A mass of the filling weighing half a ton was thrown over the fence into the enclosure. Three 730-gallon water-tanks filled with water, at the west end of the building, were broken from their fastenings and piled against the fence."

Considerable other damage was done, but this is enough to show to what a great height and with what force the waves are thrown on this remarkable rock in the *Pacific* Ocean.

(See Appendix B.)

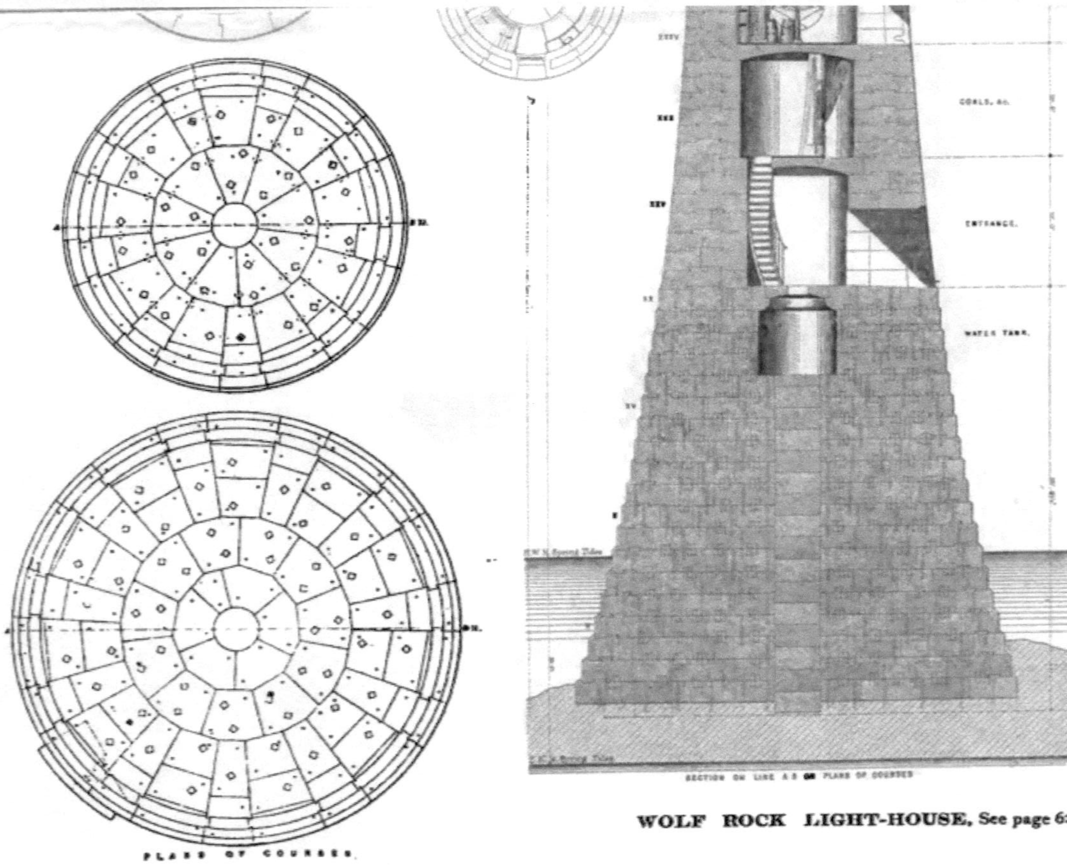

WOLF ROCK LIGHT-HOUSE, See page 62

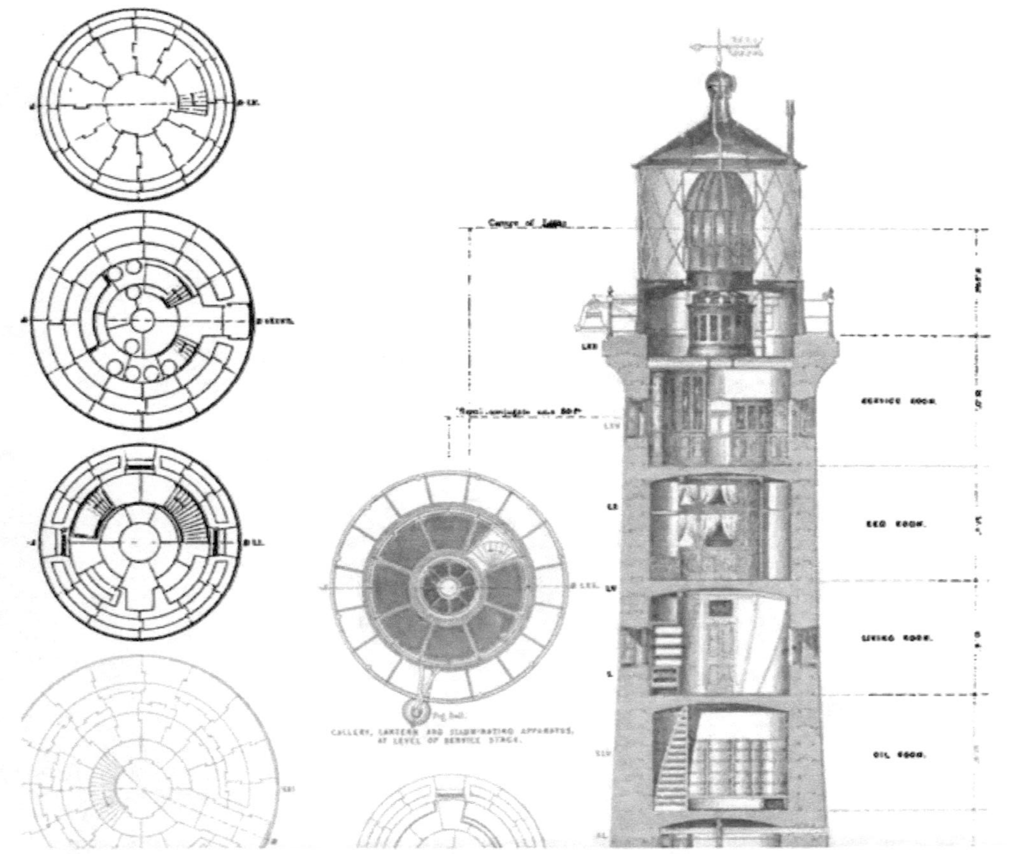
SERVICE ROOM.
BED ROOM.
LIVING ROOM.
OIL ROOM.
GALLERY, LANTERN AND ILLUMINATING APPARATUS,
AT LEVEL OF SERVICE STAGE.

CHAPTER IX.

NORTHWEST SEAL ROCK.

North-West Seal Rock, Cal.

Northwest Seal Rock, or, as it has been re-christened St. George's Reef Light Station, is now in process of construction on a small rock forming the outermost danger of St. George's Reef, opposite Crescent City, California.

Capt. A. H. Payson, Corps of Engineers, U. S. A., is in charge of this work. The high rocky coast from the bight of Crescent City to Point St. George, four and one-half nautical miles, trends in a northerly direction, and is bordered by a belt of numerous high, rocky islets and sunken dangers, nearly a mile in width.

North of the Point the coast-line turns nearly at right angles to its previous direction and becomes low and sandy, but the direction of the obstructions remain unchanged for about six nautical miles to seaward, and make what is known as St. George's Reef.

Inside the reef, close under Point St. George, is a broad and deep channel, sometimes used during heavy northwest weather by northerly-bound steamers, but only in daylight and clear weather, and probably at some risk from sunken dangers not shown on the charts.

The position of Point St. George, about midway between Capes Mendocino and Blanco, would naturally suggest it as an appropriate place for a first-order light, did not experience at Cape Blanco, an almost similar situation, show that the headland itself would but imperfectly answer the purpose. When there is not dense fog there is usually so much haze in this climate that vessels forced by the reef to give the point a berth of ten to twelve miles, would rarely see even a first-order light upon it, while a fog-signal, six miles from the danger it is designed to mark, would be practically useless.

Northwest Seal Rock is nearly two miles outside of its nearest neighbor, Southwest Seal Rock, with a clear and deep, but unused passage between, and has close to it on all sides from one hundred and eight to one hundred and eighty feet of water, with no outlying dangers. It is a mass of metamorphic material, varying considerably in character, extremely hard to drill, and brittle under the action of explosives, but offering almost the resistance of glass to the action of the sea.

The superficial area of the rock at the water-line is about forty-six thousand square feet, and its general form is an oval with a high central ridge running nearly east and west along its longer axis, sloping gently on the north, but more steeply on the sides from its crest to the sea level. To the westward is a prolongation, called Little Black Rock. The greatest height of the ridge, fifty-four feet, is at its eastern end.

The gentle lower slopes and smooth, water-worn surfaces, were plain indications that the sea at times swept over its top. Yet, to gain the requisite area for the foundation, it was necessary to excavate at a point fully thirty feet below the crest. There was no space available on the site where even temporary security of men or material could be assured, and the frequency and quickness with which all parts of the rock became untenable, greatly exceeded any previous anticipation. It is a peculiarity of this coast that a heavy sea, which results from off-shore winds and cannot be predicted from any sign, will begin to break upon the rock; and so suddenly did this happen during the working season of 1883 that in three or four hours from a dead calm the topmost surface of the rock was swept. The general features of the site for construction upon it could hardly have been more unfavorable.

Crescent City, thirteen miles away, is the nearest point at which a landing on the coast is possible. This is a shoal and rock-encumbered bight, quite open to the south and west, but offering a somewhat disturbed shelter to be relied on from the middle of June to the following September. During the remainder of the year it is exposed at any time to the entrance of the prevailing westerly swell which breaks outside the anchorage and endangers any vessel lying in it. Crescent City is a small and isolated settlement, distant by difficult mountain roads one hundred and fifty miles from the telegraph, and more than three hundred miles from a railway. The nearest harbor is Humboldt Bay, where there is a good-sized town and frequent communication with San Francisco. The depth of water on the bar varies from fourteen to twenty feet. This often causes detention, but is not a serious obstacle. Its main drawback as a depot is its distance from the rock, but this is unavoidable.

The project for the foundation consisted of an oval outline adapted to that part of the rock which included the required area, and necessitated the cutting of four horizontal terraces for the foot of the pier-wall, and the suitable preparation of the mass of rock left standing within, for a bond with the pier filling; provision was to be made for water storage in the otherwise solid mass of the pier below the top of the rock.

Since it was impossible to leave men and material on the site, it was necessary either to take them to and from the nearest landing at Crescent City, as occasion served, or to provide floating accommodations near the rock. The saving of time, so vital to success, and other evident advantages of the latter course, were strong arguments in its favor; it was, therefore, adopted, and a top-sail schooner of one hundred and twenty-seven tons, called "*La Ninfa*" was selected. She was nearly new and strongly built for carrying copper ore on the west coast of South America, and had shown her fitness for the work by being used temporarily as a light-ship to mark the wreck of the "*Escambia*" on San Francisco bar. She was altered and in various ways specially fitted for the work. Her outfit was made as complete as the large experience of Mr. Ballantyne could suggest. He had been appointed superintendent of construction of this work, owing to his success in building the station at Tillamook Rock, a work of similar character, and, besides, many of the men who had worked there were also employed here.

The steamer "*Whitelaw*" was chartered to tow the schooner to the rock and to place the moorings. After several attempts she succeeded in doing so, arriving at the rock on the morning of April 9, 1883; she placed the big twelve thousand pound mooring and attached the schooner to it, but was then, owing to the boisterous condition of the sea, compelled to abandon the attempt to place the other moorings and stood off to sea. From then until the sixteenth a continuous gale prevailed, the schooner holding on in g. eat discomfort and the steamer lying by in the offing, but the weather then moderated sufficiently to enable soundings to be made on the site of the remaining moorings. They disclosed the fact that the depths were greater than those shown on the coast-survey chart, so Mr. Ballantyne availed himself of the presence of the steamer and went in her to Humboldt Bay to get larger spar buoys, where he was detained until the 27th. Leaving on the evening of that day he arrived at the rock on the 28th only to find that the schooner and the big mooring-buoy had both disappeared. The weather becoming fine, the steamer laid the remaining moorings, and then cruised in the neighborhood of the rock until the 3d of May, awaiting the re-appearance of the schooner, when she again went to Humboldt Bay to communicate with Captain Payson for instructions.

On arrival there she found that the "*La Ninfa*" had been sighted during a gale off Cape Mendocino, on the 30th of April. The

"*Whitelaw*" put to sea in search, and on the 6th of May fell in with the missing vessel twenty-five miles south of Crescent City. She had parted her new eight-inch hawser during a furious gale on the night of the 22d of April, and had since been blown first north and then south in a vain endeavor to keep near her work. Taking her in tow the steamer, for the second time, placed her in position on the morning of the 9th of May, and the weather being favorable a landing was at once made on the rock, ring-bolts put in, a temporary traveller rigged, and the work on the rock finally and auspiciously begun.

Arrangements were made with a small coast-steamer, making regular trips between Crescent City and San Francisco once every ten days, to visit the rock on each trip.

The southerly winds, which had so far prevailed, were almost immediately succeeded by the violent northwesters of early spring, and rock-cutting made but little progress until the early part of July. In the mean time a small donkey-engine had been put on the "*La Ninfa*" to assist in handling the numerous moorings and spring lines, and to work the traveller. A new bad-weather mooring was put down to replace the one lost, various attempts to recover it having failed.

From this time forward the work went on without material interruption. There was much parting of lines and tackle, and the men often had to be taken hastily off the rock just after they had been put on, but in spite of many narrow escapes and some dangerous accidents, there was no serious injury to any one. Work on the north low bench was the most difficult, though it was twenty-five feet above the sea; the men there were almost constantly drenched with spray, and hardly a day passed when the sea did not break upon it at high water.

During a gale on the 29th and 30th of September stones, over a ton in weight, which had been rolled overboard from this bench, were swept like chips up along its whole length and over again on the east end. On September 10, while two quarrymen were drilling a hole on the lee side, just below the top of the rock, a tremendous sea swept completely over it, washing them down the steep south slopes nearly thirty feet, where they fortunately lodged on the south bench, none the worse save for a few bruises.

It was judged best to store the high explosives, of which there were at times six hundred pounds in stock, on the rock itself. The magazine, built of heavy timbers, was put in a square excavation, made especially for it, in the topmost pinnacle, fifty feet above the sea, and secured by a network of four-inch lines set over its top as tightly as possible to ring bolts in the rock; yet the magazine was several times twisted around by the sea under its rope lacing. The presence of this large amount of explosive in such close proximity to the blasting was a source of much apprehension, but the precaution was taken to wrap it in many thicknesses of tarred canvas and no accident occurred.

To avoid the delay of frequent and tedious changes in the position of the schooner she was hauled in close enough to the rock to permit the use of the wire traveller-cable, and kept there as long as the spring lines held. She was much exposed to flying fragments, which often went over her in showers, marring her appearance a good deal, but doing no serious damage.

The total distance over which the cage of the traveller passed was three hundred and fifty feet. The traveller-block was made of two pieces of boiler-plate, bolted together, and forming the bearings for the axles of four grooved gun-metal wheels, which just held the cable between the upper and lower pairs, and made it impossible to nip or bind, even were it twisted completely round the cable by the sea. The cage was a horizontal iron ring four feet in diameter, suspended from the traveller-block by three cords, attached at equal distances around its circumference, and having hung below it a piece of plank on which the passengers stood. At first the men were hauled to and fro singly in a breeches-buoy, but the cage was found much more convenient as it permitted the transport of at first four, and later of six men at a time, and allowed them to easily extricate themselves should any accident happen. The whole arrangement worked perfectly, and by the aid of the engine a round trip, taking off six men, and return, could be made in three minutes. The shore end of the cable being some sixty feet above the sea, and the lowest point of its curve not over fifteen feet, the cage, when released from the rock ran down this slope with great speed. Taking advantage of this, and standing by to haul in with the engine, the men were often taken on board dry, when every sea went over the low part of the cable; such confidence did they gain in this means of retreat that they did not think of leaving the work till the sea began to run continuously over all the working levels; then, lashing their tools to ring-bolts prepared for the purpose, the cage was put in use and in twenty minutes all hands would be in safety. But one accident occurred with it, and that was the parting of the traveller-rope in a heavy sea just as four men were being swung off the rock, but, luckily, they had only started, and so fell unharmed on the east bench. Whenever the sea would permit, the men were taken to and from the rock in a surf-boat to save the costly item of water and also time. It was extraordinary to see how, little by little, they became more venturesome, till, at the end, they would jump out one by one from the boat, holding to a life-line from the rock, with the sea rising and falling fully fifteen feet on the nearly vertical east face.

The schooner's position near the rock, the character and position of the moorings, and the manner in which the traveller was rigged, are shown in the accompanying plate.[1] About the middle of August the foundation benches had been roughly formed, and needed only the finishing touches of the stone-cutters.

The position and size, eleven thousand cubic feet, of the cistern having been fixed, the party commenced to work on this; the ten days from the 18th to the 28th of September were the finest of the whole year, and the men, warned by the lateness of the season and the ominous westerly swell, and very anxious to end their long seclusion, worked with such eagerness, that, contrary to the expectations of the foreman, everything planned for the season was finished by 2 P. M., September 28. The tools were taken on board that evening

---

[1] See full-page picture, upper half.

with the men, and by 2 A. M. next day the long-expected first winter gale had reached such violence that all the rock-lines parted, and the schooner was lying by a single line to the outer buoy. The storm continued until the 1st of October, and on the 2d the steamer "*Crescent City*" came out to the rock with instructions for closing up the work. As it was too rough to communicate there, the schooner, at 9 A. M. on the 2d of October cut her last remaining mooring-line and followed the steamer under the lee of Point St. George, where the stone-cutters and quarrymen were taken off, and she started to make the best of her way to San Francisco, where she arrived forty-eight hours after, being favored with a strong northerly gale. The steamer did not arrive at San Francisco until three days later, when the working force was disbanded and the plant stored at the depot on Yerba Buena Island.

The sketch [1] shows the appearance of the rock at the end of the working season.

The next year's work was dependent on the action of Congress in granting an additional appropriation, and, as it was a long session, no more money would be available until July or August; therefore, to save time, the steamer "*Whitelaw*" was sent to the rock to replace the moorings and to erect the big derrick in anticipation of the season's work; this she safely accomplished by July 2, but as Congress appropriated but $30,000, too small a sum to continue work at the site, it was devoted to the preparation of material at Humboldt Bay.

Before any work had been done at the rock it was first determined to get the necessary granite from the Sierra Nevada and to use sand stone for filling, but a rumor having reached Captain Payson that granite had been discovered on Mad River near the railroad from Humboldt, he at once examined the place and found a deposit of excellent quality, but no evidence of the existence of the rock in place. The side of the mountain showed, within perfectly defined and narrow limits to the right and left, but extending for a considerable distance with less-marked boundaries up and down the slope, the tops of

[1] See full-page picture, lower half.

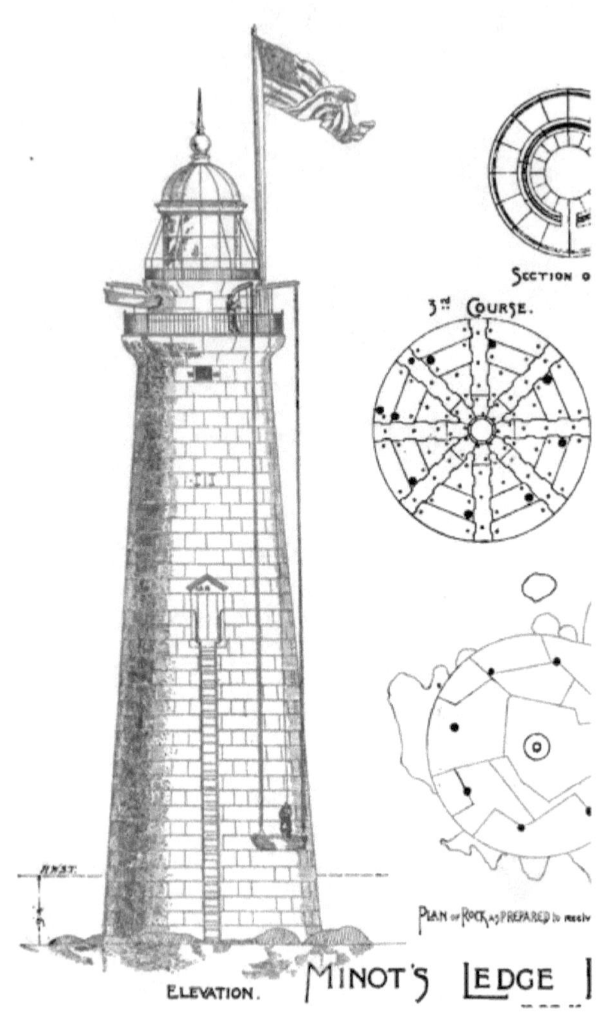
SECTION
3rd COURSE.
PLAN OF ROCK AS PREPARED
ELEVATION.
MINOT'S LEDGE

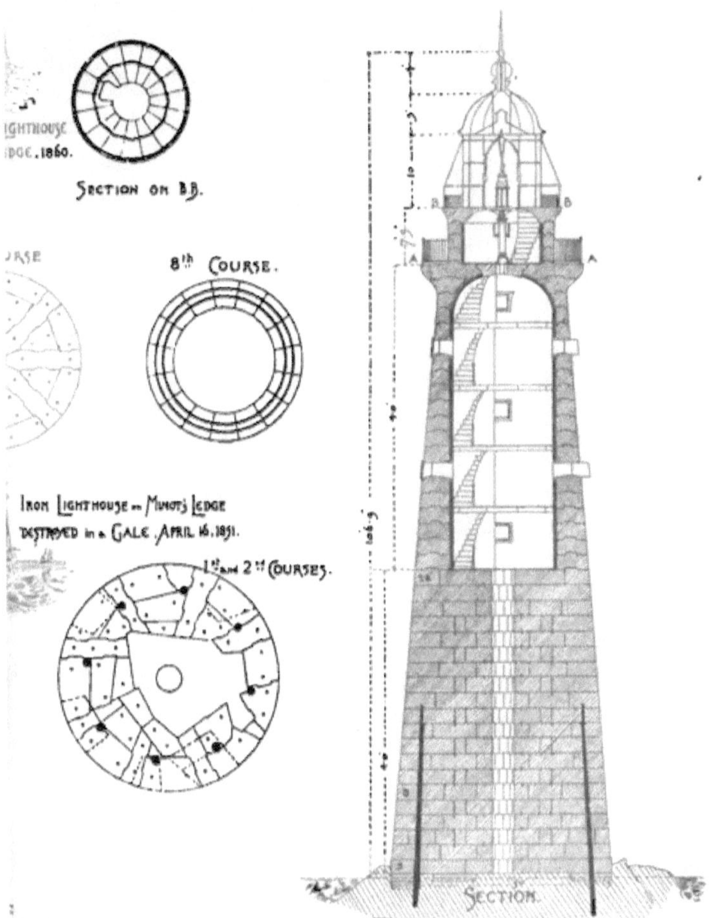

MASSACHUSETTS BAY.

See page 74

what looked like water-worn boulders, some of them of apparently several hundred tons in weight.

This discovery materially diminished the cost of the work and made the delivery of the stone more certain and speedy. Enough granite was found here not only for the facing, but also for all the interior filling. It was taken from the quarry to the depot at Humboldt to be dressed to shape.

The next year, 1885, Congress appropriated $40,000 more, which was also devoted to quarrying and dressing stone.

In 1886 there was no money appropriated.

The small appropriation of 1884–5 necessitated the abandonment of measures already taken, the waste of much money in useless preparation, and the suspension of work upon the rock.

In 1887 Congress appropriated $120,000, active preparations were at once made to commence laying the stone already prepared, and it is hoped to complete the first eight courses on the rock by the end of this working season.

The amounts so far appropriated are as follows:

August 7, 1882, ...	$50,000.
March 3, 1883, ...	50,000.
July 7, 1884, ...	30,000.
March 3, 1885, ...	40,000.
March 3, 1887, ...	120,000.
Total, ...	$290,000.

It will take about $160,000 to finish the work; had the appropriations been of adequate sums it would now be completed, and at much less expense. In a future article I expect to finish the history of this light-house, which may fairly rank among the *sea-rock* light-houses of the world.

LIGHT-HOUSE OF TRIAGOZ.

The light-house of Triagoz in the Department of Côtes du Nord, France, is also established on an isolated rock in the sea called Guen Bras. The plateau of Triagoz is of considerable extent, being about four miles long from east to west by about one mile wide, but only isolated points of rock are exposed even in the lowest tides. The rock selected as the site of this light-house is the most elevated point on the south side, and, in consequence, marks the northerly limit of the channel followed by coasting-vessels. In front it has the appearance of an almost vertical wall, and on the opposite side it falls off with a depression in the surface forming a small open creek. This is the most accessible place during the three or four hours of low tide. The depth of water, which is over sixty feet at

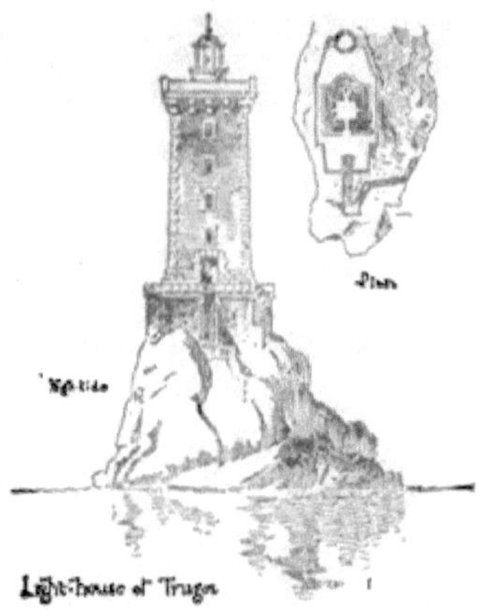

Light-house of Trugn

the lowest tides at the foot of the rock on the south side, increases rapidly as you leave it; the bottom is rocky, and the tidal currents so strong that the plan originally intended of keeping a vessel anchored here during the fine season to serve as quarters for the workmen, had to be abandoned. It was, therefore, necessary to build a hut, after having levelled off the summit of the rock, on the part corresponding to the interior opening of the tower. It enclosed a vertical post set in the centre of the structure, rigged with a boom for raising stones up to the work. The landing of the material was done by means of two derricks, one placed at the entrance of the little creek before mentioned, the other on the south-east end of the rock. They were worked with great rapidity whenever the sea was smooth enough for landings to be made. The sketch gives a view of the work when the construction had been well advanced.

The base of the tower was fixed above the level of the highest tide; the edifice consists of a square tower with a salient staircase enclosure on one of its sides. On the level of the first floor is a vestibule leading to the staircase with a store-room on each side of it. There are three rooms above the ground floor, one of which is reserved for the engineers. They are roofed over with cloistered arches and are provided with fireplaces. In the upper part of the tower is the watch-room which serves at the same time as a store-room for implements that are to be kept free from moisture. The cast-iron stairway to the lantern leads from this room. A platform conforming to the shape of the rock surrounds the edifice; it is reached by means of flights of stairs, which are built into the side of the rock, starting from the point where the landing is least difficult. Under the front part of the platform are store-rooms for fuel and other materials.

The work was executed in rubble masonry with cut-granite trimmings; the outside faces of these stones were dressed to give an appearance of rustic masonry. The work was commenced in 1861 and finished in 1864; it cost about $60,000. The tower is ninety-two feet high, the light is ninety-eight feet above high water, is of the third order, fixed, varied by red flashes, and is visible twelve miles.

THE SMALLS LIGHT-HOUSE.

Although it is not necessary to give further details of the methods employed in building sea-rock light-houses, yet before leaving this part of the subject it is proper to make reference to some incidents connected with the erection of the Smalls Light-house off the west coast of Wales. The motive which influenced Mr. Philipps, its constructor, was of a more elevated character than that of other light-house builders of his time. In lighting these dangerous rocks he proposed, above all, "to serve and save humanity." Sixty years later, when the heirs of this philanthropist ceded the structure to the Trinity House, they were awarded an indemnity of upwards of $850,000.

The task undertaken by Philipps was sufficiently unpromising. The rock selected for the site projects in ordinary weather twelve feet above the sea, but in rough weather, which is frequent in this vicinity, the rock is entirely submerged. At the time this work was undertaken, engineers were not so numerous as now, and Philipps had difficulty in finding a suitable superintendent; he did find one, however, in the person of a young man named Whiteside, a musical-instrument maker, of Liverpool, with a remarkable genius for mechanics.

In the summer of 1772 Whiteside first made the acquaintance of the place on which he was to indelibly grave his name. He disembarked on the rocks with a gang of Cornish miners, and the obstacles which they met at the commencement of the work nearly disgusted him with the enterprise. He and his companions had started the work when a storm suddenly broke upon them. The wind blew with great force, and the cutter which had brought them had to fly before the fury of the gale. The workmen left on the rock hung on the best they could for two days and nights. Whiteside, however, was not

discouraged, and finally brought the work to a successful end, but not without being exposed to many dangers.

One day the dwellers on the coast picked up on the beach a "message from the deep," that is to say, a cask inscribed "Open this and you will find a letter;" inside was a carefully-sealed bottle and in the bottle a document as follows:

"SMALLS, February 1, 1777.

"*Sir*, — Finding ourselves at this moment in the most critical and dangerous condition, we hope that Providence will guide this letter to you, and that you will come immediately to our succor. Send to seek for us before spring or we will perish, I fear; our supply of wood and water is almost exhausted, and our house is in the most sad state. We do not doubt that you would come to seek us as promptly as possible. We can be reached at high tide in almost any weather. I have no need to tell you more, you will comprehend our distress, and I remain,

Your humble servant,

"H. WHITESIDE."

Below this signature were these words:

"We were surprised on the 23 January by a tempest; since that time we have not been able to light the temporary light for want of oil and candles. We fear we have been forgotten.

"ED. EDWARDS, G. ADAMS, J. PRICE.

"P. S. We do not doubt that the person in whose hands this will fall will be sufficiently charitable to send it to Th. Williams, Esq., Trelethen, near St. Davids, Wales."

The history of Smalls has other and darker pages. It is related that at the beginning of this century there was a winter so stormy that for four months the two keepers were entirely cut off from any succor from shore. It was in vain that vessels were sent to the rock, the furious sea always prevented a landing. One of them returned one day with a strange report. Its crew had seen a man, standing and motionless, in a corner of the exterior gallery. Near him floated a signal of distress. But was he alive or dead? No one could say. Each evening anxious looks were cast at the light-house to see if its light would be shown, and each evening it shone brightly, proof that some one was still there. But were both keepers alive, and if there were but one, who was the survivor? This was learned later.

One evening a fisher from Milford who had succeeded in landing at Smalls in an intermission of calm weather, brought to Solway the two keepers, but one of them was a corpse. The survivor had made a coffin for his dead comrade, then, after having carried it to a corner of the gallery, he had stood it on end, attaching it firmly. Left alone he had done good service. When returned on shore he was so changed, so emaciated, that his relatives and friends could scarcely recognize him. He asserted that his comrade died of disease; he was believed, but after this time there were always three keepers at Smalls in place of two—a wise precaution which has since been taken for light-houses placed in similar conditions.

CHAPTER X.

LIGHT-HOUSES ON THE ATLANTIC COAST OF THE UNITED STATES.

Our Atlantic coast does not afford any examples of rocks as high as Tillamook, but there are many outlying dangers which had to be marked by powerful lights exhibited from tall towers.

At Petit Manan, for example, off the coast of Maine, is a tall granite tower carrying a first-order flashing-light at a height of one hundred and twenty-five feet above sea level, which can readily be seen at a distance of seventeen nautical miles. Clustered around the base of the tower are dwellings for the keepers and an additional

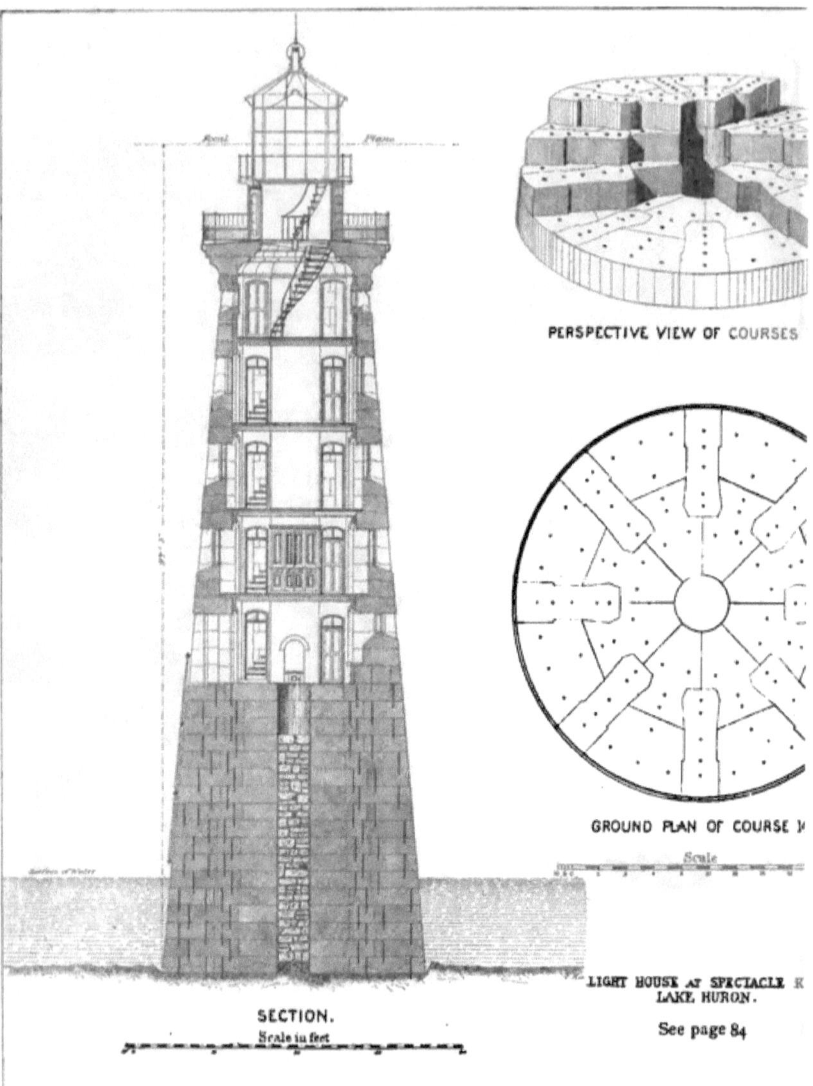

LIGHT HOUSE AT SPECTACLE R
LAKE HURON.

See page 84

dwelling has been built one hundred and fifty feet to the westward. The keepers at this station have not only to attend to the light, but also to a steam-whistle which is sounded during foggy weather.

The next important light along this coast is on Mt. Desert Rock. This tower was built with a very broad base and thick walls; at times the sea has washed entirely over the rock, and the keepers with their families have had to take refuge in the tower. The keepers succeed in raising a few flowers and fresh vegetables in earth brought by boat from the mainland and deposited in sheltered spots. The station is noted for the number of sea-birds, especially gulls, which lay their eggs there. The keepers never molest them.

Matinicus Rock is twenty-five miles out in the ocean from the mainland, directly in the pathway of the ocean-steamers plying from Boston and Portland to Eastport, St. John, Yarmouth and Halifax, and of the immense fleet of coasting and fishing vessels trading between the United States and the British Provinces. This barren and jagged rock, covering an area of thirty-nine acres at low tide, is inaccessible except during favorable weather, and on it stand the two towers, dwellings and fog-signal which comprise the Matinicus-Rock Light-station. The station was first built in 1827 and consisted of a cobble-stone dwelling with a wooden tower at each end. In 1846 a new dwelling of granite with a granite tower at each end was substituted for the old dwelling which was used for an out-house, and the wooden towers were removed. Steam fog-signals were placed here in 1856, and in 1857 the granite towers of the dwelling were cut down to the roof and two isolated towers erected farther apart than the old ones.

In the spring of 1853, Samuel Burgess obtained the position of light-keeper; his family consisted of an invalid wife, four small daughters and a son, who, though making his home on the rock, was absent much of the time fishing in Bay Chaleur and elsewhere. The eldest daughter, Abbie, fourteen years old, was the keeper's only assistant; she aided in caring for the light as well as attending to the principal household duties. In the occasional absence of her father, the whole care of the lights devolved upon her. She modestly says: "I took a great deal of pride in my light-house work and tried to do my duty"—a duty on the faithful performance of which depended the safety of many a vessel and its crew. She soon became proficient, and, as subsequent events proved, was fully competent to assume full charge. On the morning of January 19, 1856, Abbie then being seventeen years of age, the Atlantic was visited by one of those terrific gales to which it is subject. This was the same

gale that destroyed Minot's Light-house and its keepers. Her father was away, and the following letter written by her to a friend will show the dangers and responsibilities in which this brave girl was placed:

"*Dear* ——, You have often expressed a desire to view the sea out upon the ocean when it was angry. Had you been here on the 19 January, I surmise you would have been satisfied. Father was away. Early in the day, as the tide arose, the sea made a complete breach over the rock, washing every movable thing away, and of the old dwelling not one stone was left upon another. The new dwelling was flooded, and the windows had to be secured to prevent the violence of the spray from breaking them in. As the tide came, the sea rose higher and higher, till the only endurable places were the light-towers. If they stood we were saved, otherwise our fate was only too certain. But for some reason, I know not why, I had no misgivings, and went on with my work as usual. *For four weeks*, owing to rough weather, no landing could be effected on the rock. During this time we were without the assistance of any male member of our family. Though at times greatly exhausted with my labors, not once did the lights fail. Under God I was able to perform all my accustomed duties as well as my father's.

"You know the hens were our only companions. Becoming convinced, as the gale increased, that unless they were brought into the house they would be lost, I said to mother: 'I must try to save them.' She advised me not to attempt it. The thought, however, of parting with them without an effort was not to be endured, so seizing a basket, I ran out a few yards after the rollers had passed and the sea fell off a little, with the water knee deep, to the coop, and rescued all but one. It was the work of a moment, and I was back in the house with the door fastened, but I was none too quick, for at that instant my little sister, standing at the window, exclaimed: 'Oh, look! look there! the worst sea is coming.' That wave destroyed the old dwelling and swept the rock. I cannot think you would enjoy remaining here any great length of time for the sea is never still, and when agitated, its roar shuts out every other sound, even drowning our voices."

In the spring of 1857, Mr. Burgess left the rock to obtain his salary and secure needed provisions and fuel. The weather prevented his return, and the family ran short of food. Waiting till famine stared them in the face, the son started in a little skiff equipped with a sail, made by the aid of his sister, to obtain succor. Pushing from the rock in his frail craft, he was at first lost sight of in the trough of the sea, he reappeared on the top of the waves for a short distance and was seen no more for twenty-one days, during which time the mother and the four girls were reduced to a cup of corn-meal and one egg each per day. Added to risk of perishing of famine in mid-ocean was the torturing suspense as to the fate of father and son. During all this time Abbie attended to the light, cared for her sick mother, and, by her spirit and example, cheered the little family clustered together on this wave-beaten rock in the Atlantic. Fortunately, father and son finally safely returned to their ocean home.

In 1861, Mr. Burgess was relieved of his duties by the appointment of Captain Grant and son. Abbie instructed them in their duties and in the same year married Mr. Isaac H. Grant, the son. The season of 1875 found her still on the rock, the mother of four children, and, a vacancy occurring at the White Head Light, Me., her husband was appointed keeper with her as assistant. They are still at this station, though it is her ambition to retire from the light-house service to a farm.

HALFWAY ROCK, ME.

This light-house, located on a barren rock, so swept by the sea that there is absolutely no soil, contains the dwelling and living-rooms of the keepers, and forms their rather desolate residence.

From a distance the gray granite tower, showing a third-order light eighty feet above the sea, appears to stand in the water. The rock is so storm-swept that landings are almost impossible except in pleasant weather: a boat-house was built here of concrete, but the ways where first placed were destroyed by storms, so their location had to be changed, necessitating the cutting of the boat-house in two.[1]

The light-house was built in 1871.

[1] See sketch, page 160.

BOON ISLAND, ME.

Like the preceding, this light-house also seems to spring from the waves; the granite tower is one hundred and twenty-three feet high,

its base being ten feet above the sea level; alongside is the granite dwelling for the keepers. It was built in 1812 and shows a second order light visible for eighteen miles.

Before the improvement in the lenticular apparatus had reached its present perfection, by which the characteristics of adjacent lights can be made so dissimilar that there can be no danger of confounding them, the same object was secured by building two, or even three lights close together on the point to be marked. Some relics of this expensive, and, I trust, obsolescent custom still remain, notably, at Cape Elizabeth, Casco Bay, Me., at Thatcher's Island, Mass., and at Nauset Beach, Cape Cod, Mass. At Cape Elizabeth the two towers were built in 1828, and show, the one a white light, and the other a white light varied by a white flash every minute at a height of one hundred and forty-three feet above the sea level; both lights are of the second-order, and can be seen for eighteen miles.

The Cape Ann towers, on Thatcher's Island, are handsome granite structures one hundred and sixty-five and a-half feet above the sea, carrying first-order lights, visible for nineteen miles. They were first established in 1790 and rebuilt in 1861. At Nauset Beach there are three little, low towers, eighteen feet high, but situated on a bluff, so that the fourth-order lights they carry are ninety-three feet above sea level and can be seen over fifteen miles. There are double lights also on Gurnet Point, near Plymouth, Mass., and on Baker's Island, Mass., but these are of use mainly as "ranges."

BOSTON LIGHT.

The oldest light-house in the United States is the Boston Light, situated on Little Brewster Island on the north side of the main entrance to Boston Harbor, Mass. It was established in 1716 and rebuilt in 1859. The light is of the second-order, flashing every thirty seconds, is shown from a tower one hundred and eleven feet above sea-level, and is visible for sixteen and one-half miles. The following account of this light, and of some of its various vicissitudes is taken from the *Boston Evening Transcript* of August 26, 1880.

In the *Evening Transcript*, copied from the *Providence Journal*, the latter paper is mistaken in saying that the light-house built in 1740 on Beaver Tail, the south end of Conanicut, was the oldest light-house built on the New England coast, or even on the American coast; the second being the Brant light, entrance of Nantucket Harbor, in 1754, etc. Our Massachusetts records, and also those of Nantasket (Hull), give evidence of one built by the Massachusetts Colony thirty-four years previous to 1749, viz.: "The General Court of the Province [of Mass. Bay], order a Light house erected by the Province, June 9, 1715, & a committee named to build it, viz: William Payne, Colo. Samuel Thaxter, Colo. Adam Winthrop, the Hon. William Tailer, & Addington Davenport added to it. Approved by Gov'r Dudley — enacted in July, & 1*d* a ton inward & 1*d* a ton outward to be paid to the Receiver of Imposts by all ships or vessels except coasters: & an application made to Hull for little Brewster for it, £60 allowed Payne and Capt. Zac Tuthill to build and finish it. Lt Governor Tailer assented." The cost was £2,385 17*s.* 8½*d.*

Hull generously assented as "at a legal meeting of the Proprietors of the undivided lands in Hull, on Monday, Augt 1, 1715 Colo. Samuel Thaxter for the com'e on application for building a light house on Brewster Island, so called, adjoining to the Great Brewster, being present and 'censeble' of the general benefit to trade and particularly to themselves, by unanimous vote have granted the said Brewster Island in the Province of Mass Bay for the use of a Light house forever: provided said proprietors of the Great Brewster be held harmless. Hull Augt 1 1715."

"1716. A com'e of Hull petitioned the Genl Court for liberty to choose a Light House Keeper." But "June 25, 1716 the General Court appointed a committee to choose one, at £50 a year, & chose George Worthylake, husbandman, Æ. 43, as the 1st keeper." In the second year, on his petition, his salary was raised to £70 as "he lost 59 sheep by drowning in a severe storm, his attendance on the Light House preventing him from saving them."

He and wife and daughter Lucy, or Ruth, were drowned November 3, 1718, going to Noddle's Island, and were buried in Copp's Hill cemetery, Boston.

Benjamin Franklin issued a ballad on the occasion and hawked it about Boston. November 18, 1718, John Haynes was chosen the second keeper of the light; he was a mariner and pilot, and resigned August 23, 1733, and was succeeded by Capt. Robert Ball, an Englishman, on August, 1733. He married Mrs. Martha King, of Charlestown, whose daughter Martha married Adam Knox. In 1776

the town of Hull dissented from Robert Ball's proposals, paying him "£5 for 4 years past & same anualy, as long as he keeps the Light House." By this, Hull had some interest in the keeper, or, perhaps, employed his services for the beacon or watch-house. Ball was taxed in Hull, 1767, but he refused, as non-resident; it was finally abated in 1774. His son, Capt. Robert Ball, sea captain, wills, in 1772 or 1782, Calf Island, Boston Harbor, and Green Island in Hull to his son John, and to his daughter Sarah, the outer Brewster Island (which was sold in 1794 for £50).

Robert Ball, Sr., kept the light-house from 1733, under the Royal Government, to or after 1766, and one account thinks till after the British fleet left Boston Harbor in the Revolution.

June 19, 1746, John Fayerweather, a merchant of Boston, in his account-books on that date charges the "Town of Boston 50s., cash

Perspective View from the North East, showing the Station in Proc

AMOOK ROCK, OREGON.

age 94

of Construction. Sea at lowest Stage, and very quiet.

paid at ye Light House *Tavern*, for sundry meetings held there with ye committee to measure ye rocks from ye lower middle ground, for order to sink hulks, if occasion, & 8*s* 6*d* more for drink, for the boats crew in April — total £3–4*s*–8*d*." And gave an order to Henry King to receive it. He credits "received of King £2–19–8."

1751. The light-house injured by fire was repaired.

1775. The light-house in possession of the British fleet, was destroyed July 19 by the Americans; Admiral Graves of the British fleet repaired it.

July 31, 1775 the Americans again destroyed it; it was again repaired, and when the British fleet were driven from Boston Harbor Captain Bangs, of the "*Renown*," placed a train of powder under it and blew it up.

A keeper who was at the light-house with his wife when destroyed by the Americans, left his property and fled to Dorchester; there his wife saw one of her dresses on a woman in the street.

1783. Massachusetts rebuilt it, sixty-eight feet high, of stone, with four lamps of a gallon of oil each, and four burners, and on November 28th of that year, Capt. Thomas Knox, pilot, was appointed keeper by Governor Hancock. His father, Adam, and mother, Martha Knox, resided there with him; she died there January, 1790, and Adam died there December of the same year, aged eighty-one.

1790. The island was ceded to the United States. In 1829, Jonathan Bruce, pilot, was keeper, being recommended by the Boston Marine Society.

Neal, in 1719, says: "The light-house was built on a rock above water, 2 leagues from Boston, where, in time of war, a signal is made to the castle & by the castle to the town, by hoisting and lowering the Union flag so many times as there are ships approaching; if they exceed a certain number, the castle fires 3 guns to warn the town of Boston, & the Gov'r if needs be, orders the Beacon fires, which alarms the adjacent country, and gives 6 or more hours to prepare for their reception." "*Shaw's History of Boston*" (Pemberton's account), 1817, says: "Light-House Island is a high rock of 2 or 3 acres, ¾ of an acre of it good soil; a bar, dry at low water, connected with Great Brewster; a stone Lt house shows one light; it is 8¼ miles from Long Wharf, Boston, and was formerly known as *Beacon* Island, &c.; pilots here have a piece of artillery to answer signal guns."

This and all the islands and Nantasket, including its beaches, were, on the settlement of the colony, covered with dense woods.

Boston Light, 1888.

In 1676–77, the proprietors of Hull divided the wood on the lesser Brewster, as they afterwards did on the other Brewsters, to clear them for planting and grass, to be done by May 1, 1679, the land and lots to be divided by lot.

1801. Sumner's "*East Boston*" speaks of the Brewsters wearing away.

1815. Boston Marine Society petitioned to have the light-house lit in winter (probably closed in war of 1812).

1860. The old tower was heightened and had a revolving-light. There was, no doubt, quite early a beacon and watch-house erected on Beacon or Light-House Island, as well as on Point Allerton Hill, by the town of Nantasket (Hull) to look out for and warn of an enemy's approach.

On the Massachusetts archives is this: "Hull, March 9, 1673-4. A true copy of the charges of the town of Hull hath been at about the Beacon, with the persons that *warded* the said Beacon, with an account of corne that was spoyled by carting over the said corne, and what was pluct up to set up the Beacon. The ward was, first, Benj. Bosworth, Sen'r, 17 days [other names omitted here] total 66 days. In the name of the Towne Serg't Bosworth, Nathaniel Bosworth.

"Charges about the Watch-house — timber & setting up, 2s., 300 of boards, 10s. 6d.; nails, 2s.; carting to the place, 2s. is £0 16s. 6d.; more for the beacon: a kettle, 5s.; for pitch, 2s.; John Loring & John Prince for making fier bales with pitch and ocum to make the bales, 1s. 6d.; for men to go to Boston to fetch more pitch for the beacon, 4s.; sum, £0 16s 6d.; total, £1 13s. 0d. For the corne spoyled by carting of the beacon setting up, which corne Capt. Oliver had a note of, to show to authority, which was three bushels."

March 9, 1673-74. The petition of the inhabitants of Hull about the trouble of setting and warding the beacon *erected on Point Allerton*, says: "We are a small people, our employment is wholly at sea, constantly every week of summer time, so that the whole burden lay upon a few men, whereby those men not only lost their time, but by continued working and warding, made unfit to carry on our employ, which we think is not the case with any other town in the colony. You do not consider how hardly it pinched us; yet we are assessed to pay our whole rate to the county & the castle. We think it too hard, &c. Notwithstanding that at the request of the Hon'd persons betrusted with the castle edifice, who send to us to dig and have some stone quarried at Brewsters Islands, which we consented to, & gave a gratuity thereto to the number of 400 boat loads, we hear that other towns had abatement in those rates, but we have none, but the castle got our stones and we may pay for the boating of them. We request the Hon'd court to weigh well these premises, and doubt not that they will do right, and have sent this 2nd address, and we, committing you unto the Lord's direction, we take leave to rest yours, in all humble subscription, Nath'l Bosworth, Thos. Collyer, John Benson, Sen'r, John Loring, Robert Goold, Selectmen, and in the name of the rest, Hull, March 9, 1673–74."

Indorsed "The magistrates remit the town of Hull the county rate, their brethren, the Deputies, consenting, Edward Rawson."

"The Deputies consent *not* hereto, but judge meet to refer ye answer to the said petition to the next Court. The Hon'd Magistrates consenting hereto, Wm. Terry Oliver, 27-3-1674, consented to go to ye Magistrates, Edw. Rawson, 29 May, 1674."

Hull's county tax for 1674 was £8 4s. The beacons on Point Allerton and Beacon Island were, no doubt, the origin of the lighthouse on the latter.

CHAPTER XI.

THE ROTHERSAND LIGHT TOWER.

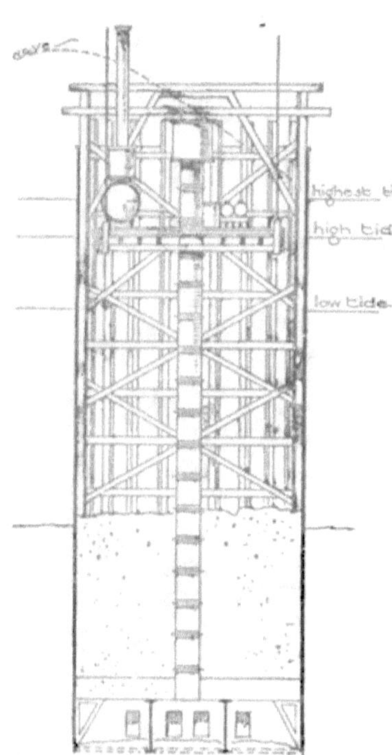

The light-houses so far described were built upon solid rocks; the engineers found a stable foundation on which to erect their structures, and if the towers were properly rooted to the rock there would be no fear of their destruction from the undermining or changing of their bases.

But there are many cases where the safety of life and commerce imperatively demands the erection of these guides to mariners on shifting shoals at long distances from shore: then are the difficulties and dangers multiplied many fold, and the skill and ingenuity of the engineer severely taxed. In many localities in this and other countries dangerous outlying shoals are marked by light-ships, but wherever light-houses can replace them, even though a great outlay may be necessary, it is advisable to erect the latter, which need but a few men to attend them, and which make a much more reliable signal, as it is not uncommon for light-ships to be driven from their moorings, thus depriving mariners for a time at least of their friendly light. As examples of how such works have recently been built, I will give a description of the construction of the Rothersand (red sand) light tower in the North Sea, Holland, condensed from a paper read before the Society of Civil Engineers and Architects at Hamburg, the 21st of April, 1886, and also of a similar structure just completed in this country at a shoal called Fourteen Foot Bank, Delaware Bay.

THE ROTHERSAND LIGHT TOWER.

The construction of this tower has a history of many years. The best way to enumerate the many difficulties under which the work was carried on and finally completed is to relate how the project was originated and developed and how at first a failure and later a success was attained.

By an agreement, the bordering states of Prussia, Oldenberg and Bremen bound themselves to mutually regulate the construction and maintenance of the aids to navigation of the Weser, and to meet the necessary expenses by a tax levied upon all the vessels entering the mouth of the river. An inspection tour was to be made annually under Prussia's authority.

In June, 1878, the first inspection drew attention to the imperfect manner in which the entrance to the Weser was lighted, and a light vessel was recommended. But as it was found impossible to moor a vessel securely, it was concluded to attempt the erection of a light tower.

The three above named allies gave Bremen the authority to build it; the matter was referred by the Light-house Establishment of Bremen to its Senate, which detailed Herr Hanks to execute the work.

This gentleman entered into correspondence with the Harkoort

Company of Duisburg on the Rhine, in August, 1878, and inquired if this company would undertake the erection of the tower at its own risk, and requested it to submit a proposal.

The tower was to be built on a sandy bottom twenty feet below the surface of the water, was to have a height of ninety-three feet above low water, and to be strong enough to resist heavy seas and floating ice. Herr Hanks suggested a screw pile foundation such as are used in England.

The company expressed its willingness to undertake the work, but proposed a very massive foundation to be sunk by the pneumatic process as preferable to one built of screw piles.

Considerable correspondence ensued and an inspection was made of the site. The latter is thirty-one miles from Bremerhaven, nearly in a straight line to the island of Heligoland, a little nearer the latter, distant from any harbor, and in a locality where winds from the west and northeast get up heavy seas.

In addition, it was required that the tower be built close to the fifty-foot channel, which is constantly changing; this precluded the use of any type of foundation except the one proposed by the company, and even this had to be sunk to a considerable depth. Under the circumstances it seemed impossible to erect a working platform, nor would it be prudent to attempt to transport a caisson to the site suspended between two vessels.

Herr Hanks proposed to float the caisson to the locality, to sink it there, and then to fill it with concrete. The company believed this to be a brilliant and practical method, and perfected it by proposing to sink the caisson *on* the sand by filling it with water, and *into* the sand by the pneumatic process, the necessary machinery; namely, boiler, air-pump, air-lock, etc., to be placed within the caisson.

Plans and specifications conforming to the above were submitted on the 7th of February, 1879. The requirements at that time were different from the present tower; it was contemplated to sink it only thirty-eight feet below low water, and to be filled with concrete 13.6 feet above the same level.

While the drawings were being prepared, the Company's engineer who had been engaged on the work unexpectedly resigned. Shortly afterward he and two other engineers formed a company with the intention of competing for the construction of this tower. They were rather premature, however, in their action, as eighteen months elapsed before the fund accumulated from the light dues was large enough to begin the work. On September 15th, 1880, proposals were invited and bidders were furnished with plans and specifications, which, however, were not binding in all their details. The young company mentioned above were very anxious to get the contract, believing that its successful execution would secure them a glorious future.

The Harkoort Company bid 480,500 marks (about $120,125) not including the brush mattresses and rip-rap protection against scour; their competitors bid was 450,000 marks (about $112,500) including the above protection. As after experience showed, this protection cost 110,000 marks, so according to these figures the two estimates differed by 140,500 marks ($35,125.)

The low price at which the contract was taken was the principal cause of its failure. The contractors were compelled to save in the construction of details which should have been executed in the best manner, and were forced to neglect important preparations for which they had neglected to estimate.

The construction of the floating caisson was commenced and completed during the winter of 1880–81. On the morning of May 22, 1881, when there was a dead calm, two tug-boats towed the caisson from the harbor (Kaiser's haven) in Bremerhaven, down the Weser to the site. The caisson was not under good control; rolling heavily, it parted its tow-line in the following night, and went ashore at ebb tide. Next morning at high tide it floated off again, the hawser was refastened, and on the evening of the fourth day from leaving the harbor it had reached the site, and was sunk to the bottom by the rather primitive method of removing a large wooden plug six inches in diameter, located two and one-half feet above the bottom of the

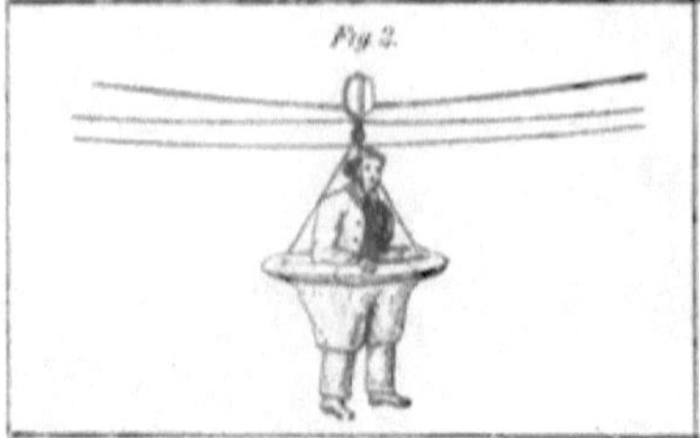

TILLAMOOK LIGHT.

See page 95

Perspective View from the Northeast, showing t

Station completed. Rough southerly Sea.

caisson. This nearly caused the caisson to upset, but finally at nightfall it reached the bottom.

All this unexpected trouble worried and discouraged the men, who had hardly slept since leaving the harbor — a few of them, under charge of one of the engineers, remained on the caisson; the rest found quarters on the steamer provided for this purpose, and moored at a safe distance from the caisson.

The next morning, when all except the mate of the steamer were sound asleep, he saw through the lifting fog that the caisson was much inclined. It took considerable trouble and time to rouse the tired men and to start the fires under the boilers so as to go to the relief of the excited party on the caisson, who had been awakened at daybreak by being rolled involuntarily from their berths. "That is caused by the ebb current," said the engineer, to encourage his men. "It scours on the south-east side; when the flood sets in and scours the north-west side, everything will be all right." But when the latter came, contrary to his prediction, the caisson inclined still further, until it reached twenty-one degrees from the vertical. The engineer, as well as the men, were greatly relieved when the steamer sent life-boats to take them off; they got on board without loss of time by sliding down a rope. For four days the caisson was left to its fate, and no work could be done on it, as during flood tide the water entered from above (see following cut).

Later, by the counter action of the flood-current, the caisson took a more upright position, about ten degrees from the vertical. Its height was increased six and a half feet before the May storms commenced. When they abated on June 14th, and the working-party returned, they found that the scour caused by the storms had acted favorably; the caisson stood perfectly plumb and had sunk into the sand from seventeen to eighteen feet.

The concrete filling was now commenced and the machinery put in order. A month later the water in the air-shaft and working-chamber was displaced by compressed air, and on August 4th the sinking of the caisson began. During the next two months the weather was fine, and the caisson was sunk nearly twenty-six feet farther into the sand, bringing it seventy feet below low-water mark—a considerably greater depth than the original plan contemplated.

But while this work was going on, the height of the caisson and the amount of concrete filling was but slightly increased, and little was done to protect the caisson from the approaching October storms. During the May storms, when the upper edge of the caisson was twenty-two and one-half feet above low water, the seas ran so high as to entirely submerge it, yet the iron was carried only twenty-

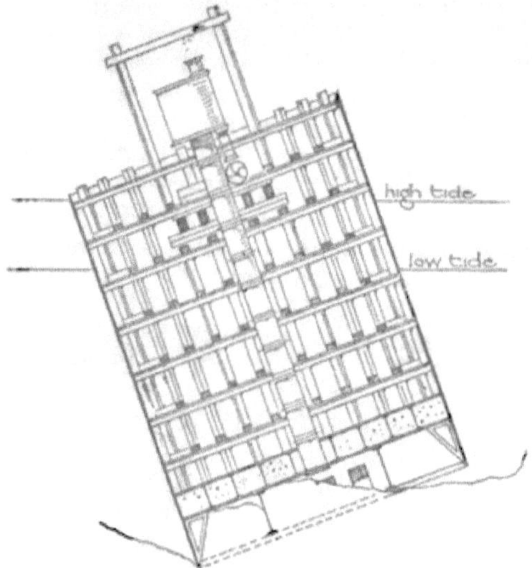

six feet above low water, and worse than this was the delay in the construction of the brick lining and concrete filling, difficult operations, necessarily consuming much time. In the early part of October the brick lining had not been commenced, the concrete filling was only up to a level with the bottom of the sea, and the brush mattresses and rip-rap were still over thirty feet below low water.

In addition, the weak wrought-iron sides were only braced with timbers not strong enough to resist the combined action of the wind and sea.

The contractors were warned of these defects and deficiencies, but did not remedy them, preferring to continue the sinking of the caisson, as, according to agreement, they could draw money by partial payments, the amounts being proportioned to the distance the cutting-edge penetrated the sand.

Of course it was impossible to leave men on this insecure structure, so when bad weather caught them on October 9th, the working-party was compelled to run for a harbor. About three or four miles from the site, and toward the shore, the light-ship "*Bremen*" was moored on the Weser. At noon, on October 13th, 1881, when the lookout accidentally sighted the structure, it seem to him to suddenly disappear. He could not believe his eyes. Grasping his telescope, he scanned the horizon closely, but could find nothing. The tide had risen to a height of sixteen and one-half feet, so that the ironwork projected only a little more than eight feet above the sea. The waves rolled heavily over the structure, breaking or knocking out the iron braces, and the whole work, with the boilers and machinery collapsed. It was reported that the caisson, after penetrating forty feet of sand, had struck a layer of semi-fluid silt, and dropped out of sight. Pictures illustrating this story were printed and circulated.

When fine weather permitted an examination of the site by divers, it was found that the iron mouth of the caisson had been broken off seven feet above the bottom of the sea, and that the boiler and machinery had fallen toward the lee side (south east) of the structure.

The expenditures had been $97,500 to date; of this amount the contractors lost $31,250, their own capital; those who furnished the materials and loaned money lost $46,250, and finally, the Government $20,000, for the total amount ($45,000) of all installments previously paid was only secured by a bond of $25,000.

So ended the first attempt to erect a light-house in the breakers of the "Red Sand" Shoal.

The following March (1882) Herr Hanks asked the Harkoort Company if they would make a trial to erect a light-house at this locality, and this company, in June, submitted a bid in accordance with their original project. The contract was signed on September 21. The total price for the complete structure, ready for occupancy, but exclusive of the lens and illuminating apparatus, amounted to $213,500, which was later increased by $3,250 on account of alterations made in the height and construction of the upper part of the tower.

The mistakes and errors of omission made at the first trial were of great value to the Harkoort Company — the general plan remained the same and it only remained to execute the details in the proper manner to ensure success.

While the contract was under discussion all the necessary drawings for the details of the caisson and of the special apparatus were prepared, so the work was commenced immediately after the signing of the contract.

The structure consisted, generally speaking, of two parts — the foundation and the tower. The first, of course, was the only part which offered any engineering difficulties.

To build this foundation a caisson was used which, after being sunk to the required depth, was to be filled with masonry and concrete, on which the tower could be erected. The caisson, in plan, resembled a section of a bi-convex lens. It was thirty-six feet eight inches wide, forty-six feet eight inches long, and sixty-one feet eight inches high when it was towed to the site; this height was gradually increased during the sinking to one hundred and seven feet six inches.

The caisson was made of boiler iron four-tenths inches in thickness, was well braced vertically and horizontally, and none but the best material was employed in its construction. It was calculated to withstand a hydrostatic pressure produced by a column of water twenty feet high.

Eight feet four inches above the cutting edge of the caisson was an iron diaphragm, forming the top of the working-chamber, carried by two longitudinal and twelve cross girders. This was also very strongly braced to the walls by a great number of iron brackets. From its centre rose the cylindrical air-shaft, three feet four inches in diameter, provided with an air-lock.

This air-lock had four chambers — two for the use of the men and two for the supply and discharge of material, and was provided with a steam winch for hoisting the sand. Besides, there were six pipes to be used for blowing out the sand if it were found practical to use this more expeditious method.

The upper part of the caisson was divided into four stories. The first, or lowest, was for mixing concrete; the next was the machinery floor, and carried two boilers, one air-compressor, a surface condenser, a centrifugal pump, the coal, and fresh water, and the steam-pipes leading to the two steam hoisting-cranes, to the compressor, and to the winch of the air-lock.

On the third floor were two sleeping-rooms and store-rooms; from this floor access was gained to the air-lock. The top story carried two revolving steam cranes.

As the work progressed the upper three floors would have to be raised from time to time, and it was important that this should be done without interfering with the other work.

This was accomplished by suspending the two upper floors by four long and strong screws to the vertical ribs of the caisson, which were made higher for this purpose. The second floor was suspended from the fourth by four other screws, and there was another screw in the centre of the fourth floor for raising the air-lock.

By means of these nine screws, all worked from the top floor, the raising of the floors, with everything on them, was effected by a few men without delay to the work.

This was a far superior arrangement to that previously adopted, which required the cessation of all work while the platform was being raised, and in addition, the interior wooden bracing of the caisson was always much in the way.

When the caisson reached the Red Sand Shoal it was to be sunk to a depth of about seventy-three feet below mean low water, and then filled with concrete and masonry to six and two-thirds feet above the same level.[1]

This foundation was to support a tower with a circular base of thirty-four and two-thirds feet, the offset round the foot of the tower being covered with strong cast-iron plates securely fastened to the foundation. To a height of twenty-six and two-thirds feet above the foundation the tower is trumpet-shaped. At this height its diameter is reduced to twenty-three and one-third feet, and this part is solid masonry except the spaces left for cisterns and for the float of the tide-guage.

The portion above the cellar was to be lined with a twenty-one inch brick wall, and have a fireproof ceiling of corrugated iron and concrete.

The upper stories were to have an iron shell with a double wooden lining, lathed and plastered.

Above the living-room is an iron gallery eighty-one and two-thirds feet above low water, and at this height the tower is reduced in diameter to seventeen feet.

Two of the three semicircular dormers, or small towers, at the gallery level contain range lights, and the third is used as a watch-room. One also contains the stairway leading to the gallery and lantern of the main light. The latter is eleven feet in diameter, and is covered by a copper roof on which is the ventilator one hundred and two and two-thirds feet above low water.

The following is the method employed in transporting the caisson to the site:

The depth of water in the harbor and on the shoals, over which the caisson was to pass on its way to the site permitted a draft of only twenty-three and one-third feet, and in calculating the stability of the caisson the probability of encountering a moderate storm was taken into account.

It was assumed that the caisson would be safe and not capsize when subjected to a wind pressure of about two hundred pounds to the square yard — corresponding to a wind velocity of one hundred

[1] See page 139.

feet per second. The caisson was to carry all the machinery previously mentioned, which was to be so arranged that work could be commenced as soon as the caisson was sunk on the shoal, and at the same time it was to be placed as low as possible so as to lower the centre of gravity of the floating mass.

To accomplish this the bulkheads on which the machinery floor rested were provided with four hinged rectangular frames which, when raised vertically, supported the floor in a position ten feet higher.

It was also important to build the iron shell as high as possible so

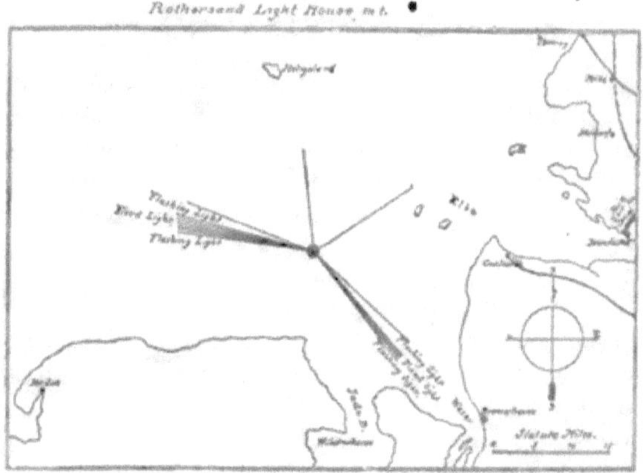

that after the caisson was sunk it would project sufficiently above the water to prevent the entrance of the sea. Owing, however, to its great weight, this height did not exceed sixty-two and one-half feet, four and one-sixth feet higher than at the first trial.

Sufficient ballast was added to bring the draft to twenty-three and one-third feet, but a careful calculation showed that the stability, with reference to the assumed wind-pressure, was not sufficient. The elongated shape of the caisson required more support at the

[1] See page 142.

sides, and to attain this two pontoons were used. They were made of boiler-iron, air-tight, twenty-six and two-thirds feet long, six and two-thirds feet wide, and ten feet high, and had strong lugs fitting into concavities in the shell. Each was provided with a pump for admitting water and with an air-cock, which were so arranged as to be operated from the caisson.

When the latter floated at twenty-three and one-third feet draft the pontoons sunk three and two-thirds feet into the water. When the caisson rolled, one pontoon sunk deeper than the other, counteracting the tendency of the structure to leave a vertical position.

It will be seen from the preceding that the most important part of the execution of the work was the construction of the caisson with all the requisites for transportation, sinking by the pneumatic process, etc.

The contract with the Government was signed in October, 1882, and on the 1st of April, 1883, the caisson was completed as described, and moored at Kaiserhaven ready for transportation.

In the meantime, the necessary vessels and steamers required had been chartered; they consisted of the "*Palme,*" on which the men were to be quartered, and which was to be moored near the work. The "*Solide,*" a tug which was to tow all vessels to Bremerhaven, in case the weather compelled them to make a harbor. Two solidly built sail-boats, the "*Leopoldine*" and "*Maria,*" carried the men between the "*Palme*" and the structure. In addition several vessels and the tug "*Otto*" were employed for carrying material, and kept a constant communication between Bremerhaven and the site.

For the transportation of the caisson to the site, the "*Samson*" and the "*Nord See,*" the two strongest tugs of the North German Lloyd were chartered, and in addition the tugs "*Solide,*" "*Herkules*" and "*Otto,*" were to assist if required. Three special tow lines, 4 8-10 inches in diameter, were constructed for the purpose; two were attached to the stem and one to the stern of the structure, about eleven feet below the surface of the water.

The meteorological station at Hamburg had kindly promised to

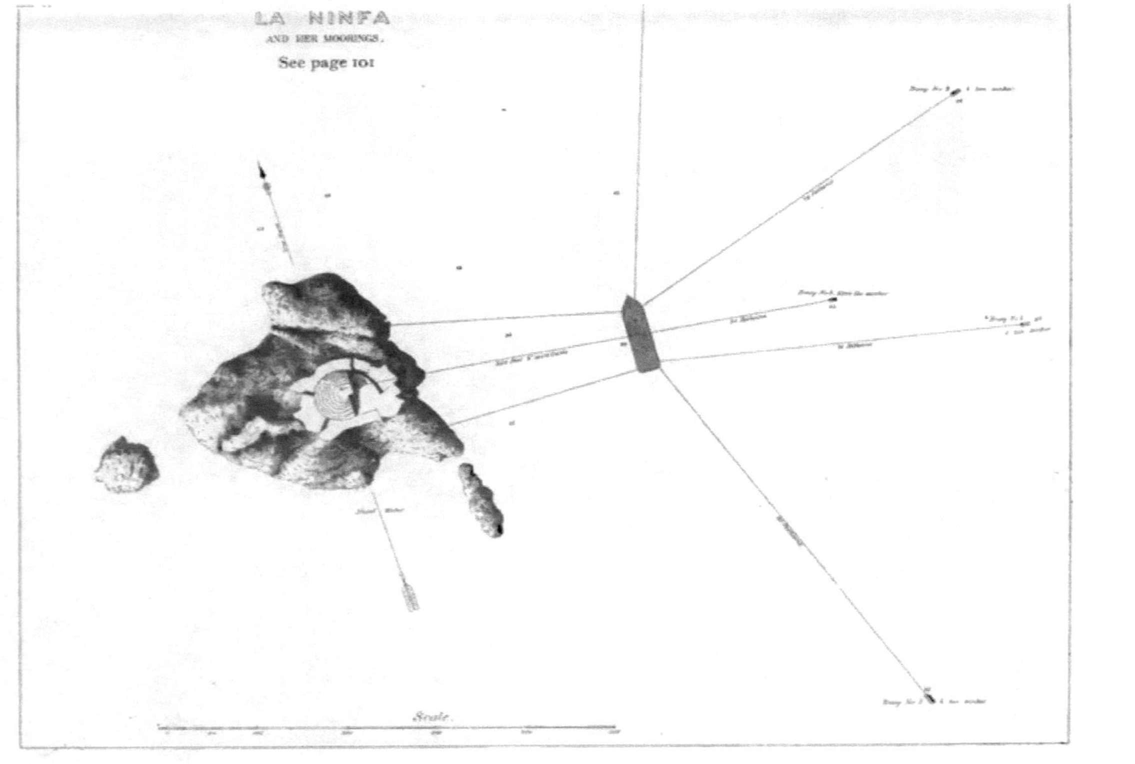

LA NINFA
AND HER MOORINGS.

See page 101

ST. GEORGE'S REEF LIGHT STATION.

View from the South-West, showing the Rock as it appeared at the End of the Working Season, and the Method of Landing Men from the Schooner "La Ninfa."

ST. GEORGE'S REEF
LIGHT STATION.

PLAN OF ROCK
and
RELATIVE POSITION OF THE MEN'S QUARTERS.

telegraph daily the weather indications during April and May, and the state of the wind at Wangeroog and Neuwerk, two stations in the neighborhood of the shoal. The weather in April was so unfavorable that the station at Hamburg advised not to start until May 14; this delay was very expensive to the contractors, as they had all the vessels and eighty men under pay during this time.

On the 15th of May good weather was prophesied, but the flood-tide did not rise high enough to float the structure out of the harbor, and then the weather became bad again.

Finally, on the 25th of May favorable news was received from Hamburg, and everything was got ready to start at 2.30 A. M. on the 26th. At 3.30 A. M. the tide had risen high enough to open the gates of the basin, and soon after the caisson, which nearly touched the sills and jambs of the gates, was towed into the Weser. Immediately afterwards the German flag was hoisted on the colossus. The tug "*Nord See*" was ready to take the hawser, and though it was difficult to overhaul the latter on account of its great weight and stiffness, this was quickly done. Then the "*Samson*" fastened its hawser to the "*Nord See*," and both headed for the site. The other steamers and sailing vessels, nine in all, accompanied the tow, making quite a fine naval pageant. The contractors' steamer headed the procession, indicating the deepest channel, and thus all shoals were passed in safety. Quietly and majestically the caisson floated down the Weser with the ebb-current, and so quickly that it arrived at Droorgat at 7.15 A. M. The strength of the ebb had greatly diminished, and as it was impossible to reach the site before the tide changed, the caisson was anchored near the Eversand shoal to wait for the next high water at 4 P. M.

The flood-current increased so much by 11 A. M. that the anchors of both tugs commenced to drag. Their engines were quickly started and the "*Solide*" was called to their assistance, but as all three could not prevent the caisson from drifting, the "*Herkules*" was also called upon. The combined strength of these four steamers, about 350 horse-power, held the caisson and when the flood diminished they were enabled to proceed, so that at 2.30 P. M. the caisson reached the Hohewey Light-house and came to anchor again. Hardly had it arrived when a signal from the Light-house announced the arrival of a telegram from Hamburg, stating that the wind would change to north, and that squalls were approaching from England. In a short time clouds commenced to rise, the sky turned the color of sulphur, the sea got rough, rain and wind followed, and at 4.50 P. M. the fleet was in the centre of a storm, which caused great anxiety. However, the caisson stood the storm remarkably well, rolling very little as the pontons gave it excellent support.

This storm prevented the continuance of the journey, the watch on the caisson, twelve men, were relieved by others, and by 8 P. M. the whole fleet was got ready for the night.

The delay was troublesome, as at every change of the tide the caisson swung round and had to be guided by the tugs; this manœuvre was difficult to execute in the darkness, but was successfully accomplished.

The following day the weather was bad, and the start was postponed until the succeeding one at 7.30, A. M. when the anchors were weighed and the seaward journey re-commenced. When, as the report has it, "in spite of the rough sea, the colossus parted the water with ease, wind and water did not affect his majestic dignity."

At 9 A. M. the Bremen Light-ship was passed, at 9.30 the dangerous "Rothen Grund," and at 10 the tow arrived at the place where a wreck buoy located the position of the former ill-fated caisson.

A little over twelve hundred yards below where this caisson was wrecked a buoy, painted black, white and red marked the spot where the tower was to be erected.

The Harbor-Master and the Chief-Engineer boarded the caisson; slowly and carefully the tugs brought the structure nearer and nearer, and when about one hundred yards distant from the buoy — exactly at eleven o'clock — the raising of the flag on the caisson gave the signal for all anchors to be dropped overboard. Both valves for admitting water to the caisson were opened, and the latter slowly and steadily, and perfectly plumb, sank to the bottom of the sea. A slight shock, at 11:15, indicated that it landed on the shoal. A second time the flag was raised and was greeted with loud cheers by all who witnessed the performance.

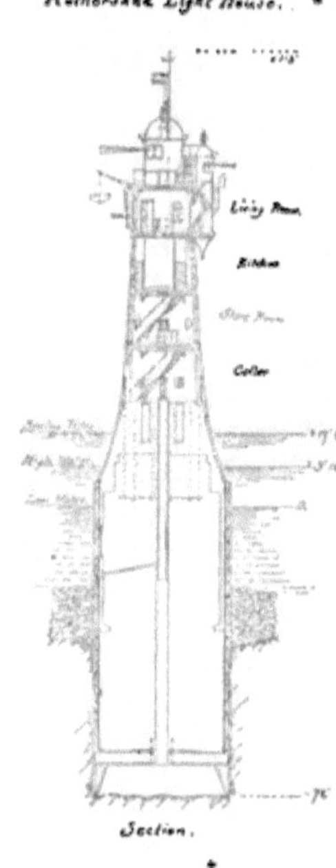

The heavy hawsers were removed, and the large tugs left the site and returned to Bremen. The most pressing work was now to release the pontons which were invisible, being about two yards below the surface of the water. By opening the valves sufficient water was admitted into the pontoons to overcome their buoyancy, they then began to sink, thereby disengaging themselves from the caisson. As soon as they were free the valves were closed again and both pontoons were sunk in the neighborhood where they soon after disappeared in the sand of the shoal. The increased current which was produced in the vicinity of the caisson at once scoured the shoal to a depth of three feet near by, diminishing to nothing at a distance of one hundred yards.

In addition, the first flood-current scoured a hole alongside of the caisson facing the current, inclining the caisson toward the north four degrees; during the following ebb current the south side was undermined, and the caisson inclined the same amount to the south. In

[1] See page 131.

this manner, moving like a pendulum, the caisson sunk itself in four days more than six feet in the shoal. On the first of June the cutting edge was thirty-five feet below low water and the ceiling of the working-chamber commenced to bear upon the surface of the shoal. This self-sinking finally ceased entirely at thirty-seven feet below low water, when the large number of brush mattresses which had been sunk on the shoal prevented further scour.

The remainder of the working season was devoted to sinking the caisson by the pneumatic process, to filling it with concrete and masonry, to placing additional mattresses and rip-rap around it, and to building the iron shell as high as possible. On October 15, 1883, the cutting edge was fifty-two feet below low water, the concrete level was thirty-six-and-two-thirds feet above low water, the top of the masonry was eight-and-two-thirds feet above low water, the upper edge of the highest completed section of the iron caisson, and also the height of the floor of the quarters for the temporary keepers was thirty-seven-and-one-quarter feet above low water, and finally the uppermost floor with the steam cranes, and also the upper edge of the unfinished section of the caisson was forty-seven-and-one quarter feet above low water, or ninety-nine-and-one-quarter feet above the cutting edge. On this day the workmen were compelled to leave the station as the strong southeast wind made it impossible to go near the caisson. The vessels anchored at the Eversand shoal to wait for better weather, but on October 16th the weather became worse, and the wind and sea increasing in violence, they returned to Bremerhaven. On the 17th and 18th of October, 1883, it was storming as it did on October 13, 1881, when the first caisson was destroyed. This time, however, but little damage was done. According to the reports of the two temporary keepers, stationed on the structure, a single wave, on the 18th of October, tore asunder one of the plates of the top section of the caisson and bent up two others which had not been bolted together, and were consequently liable to such destruction. Two heavy boxes of bolts were blown from the upper floor, the caging around one of the steam cranes was greatly damaged, and one of the keepers was violently thrown by a wave to the floor of his room as he attempted to leave it.

After this storm, which was followed by others of equal violence, but little work could be done during the winter. The air-lock and the machinery floor were raised so that the latter stood at a level twenty feet above low water. The masonry and concrete were also raised twenty and forty inches respectively, and a Pintsch gas apparatus with lantern and light visible six to seven nautical miles was erected.

Work was commenced in February, 1884, and continued until November, with many interruptions from wind and weather. The required depth, seventy-three feet below low water, to which the caisson was to be sunk, was attained on the 21st of May, 1884, one year after the caisson was launched at the site, and at the same time the level of the concrete and masonry had reached a height of three feet four inches above low water. Over two thousand cubic yards of sand, in addition to that which had leaked into the working-chamber from without, was all removed from the latter by the sand blast. The sand was very fine and mixed with small shells. A layer of stones was reached when near the required depth, but as it was not necessary to remove them; no use was made of the steam crane in the air-lock.

In June the machinery and boilers were removed, and by November the solid substructure of the tower, the cellar, the storerooms and kitchen were completed, and a part of the exterior walls of the living-room was put up.

Good progress was also made in securing the sand around the foundation. According to contract, the latter was to be covered with brush mattresses thirty inches thick and over a width of fifty feet around the tower, held down by a layer of rip-rap twenty inches thick, first filling all depressions caused by the scour during the construction of the foundation. This scour was much greater than had been anticipated.

This work was accomplished with great difficulty, and it was not until the middle of the following year that it was completed: sixty-six hundred cubic yards of mattresses and eight hundred cubic yards of stone were needed.

On December 2, 1884, Herr Kröte, who represented the Government during the construction of the tower, wished to inspect it once more prior to a pleasure trip during the Christmas holidays, and left in company with the Constructing Engineer to stay but a short time. They had hardly made a landing when a storm arose which made it impossible to take off the inspecting party. At first they rather enjoyed their detention, but when days lengthened into weeks and there was still no possibility of release, the situation became grave, especially as they signalled that one of the men was seriously ill. Finally, on December 21, with the sea still running high, all were successfully taken off except two men who were left to act as keepers during the winter.

Work was recommenced on April 12, 1885, the living-room and its three dormers, the lantern and the interior finish completed by August 10th and the main lens set up.

The main light of the fourth order, with Otter's revolving shutters, guides the incoming vessel first to the tower, and from there into the narrow channel leading to the Hoheweg Light-house. Each of these courses is marked by a fixed light, illuminating an arc of seven degrees toward the sea, and an arc of three-and-one-half degrees toward the river (see chart).[1] In passing the limit to either side of these courses the fixed main light changes to a flashing light. The distance from the tower, where a vessel approaching the light has to change its course, is indicated by two fifth-order lights, one in the northwest, the other in the south dormer, about seventeen feet below the main light. The intensity is so regulated that they only appear to the naked eye as separate lights at a distance of two-and-one-half nautical miles from the tower; at a greater distance they cannot be distinguished as they are overpowered by the main light. Finally, another light of the fifth order was placed in the dormer containing the stairs, to locate the range on which vessels, coming from the Island of Heligoland, enter the mouth of the Weser.

[1] See page 135.

The base of the structure, for a height of twenty-seven feet, is painted black, and the tower above, with alternate red and white bands fourteen feet wide. This makes the tower so conspicuous that it can be seen on a clear day for a distance of twelve nautical miles.

By the end of August the upper part of the caisson was taken down; in September the tower was connected to the shore by an electric cable, and on October 23, 1885, the tower was accepted by the Government.

This is, I believe, the first light-house erected at a long distance from land which does not rest on a rock foundation.

CHAPTER XII.

FOURTEEN-FOOT BANK LIGHT-HOUSE, DELAWARE BAY.

Fourteen-foot Shoal Light.

FOURTEEN-Foot Bank Shoal is situated on the west side of the main channel, about 3½ miles from the Delaware shore, 10¼ miles northeast of the mouth of Mispillion Creek, and 14½ miles north 51° 15′ west from Cape May Light.

This shoal, which is a turning point in the navigation of the bay, was marked in 1876 by a ght-ship. Owing to floating ice, the light-ship could not remain at her station during the winter months, when it is very important to have the location of the shoal defined.

In 1882, the year after the disaster to the first caisson attempted to be placed on the Rothersand shoal, the Light-house Board of the United States considered the desirability of replacing the light-ship by a permanent structure, and several projects for the foundation pier were entertained. They all embraced the general features of a cast-iron pier filled with concrete. Different forms of vertical section for the pier were proposed and discussed; finally in 1883, a cylinder, 73 feet in height and 35 feet in diameter, was adopted by the Board, on the recommendation of Major D. P. Heap, Engineer Secretary of the Board.

This cylinder was to be composed of 1½ inch cast-iron plates.

BOTHERSAND LIGHT. (SECTION.)

See page 137

feet in height, with 6-inch horizontal and vertical flanges, 1¾ inches in thickness; it was also required that these flanges be planed so that the joints could be made water-tight.

A cylinder such as recommended presented the advantage of simplicity of construction; all the plates, being of the same size, would be interchangeable, a decided help in putting the cylinder together at the site.

By Acts of Congress, approved August 7, 1882, and March 3, 1883, the Board had, at its disposal, the sum of $175,000 for the entire completion of this work.

The contract for furnishing the metal-work of the cylinder was awarded to the G. W. & F. Smith Iron Company, of Boston, Mass., who delivered it on the Government Pier at Lewes, Del., on July 19, 1884.

The general figure of the shoal is oval in plan; its length, measured up and down stream between the 24-foot curves, is 5,720 feet, while its width is 1,300 feet. The least water at low tide was 20 feet. Borings were made to the depth of 26 feet. The material penetrated was very fine, dark sand, mixed with shells, and was so compacted that a strong water-jet was necessary to force down the 4-inch wrought-iron tube used in making the borings. It will be noticed that the depth of water and the nature of the bed of the sea were nearly the same here as at Rothersand.

The average rise and fall of the tide were found to be 6 feet, and the maximum velocity of the current about 2 miles per hour.

On the 20th of December, 1884, bids were invited to build and sink the cylinder so that its bottom would be 23 feet below the surface of the shoal: this would place it on the same level as the bottom of the adjacent main channel in its deepest part; bidders were not restricted to any one plan for sinking the cylinder, but were allowed to use any process they pleased subject to the approval of the Board, and were required to give security that in case the metal-work was lost or injured from any cause while in their hands, they would make good the loss to the Government.

The bid of Messrs. Anderson & Barr, of New York City, in the sum of $38,900, was accepted, and as security they deposited $20,000 with the Treasurer of the United States; they proposed to use the pneumatic process, the Government furnishing the cylinder and the cement required for 2,000 cubic yards of concrete.

For a working-chamber they built a square wooden caisson on which the cylinder was to rest, its details are shown in the drawing, [see illustrations] as this caisson was 10 feet high its lower edge had to penetrate the sand to a depth of 33 feet, in order to bring the bottom of the cylinder to the stipulated depth.

It was built of 12 x 12 inch yellow pine, and lined with 1½ inch tongued-and-grooved stuff, laid in white-lead. The joints of all adjoining timbers were caulked and filled with mineral pitch; a sheathing of 2-inch yellow-pine planks was placed on the outside. Work on the caisson was commenced on the beach at Lewes, Del., in the latter part of May, 1885; to facilitate launching the caisson in shoal water a temporary water-tight bottom was built; in launching, this bottom leaked, and compressed-air was used to keep out the water. When launched, the caisson was moored alongside the Government pier, and three sections of cylinder plates put on by means of a boom-derrick, which was secured to the air-shaft and the roof of the caisson. The lowest section was securely bolted to the woodwork below, and the joint caulked with oakum. The joints between the plates, which had been accurately planed, were coated with red lead before being bolted together. About 9 inches of concrete were then placed on top of the caisson to depress the centre of gravity. The displacement was then about 400 tons, and the draught was 15½ feet; the caisson was then towed by two tugs, in six hours, to the site, distant nearly 20 miles.

The contractors had chartered the hulk of the old steamer "*Moro Castle*," and had moored it at the site by 6 anchors; this vessel was 200 feet long, 30 feet beam, and drew 14 feet of water; 80 tons of coal, 600 barrels of cement, 3 sections of cylinder plates, and the sections of the air-shaft were stowed below deck. The deck carried all the machinery, sand, broken-stone, timber, and kitchen and quarters for the officers and men. A boom-derrick, with a reach of 30 feet and lifting 2 tons, was secured amidships.

The following is a list of the machinery on board:

1. A locomotive boiler, with 18 square feet of grate and 400 square feet of heating-surface, and carrying 60 pounds pressure: this proved too small.

2. A feed-pump, connecting with the hot-well of the surface-condenser, with the fresh-water tanks and with the sea.

3. A surface-condenser, connected with all the engines and pumps.

4. A 2-cylinder hoisting-engine, with cylinders 6½ inches in diameter and 9 inches stroke: the diameter of the rope-drum was 16 inches, and was geared to the engine in the ratio of 1 to 5.

5. A Delamater air-compressor, having 2 steam-cylinders of 8 inches diameter, and air-cylinders, 10 inches diameter and 16 inches stroke. A maximum velocity of 120 revolutions per minute was required to blow the sand out of the caisson.

6. A Clayton air-compressor of the same capacity as the one above named; this was used to relieve the other while under repair. Both compressors were provided with water-jackets around their cylinders. The air was forced through water in a cylindrical cooler 2 feet 9 inches in diameter and 5 feet 4 inches high, and through a 2½-inch rubber-hose, to the upper end of the air-shaft. Gauges on the cooler indicated the water-level in it and the air-pressure. There was a check-valve also where the air entered the shaft. The air in the air-lock and in the upper part of the shaft became intensely hot, because no provision had been made for circulating water through the cooler; the workmen suffered considerably on this account.

7. A portable centrifugal pump, with 4-inch suction and discharge, and connected to the boiler and surface-condenser with hose. This pump was used as a bilge pump.

8. A duplicate of the above was used to furnish water for mixing concrete.

9. An air-lock large enough to admit 4 men at one time; it was

made of boiler-iron, and had a cast-iron cylinder supply-lock of one cubic yard's capacity.

After the caisson was moored at the site it was quickly sunk by letting water into the cylinder through 6-inch valves. This water was partly replaced by broken stones as the latter were supplied by the schooner, and when the weight became sufficient the water was pumped out by the centrifugal pump, and the broken stone in the cylinder was made into concrete.

On July 17 the regular mixing of concrete was commenced; this work was done either on the hulk or on the schooners that brought the broken stones: on July 23, when the weight of the structure was about 500 tons greater than that of the displacement, the air-lock was bolted to the air-shaft, connections were made with the compressor, and the water was forced from the shaft and working-chamber.

The current produced a considerable scour as soon as the caisson was grounded; this continued until the caisson had sunk about 8 feet, and until its roof rested upon a mound of sand. The cutting edge of the caisson did not rest upon the shoal for a considerable part of its length, and at times the cylinder was 12° out of plumb; the scour was 10 feet deep near the caisson, and extended over an area of 70 feet in diameter. It will be noticed that the action of this cylinder was almost identical with the one sunk in the "Rothersand."

The working party in the caisson consisted of three gangs of eight men each, each gang working for eight hours, with a rest for meals after four hours work; they carried paraffine candles in their hats to light them at their work.

The sand was collected at the bottom and blown by the air-pressure through a 4-inch wrought-iron pipe which connected the working-chamber with the outside air, and which was provided with two cocks, one in the chamber, the other on the outside of the shaft. The sudden diminution of the air-pressure when blowing out the sand caused such a condensation of the moisture in the air in the working chamber as to make it so foggy that the men could see but 2 or 3 feet, and the blowing had to be limited to a half or a quarter of a minute's duration at a time. The blow-pipe was at first made with a bend to throw the sand into the sea. This caused the pipe to choke and occasioned much delay. Afterward the sand was blown out vertically and either fell into the sea, the cylinder, or the hulk, where it did much damage to the machinery. This was remedied later by stretching a stout canvas over the pipe.

Sinking was continued at the rate of from 1 to 2 feet a day until July 31, when the cutting edge of the caisson had penetrated 18 feet and when the door of the air-lock was nearly at the level of high tide. The air was then allowed to escape, the shaft extended, the air-lock replaced, and the concrete increased to a depth of 37½ feet. The water was then forced out of the working-chamber, and on August 18 the work of sinking was resumed, and by the 28th, the cutting edge had reached the required depth, viz., 33 feet 4 inches below the original surface of the shoal. The kind of material penetrated changed at the level of 29 feet, the remaining 4 feet being clean, coarse, sharp, yellow sand mixed with considerable coarse gravel.

The resistance to sinking was so great during the latter part of the time that it was found necessary to diminish the air-pressure suddenly in order to facilitate the descent. The men remained in the working-chamber at these times.

The cutting edges were then tightly under-rammed, the working-chamber and air-shaft packed with sand, and the latter sealed with concrete at a level of 30 feet 4 inches above the caisson roof. The air-shaft was then taken off at a height of 38 feet 7 inches above the caisson, and the remainder of the 2,000 cubic yards of concrete were put in place, raising the concrete to a level of 13 feet 11 inches below the upper edge of the cylinder. The contractors, after erecting a mast from which the crew of the Fourteen-Foot Bank Lightship were to show a lantern at night, left the site on September 16. Three foremen, two engineers, two firemen, thirty laborers and one cook were employed on the work.

At one time a rather curious accident occurred. During a heavy blow from the southward, the old bulk parted her moorings and commenced drifting directly toward the cylinder, which was then 8 or 10 feet above the water, but only filled with concrete to the water-level. Several of the men immediately jumped on the cylinder, and, sitting on the upper flange, which was about 6 inches wide, dropped fenders between the cylinder and the sides of the hulk to soften the blow. The hulk came against the cylinder so as to give it a glancing blow or push and then sheered off. The men essayed to jump on board, but to their astonishment several were unable to do so. When the hulk struck, she forced open the joints between the plates of the cylinder, which, immediately closing when relieved from the pressure, caught and securely anchored the men by the seats of their breeches. The involuntary prisoners had to decide promptly, for their home was drifting from them, so they, with one accord, gave one *arrière pensée*, tore their trowsers and jumped on board.

The bids received for finishing the cellar story in accordance with the approved plan not being reasonable in amount, the Board decided to build a temporary frame house of two rooms and a platform, from which to show a fourth-order light, until the work on the superstructure should begin during the following season. This light was first shown on October 24, and during the winter was maintained by two men employed as temporary keepers. It proved of much value to navigation, as its range and visibility were greater than those of the adjacent light-ship, which besides in winter was necessarily off her station.

One thousand tons of rip-rap were placed around the cylinder to prevent any additional scour. Soundings made the following March showed no change in the shoal around the pier; an unequal settlement of one inch had taken place during the winter. Brush mattresses were not used here; they would not only have been costly, but they would also have prevented the stone from sinking through the sand, and thus holding the pier securely in place.

During the winter plans were prepared for the superstructure under the direction of Major Heap. This superstructure consists of a two-story cast-iron dwelling, surmounted by a fourth-order lantern, secured to a cast-iron gallery floor, supported by iron columns and girders and brick arches and walls, resting upon the concrete filling of the pier.

The cellar story is arranged for a Daboll trumpet and duplicate hot-air Ericsson engines, cast-iron water-tanks, brick compartments for fuel, provisions and oil, the latter having iron doors and ventilators so arranged as to close automatically in case of a fire and thus smother the conflagration.

It was found that the structure trembled somewhat from the shock of the waves, so 2,000 additional tons of rip-rap were placed around it to increase its stability.

This Light Station was entirely completed in the spring of 1887. Its entire cost, including examination of site, experimental work, rip-rap, lens, fog-signal, superintendence and contingencies of every nature, amounted to $123,811.45, more than $50,000 less than the sum appropriated.

A red sector indicates the location of the Joe Flogger shoal; this sector, combined with red sectors of Cross Ledge Light, clearly defines the main channel as far as the Ship John shoal light. Another red sector marks the Brown shoal; it is to the south of the Brandywine shoal light, and materially assists the navigation of the lower bay.

Cast-iron cylinders filled with concrete have also been successfully used on rocks nearly awash and on sub-marine sites in shallow water where the foundation was stable; they are less costly and in some respects superior to masonry piers, as they are easily and quickly placed in position, and they have no joints into which water can penetrate and freeze, thus forcing out the mortar, as is the case with piers built of stone. Their circular form also simplifies their construction and adapts itself perfectly to a circular tower.

The sketches show several light-houses of this type; the towers are also of cast-iron lined with brick; they are three stories high exclusive of the cellar, and contain all the necessary room for the accommodation of two keepers.

The Stamford light rests on the south-west extremity of Harbor Ledge in Stamford Harbor, Conn.; the pile pier shown in the sketch is a temporary structure used in the construction of the light.

The Whale Rock light is on a rock at the entrance to Narragansett Bay, Rhode Island; the sea is frequently so violent here as to throw solid water as high as the top of the pier, while the spray flies entirely over the tower.

The one at Sharp's Island, Md., is in the much quieter waters of Chesapeake Bay and rests on sand, the scour being prevented by rip-rap.

One great advantage of this type of foundation over screw-pile structures is that the former can successfully resist the impact of ice.

CAPE HATTERAS.

For many years the subject has been agitated of establishing a light-house on the Outer Diamond Shoal, off Cape Hatteras. This shoal is about eight miles from land, and in such stormy waters that it is next to impossible to maintain a light-vessel on or near it. All the sea-going commerce between the Northern and Southern States has to round this point, and it is proverbially the most dangerous place on the Atlantic coast.

There is, of course, a light on Cape Hatteras, but the shoal is so distant that it is very difficult to estimate its locality, south-bound vessels to avoid the current of the gulf-stream have to pass close to it, and it has the gloomy reputation of causing more wrecks and disasters than any other place in America.

The success with the Rothersand and Fourteen-foot Bank Light-houses, in my opinion, point the way to obtaining a secure foundation in these shifting sands, and I believe that the solution of the problem consists in building a steel or cast-iron cylinder forty-five feet in diameter, sinking it on the shoal so that its base will be below any possibility of wave-action, filling it with concrete, and protecting it on the exterior by the liberal use of rip-rap in large blocks.

ROTHERSAND LIGHT. (VIEW.)

See page 142

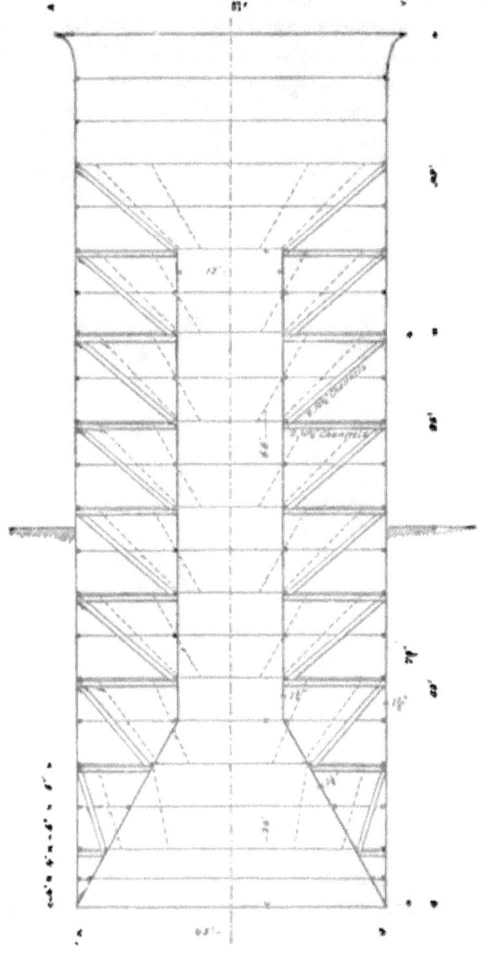

The cylinder should be double, the inner cylinder being fifteen feet in diameter and very strongly braced to the exterior one, the connection between the interior and exterior cylinder at the bottom should be conical in shape, and would answer for the working-chamber if the cylinder were to be sunk by the pneumatic process,

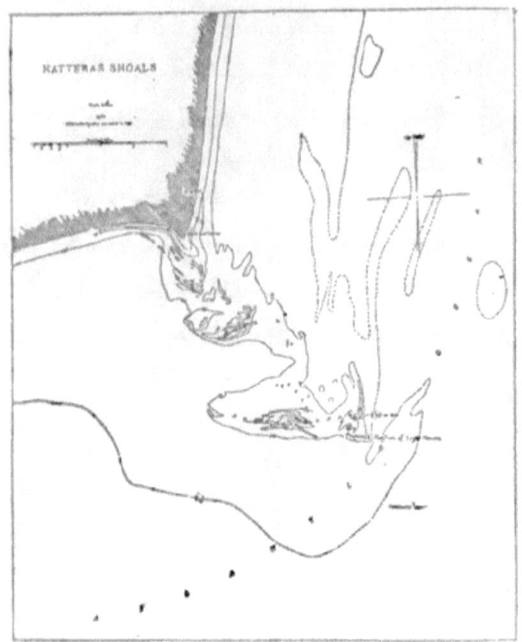

though I believe it possible to sink it rapidly by dredging from the interior. The cylinder could be so built as to admit of either plan being used.[1]

At a suitable locality on the Outer Diamond, there is a depth of about twenty feet; the cylinder should be put together at some safe

[1] See sketches, pages 153 and 155.

harbor, floated to this point and sunk as quickly as possible. I estimate that when the bottom of the cylinder reaches fifty feet below the surface of the shoal and the rip-rap is placed around it, it will be safe from the scour of the waves.

One of the many difficulties attending this work is that the nearest

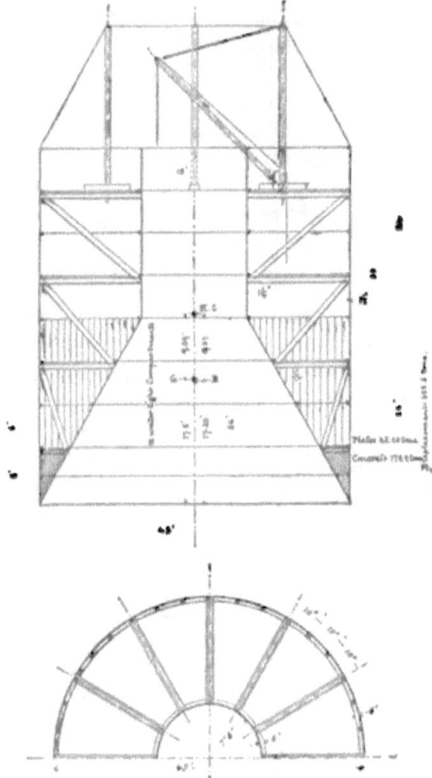

available harbor is Cape Hatteras Inlet, only fifteen feet deep and fifteen miles away. Should a storm overtake the cylinder while being towed to the site, it would, in all probability, be lost, and the same catastrophe might occur if there were a heavy blow during the first part of the sinking of the cylinder; after it had gone down ten or fifteen feet the danger would be much less, and if the attending vessels were driven away by stress of weather, they might have a reasonable assurance of finding the cylinder in place on their return. The power of the cylinder to resist the waves, before it was filled with concrete, would depend entirely on the strength of the interior bracing, and too much pains could not be expended in making this of the best design, material and workmanship.

With the foundation once secured, it would be of no great difficulty to erect a suitable superstructure.

Should this light-house be successfully established, it will be a remarkable feat of light-house engineering, and be of benefit to more commerce than any one light-house in the world.

Barring accidents, the cost should not exceed $300,000 for the foundation, but it would not be safe to commence work without having at least $500,000 available. The accompanying sketches give a general idea of the plan and elevation of the kind of cylinder proposed.

Congress will be asked this session to appropriate the necessary funds for this important work.[1] Should the appropriation be made, the foundation could be built and placed, barring accidents, in less than two years.

[1] Congress has not voted the necessary funds for this work up to the present time (Dec. 1, 1888).

CHAPTER XIII.

SKELETON IRON LIGHT-HOUSES.

Another type is the skeleton iron light-house: this is especially adapted to sites where it is desired to erect a lofty structure without too much weight; it may rest on iron-piles, screw-piles, grillage or other foundation, depending on whether the light-house stands in the water or on land, and whether the site is rock, stiff clay, sand, earth or mud.

The two finest light-houses of this kind, which rest on iron-piles driven in coral rock, are those erected on Fowey Rocks and American Shoals, Florida. They are duplicates of each other, the first one built being the one at Fowey Rocks on the east coast of Florida, at the northern extremity of Florida Reefs.

Examinations to test the character of this reef were made in 1875; the engineer reported: "It was with the greatest difficulty and delay that a sailing vessel could reach the spot in weather sufficiently calm to do any work. The rock composing the reef is harder than that farther south and west, and it is believed will furnish a secure foundation for the kind of structure decided upon." During the same year the designs for the light-house were well advanced, and preliminary works connected with the erection of the light-house were begun. These consisted in building at Soldier Key, four-and-one-half miles distant from the reef, a substantial wharf with track, storehouse and quarters: all these buildings had to be raised six feet above the surface and strongly secured, as during hurricanes the sea sweeps entirely over the surface of the Key. At the site the working platform was completed, and contract was made for the delivery of the ironwork for the foundation and first stories of the light-house, which was delivered at Soldier Key in the spring of 1867, and during the same year all the foundation-piles were driven as follows:

The disc for the central foundation-pile was first lowered to its place, and through this disc the first iron-pile was driven. One of the perimeter discs was then placed in position and located by a gauge consisting of a heavy iron I-beam, lying on the bottom between and in immediate contact with the edges of both discs, and then the first perimeter-pile was driven through the centre of this disc. The greatest precaution had to be taken to drive these piles vertically; hence, after each blow of the hammer the pile was tested with a plummet, and the slightest deviation from the vertical was rectified by tackles, used as guides, fastened to the top of the pile. Each iron-pile was driven about ten feet into the rock. In locating the disc for the next perimeter-pile, two gauges were necessary, one to obtain the proper distance from the central pile, the other to maintain the proper distance from the perimeter-pile just driven; and these two gauges were alike except in length. The discs were dragged along the bottom until their outer edges just touched the free edges of the gauges. Each pile was then driven through the centre of its disc. After all of them were driven, their tops were levelled by cutting off each to the line of the lowest. The piles were then capped with their respective sockets; the horizontal girders were inserted, the diagonal tension-rods were placed and screwed up, and the foundation series was completed. This work, including the building of the temporary platform occupied just two months, during which time the sea was quite smooth.

Owing to various delays in the manufacture of the superstructure it did not arrive at Soldier Key until November 12, 1877. The weather preceding its arrival and for three months after was unfavorable for its erection. Gale followed gale, and though a large force of workmen was at Soldier Key ready to work when weather permitted, nothing could be done. For six weeks there was but one day on which a landing could be effected at the light-house site. This day was utilized by laying a decking of four-inch plank on the wooden platform. Finding the weather still unfavorable, with no immediate prospect of getting to the site, and all the shore-work completed, it was decided on December 13, 1877, to temporarily suspend operation.

On February 24, 1878, the weather appearing more favorable for reef-operation, work was resumed; the party arrived at the site on the 25th February, and encountered a tornado which considerably damaged the vessels.

One of the lighters, a small schooner, capable of carrying twenty-five to thirty tons of freight on four feet draught of water, was loaded with the portable hoisting-engine, derrick, tackles, shear-poles and a small quantity of iron. The sea continued so rough that this load could not be landed until March 12, when a landing was effected through the breakers by means of small boats, and the derrick and shears erected on the platform. During the next sixteen days five more cargoes of iron were landed, and the first series of columns, girders, sockets and tension-rods placed in position.

It became evident from the slow progress thus far made, owing to stormy weather and the danger attending frequent landings through the breakers, that, unless a lodgement could be effected on the platform and the men be made to live thereon, the structure could not be completed within a year. Therefore, on March 29, the lighter was loaded with one month's supply of provisions, water, etc., towed to the platform and its freight landed; two large tents were set up on the platform, a temporary kitchen built, and twenty men left to continue the erection of the light-house. The advantages of this arrangement were very great. No matter how high the sea might be running, the men were there out of water, on a safe and steady foundation, and they could continue the work so long as they could be kept supplied with material.

The remainder of the force was employed in loading the lighter and steamer, and when the weather was favorable, in unloading the lighter at the platform On days that were too rough to unload the lighter, all hands would land at the site in small boats, if a landing was practicable, and assist in erection. By keeping the lighter loaded and steam on the tender day and night, no available time was lost.

On June 15, 1878, the tower was completed and the light was exhibited.

The cost of this light-house was about $175,000

Another advantage of this type of light-house is the quickness with which it can be erected. At American Shoals the ironwork was completed at the North, shipped to Key West, Florida, and the light-house completely erected and lighted in one year.

Both Fowey Rocks and American Shoals Light-houses are first-

FOURTEEN-FOOT BANK LIGHT.

See page 149

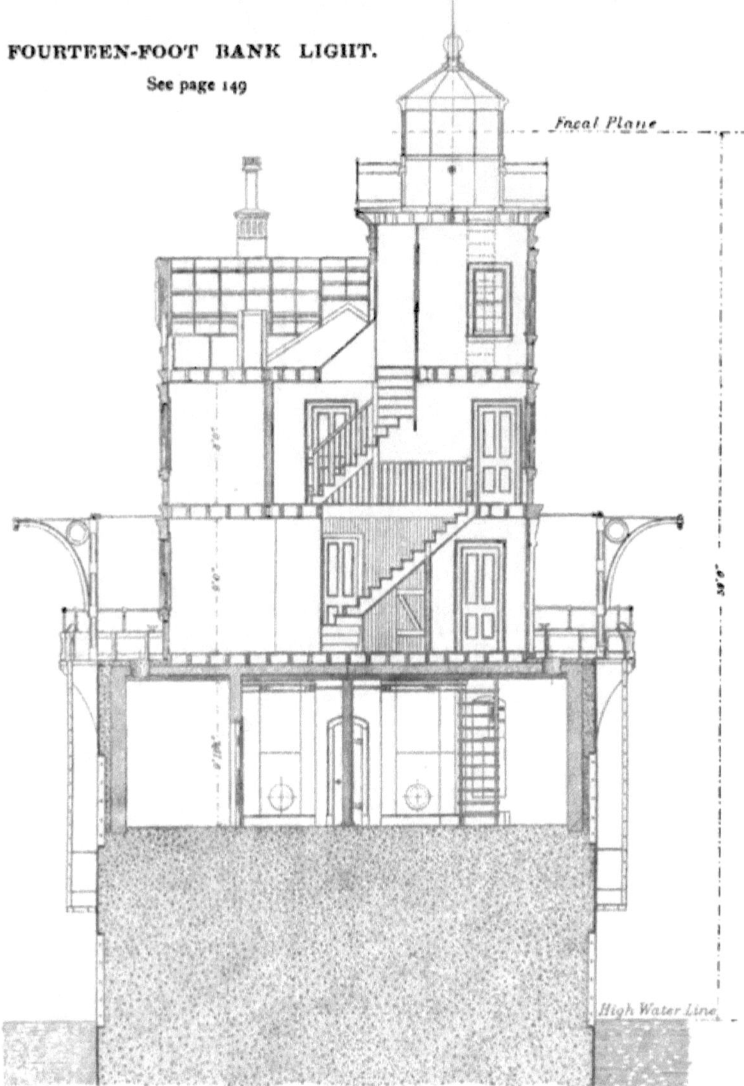

Sectional Elevation

order lights, one hundred and fifteen and one-half feet high, and visible sixteen and one-fourth nautical miles.

There are several other light-houses of this type on the Florida Reefs, such as Carysfort Reef, Alligator Reef, Sombrero Key and Sand Key, all first-order lights, from one hundred and ten to one hundred and forty-four feet high.

Florida is rich in first-order lights; she has twelve in all, as many as Maine, Massachusetts, Rhode Island, Connecticut and New York combined.

In 1873 the old brick tower at Southwest Pass, Mississippi River, built in 1831, was replaced by a skeleton iron structure. The old tower was in a dilapidated condition, had sunk several feet into the soft ground, was three or four from the perpendicular, and its light was of an inferior order compared with its importance. At this place, the great difficulty was to obtain a secure foundation on the soft and treacherous alluvial formation of the Delta of the Mississippi. The plan adopted was as follows:

The foundation is octagonal in shape and fifty-eight feet eight inches lesser diameter. It consists first of one hundred and eighty-five square piles driven four feet apart to a depth of thirty-three feet. At six feet below the tops of the piles, which are one foot below low water, a horizontal course of twelve-inch square timbers are notched into them. Below the timbers a mass of shell concrete two feet thick is rammed about the piles, and on the timbers rests a floor of three-inch plank. Above this floor are a second and third course of timbers notched into the piles and laid at right angles to each other and diagonally to the first course. A mass of concrete is forced into the interstices of the timbers and filled up to a height of four feet above the third tier, bringing the top of the foundation eighteen inches above the main level of the water. The superstructure is a skeleton iron tower composed of six series of eight cast-iron columns placed at the angles of an octagon and strongly braced and

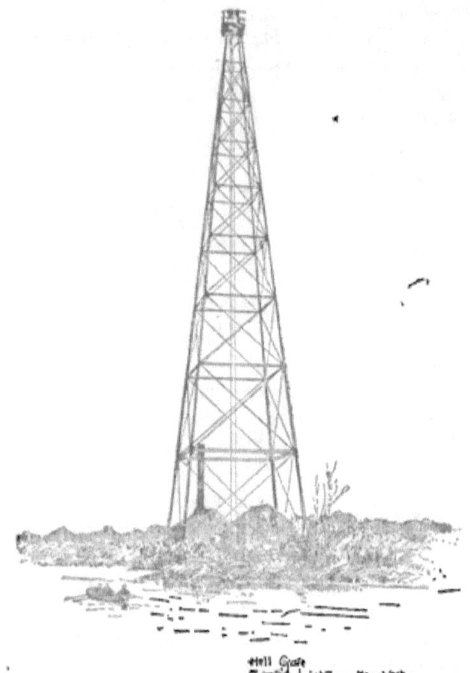

Hell Gate
Electric Light. . New York.

tied by wrought-iron rods. On the sixth series stand the watch-room and lantern, access to which is gained by a stairway winding round the axis of the tower and inclosed in a wrought-iron cylinder. The keeper's dwelling, two-stories high, rests on the first series of columns.

The tallest skeleton tower in the Light-House Service was erected at Hell Gate, Astoria, N. Y., in 1883–84. It is two hundred and fifty feet high and was intended to display nine electric lights of six thousand candle-power each to illuminate the channel. Its construction is sufficiently well shown in the sketch. Within the legs of the structure are seen the engine and boiler house. When the lamps were lighted the effect was very beautiful. The tower was invisible and the lights had the appearance of an immense chandelier suspended in the heavens and flooding the scene with their brilliant light.

At the explosion at Flood Rock in 1885 advantage was taken of this tower to photograph the explosion and get a plunging view on the rock.

In 1886 this light was discontinued, as the pilots complained that it was so brilliant that it dazzled their eyes and prevented them from seeing objects beyond the light; also that the shadows were so heavy that they often assumed the appearance of obstacles.

SCREW-PILE LIGHT-HOUSES.

As previously mentioned, the principle of the screw-pile was invented by Alexander Mitchell, of England. The way the foundation screw is made is shown in the accompanying sketch. The screw is fastened to the lower end of an iron pile and forced down by turning the pile. It is sometimes assisted by a water-jet. This style of foundation is especially adapted to sandy bottoms under water, but in my opinion iron-pile structures should only be used in southern waters where they would not be exposed to floating ice.

There are a number of such structures in Chesapeake Bay, and the method of building has been the same in each case, the only difference being in the number of piles used, the bracing, and the style of superstructures. In several cases these light-houses have been threatened with destruction by the ice, and it has been necessary to protect them with a ring of rip-rap placed at such a distance from the light-house that it would act as an ice-breaker.

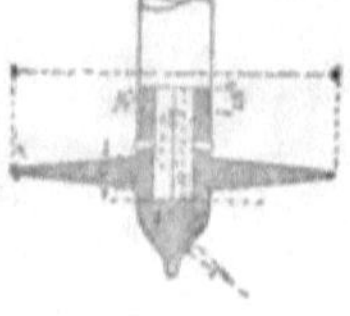

Section.
Foundation Screw.

Plan.

Elevation.

The accompanying sketches show several of these structures.[1] The general plan of all is a one-story dwelling with lantern in the centre. Most of them are also provided with fog-bells rung by clock-work. The projecting piles, shown in some, partially serve the purpose of ice-breakers. A time-honored joke of the light-keepers is that they have fine fishing privileges and that they raise all their own vegetables.

The "Bug Light"[2] in Boston Harbor, officially known as "The Narrows Light," built in 1856, is another example of this style. Fortunately for its stability the shoal on which it was erected has so changed since the light was established that it is now seldom covered with water and the piles have been spared the shock of floating ice.

On the east side of the dredged channel in Mobile Bay, Ala., an hexagonal screw-pile structure was built during the years 1884–85. The bottom is soft mud, and on September 12, 1885, when the light-house was nearly completed, it commenced to settle, and went down bodily seven and a half feet. The subsidence was so nearly equal on each column that the inclination of the structure cannot be detected by the eye. The actual difference in level between the extremes at the top of the foundation series is between three and four inches. No part of the structure was strained in the least. In

[1] See pages 161 and 165. [2] See page 153.

order to prevent further subsidence, twelve creosoted piles were driven into the mud alongside of the structure and bolted to it. They

were then cut off at about the water level. Since then the light-house has sunk no further.

LIGHT-HOUSES ON THE GREAT LAKES.

On our "unsalted seas," the great lakes, light-houses are as necessary as on our sea-coasts; on their shores timber of excellent quality is plentiful and cheap, and when submerged is practically indestructible as it is not exposed to the greedy tooth of the ship-worm which so soon destroys any wooden structures, especially in our southern waters and in the Pacific.

Advantage has been taken of this by army engineers in building numerous wooden piers, composed of cribs filled with stone, in their harbor improvements; and similar plans have been adopted in making the foundations for light-houses when the latter have to be placed in the water; an excellent type of light-house on a crib foundation is the one built in the mouth of Detroit River, Mich., during the years 1884–85.

The Canadian Government had maintained a light-ship on Bar Point since 1875, but though useful, it was not adequate to the needs of commerce. It could be seen only a short distance, its lights were with difficulty distinguished from vessel lights near by, its location was of little service as a guide between the difficult shoals at the entrance to the river inside its position, and it was liable to be driven from its station by ice or other causes.

Congress made appropriations to the amount of $68,000 in the years 1882–83 and 1885 for establishing a light-house and steam fog-signal at or near the mouth of Detroit River.

The site was so selected that vessels from the Eastward passing Point Pelée and sighting the light, could steer directly for it and clear the dangerous shoal marked by the light-ship; that vessels from the south-west could use it as a range with the Bois Blanc (Canadian) light to clear the long spit off Point Mouillée, while there would be no dangers in front for vessels approaching from any intermediate point; and finally, that this same range with Bois Blanc light would also lead through the narrow buoyed channel in the mouth of the river.

Soundings at the site showed that the bottom was generally quite level with a uniform depth of 22 feet. Borings gave approximately uniform results, the first three or four feet being composed of hard limestone, gravel and sand, very compact and difficult to penetrate,

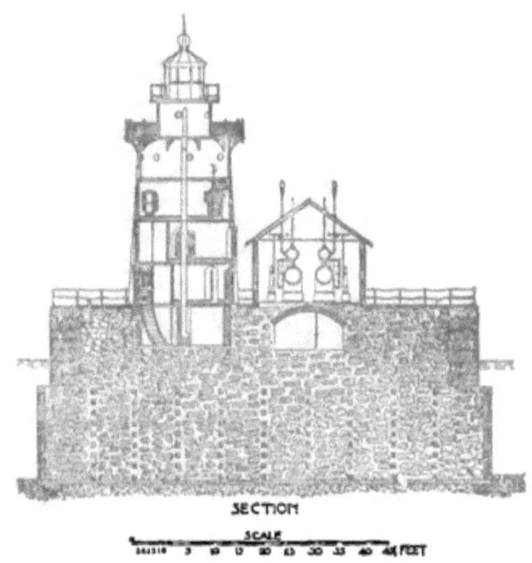

then twelve feet of soft clay and fine sand, easily penetrated, and finally underlying the whole a bed of tough, hard blue clay, very difficult to bore. No boulders were encountered.

The general plan of the foundation is a crib of heavy timbers with a tight bottom; this crib is 90 feet long, 45 feet wide and 18 feet high, thus bringing its top to four feet below high water; it is filled with concrete flush to its top.

This crib supports a pier 15 feet high of cut-stone masonry backed with concrete, the foot of the pier is nine inches back from the edge of the crib.

On the southern end of the pier is a cast-iron conical tower surmounted by a fourth-order lantern; in this tower, the keepers live.

The fog-signal house, containing duplicate steam fog-signal apparatus, is built of heavy framed timber covered on the exterior with two-inch planking and with inch boards on the inside, the space between is filled with mortar made of lime and sawdust. The roof and sides are covered with No. 18 corrugated iron, and the interior with No. 26 plain sheet-iron.

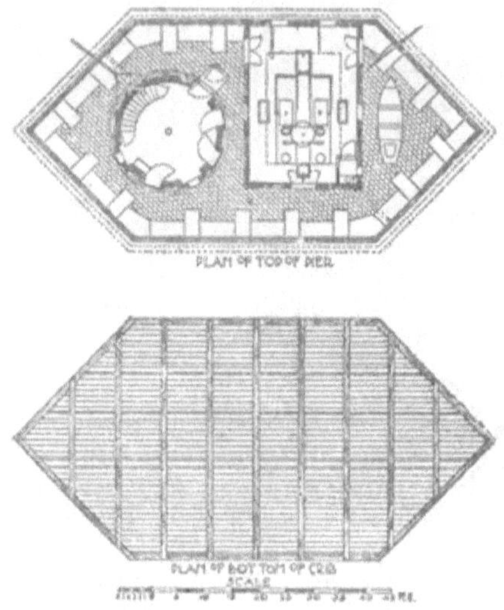

The coal cellar is underneath the fog-signal house.

Amherstburg, Ontario, was the most convenient point at which to

FOURTEEN-FOOT BANK LIGHT.

See page 150

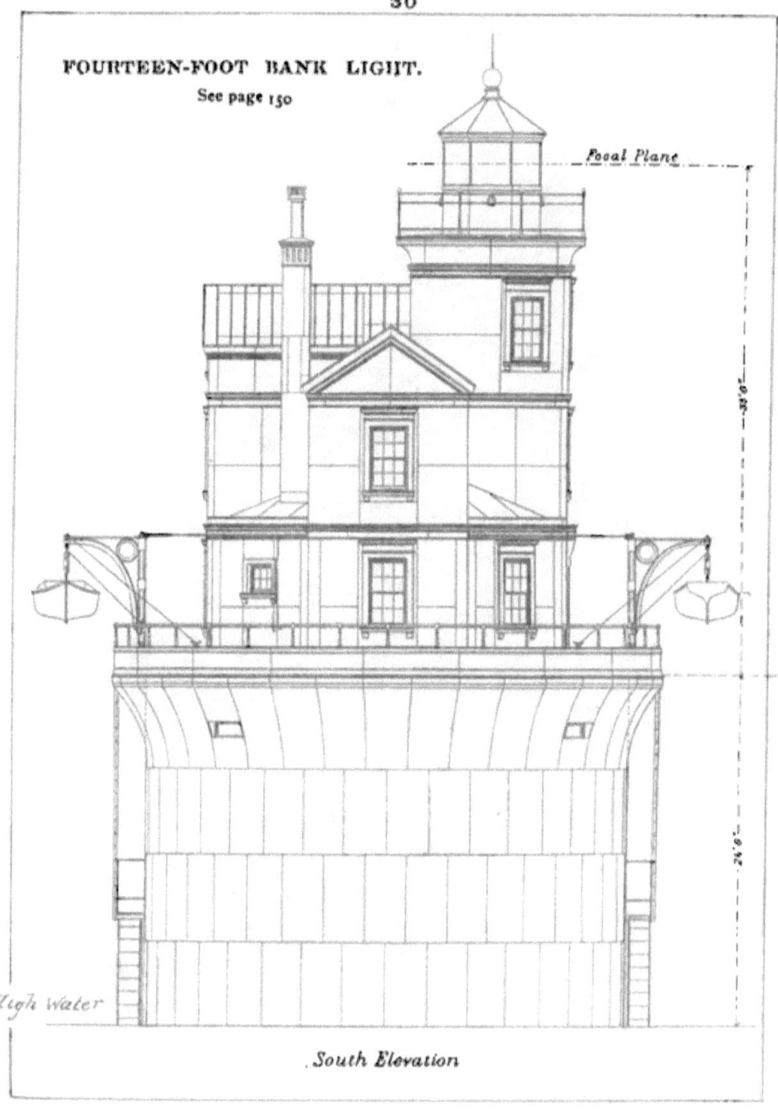

South Elevation

build the crib, and permission was obtained from the Governor-General of Canada to construct the crib there and to introduce the necessary tools, materials, etc., free of duty.

Framing the crib commenced on March 19, 1884, on July 1 it was completed and partly filled with concrete while floating at the wharf, on July 3, it was sunk in place, by September it was filled with concrete, on November 21 the last course of cut-stone was in place and backed with concrete; work was then suspended for the season, a temporary shelter was built and two men were left to display warning lights until the close of navigation.

During the filling of the pier the settlement was uneven, and at the close of the working season it had reached nearly 16 inches.

It was therefore decided to load the pier and leave it loaded during the winter with a much greater weight than it would ultimately have to stand. For this purpose 550 tons of rubble stone were distributed over the pier with a preponderance on the high side. The calculated weight to be borne ultimately was but 160 tons.

The settlement continued slowly for a while and then ceased; when the men in charge of the lights left it was 18 inches, the pier was level and since then there has been no change.

Work was resumed in May, 1885, the pier was paved, the various structures erected and the station entirely completed and lighted by August 20, of the same year.

This light-house was built under the immediate direction of Captain C. E. L. B. Davis, Corps of Engineers, from plans prepared by him.

On the completion of this light-house the Canadian light-ship at Bar Point was removed from her station.

CHAPTER XIV.

CHARACTERISTICS OF LIGHT-HOUSES.

It is evident that if all light-houses exhibited the same kind of light, fixed white, for example, it would lead to confusion. A mariner, when he saw a light, could not determine which one of several

it might be, especially if he were uncertain as to his reckoning. This difficulty was overcome by having different numbers of lights at neighboring light-stations. For example, on Little Brewster Island, Boston Harbor, there is one light, at Plymouth there are two lights, at the Gurnets, at Nauset Beach, Cape Cod, there are three lights, at Chatham two and at Monomoy Point one light. This device is both expensive and clumsy, and as the needs of commerce require intermediate lights to be established from time to time these groups of lights lose in a measure their distinctive character.

More modern science has devised other and better means for making the lights distinctive. This is done by changing the colors of the lights and by making them fixed or flashing or a combination

of the two. But two colors are used, white and red; the latter color is obtained by using a chimney of ruby glass on the lamp or a pane of red glass outside the lens. Red light penetrates fog better than any other color, and it is for this reason that it is used to the exclusion of the rest.

Formerly the intensity of the light was increased by placing a slivered parabolic reflector behind the flame of the lamp, and in some light-houses reflectors are still used, but in most cases the lenses designed by Fresnel have been substituted. His original idea was to use a large central flame three and one-half inches in diameter and to arrange around it eight large plano-convex lenses three feet three inches high by two feet six inches wide, so as to refract the light.

This form of lens was improved by Condorcet for burning-glasses in 1788. If a lens three feet three inches in diameter were ground to a continuously spherical figure it would attain a great thickness at the axis and the loss of light by absorption in its passage through the thick glass, as well as by spherical aberration, would be considerable. But light-house lenses are so formed as to avoid these disadvantages. The figure shows a section and elevation of one panel of a lens.

If a lens has eight of these panels it will send out radially eight beams of light, and if the lens is made to revolve the observer would see flashes alternated by dark intervals. This is known as a *flashing white light.* If alternate panels are covered with panes of red glass it would be *flashing red and white.* It will readily be seen that quite a number of characteristics can be made by altering the number of panels and by covering up more or less of them with red glass.

The above is only suited to flashing lights. It was not until Fresnel extended his researches to the improvement of fixed lights that he completed the system of light-house illumination. He conceived the idea of forming a barrel of glass having the same profile as a vertical section through the axis of the lens just described. Such a lens allows the rays from a lamp in its centre to spread freely in a horizontal plane, while it only refracts them vertically, thus producing a powerful band of light equally all round the horizon.

If flash panels, consisting of a set of vertical prisms, be made to revolve around the above lens, it becomes fixed white varied by white flashes; if half of the flash panels are alternately covered with red glass, the characteristic would be fixed white, varied by red and white flashes.

The flashing lights are further distinguished by the interval of time between the flashes. For example, Boston Light is flashing white every thirty seconds; Gay Head, on the western point of

Martha's Vineyard, is flashing white and red, interval between flashes, ten seconds, every fourth flash red; Sakonet, on little Cormorant Rock, R. I., fixed white for thirty seconds, followed during the next thirty seconds by three red flashes at intervals of ten seconds.

Dangerous shoals or rocks in the vicinity of light-houses are frequently indicated by changing the color of that portion of the light covering the danger. This is done by setting a piece of red glass of the proper width against the lantern glass. Fourteen-Foot Bank Light is a case in point. It shows a white flash every fifteen seconds between the bearings N. N. W. through E. to S. S. E. ⅛ E. (from seaward) and a red flash every fifteen seconds throughout the remaining arc, covering Brown's Shoal to the southward and Joe Flogger's Shoal to the northward.

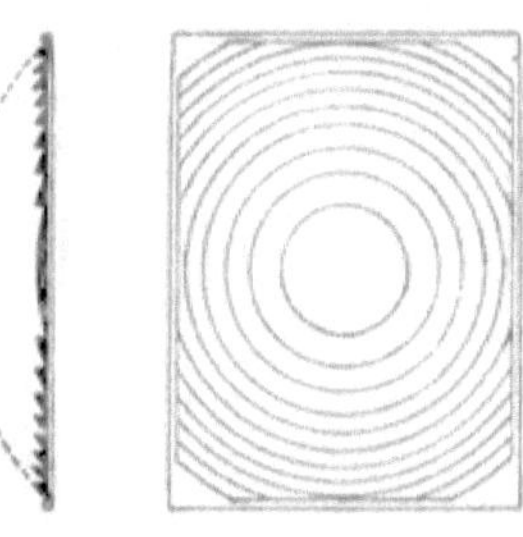

Section and Elevation of an Annular Lens.

It has been proposed that all important lights should be flashing and that they should spell out the initials of their name by the Morse alphabet, by using long and short or red and white flashes, and that the fog signals should do the same by long and short blasts. I fear, however, that such a system would tend more to confuse than to aid the ordinary mariner.

The various characteristics in use on our coasts are:

Fixed White	F. W.
Fixed Red	F. R.
Flashing White	Flg. W.
Flashing Red	Flg. R.
Fixed White varied by White Flashes	F. W. v. W. Fl.
Fixed White varied by Red Flashes	F. W. v. R. Fl.
Fixed White varied by Red and White Flashes	F. w. v. R and W. Fl.
Flashing Red and White	Flg. R. and W.

It is also desirable that the light-houses should be conspicuous during the daytime, as they make excellent day-marks; this is done

either by their shape or by some peculiarity in the way they are are painted. When the background is dark they are usually painted white, and when the background is light, the towers are either left the natural color, if built of brick or stone, or are painted some dark color. Sometimes both white and some dark color are used in horizontal bands, spirals or checkers. West Quoddy Head, Maine, has alternate red and white horizontal stripes. At Sankaty Head, Mass., the tower is white near the top and the bottom, with a red band in the middle. Fourteen-Foot Bank is brown. At Cape Henry, Va., the base, service-room and lantern of the octagonal tower are black; the shaft is colored on each face half white and half black, alternating so that the upper and lower halves of the faces show alternately black and white. At Cape Hatteras the tower is colored in alternate zones or belts of black and white, each zone twenty-two feet wide. Cape Look-

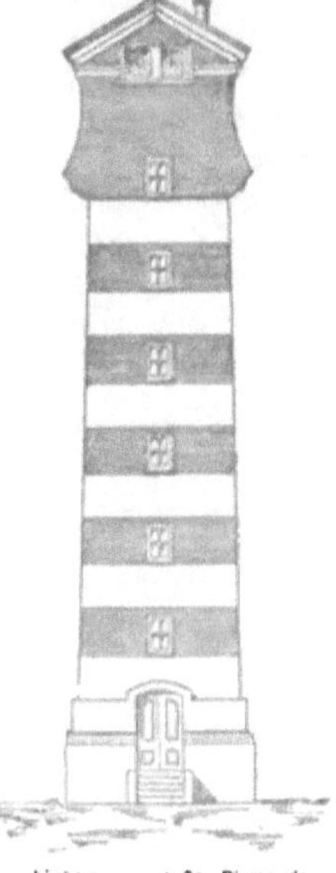

Light-house at St. Pierre de Royan, France.

out, N. C., is in black and white checkers. At Hunting Island, S. C., the tower is white from the base to the height of foliage of the background, the portion above this being black. At St. Augustine, the foundation of the tower is white, with a black cornice; the shaft is colored with black and white spiral bands. At St. Pierre de Royans, France, the plan of the light-house is a square. As it is intended as a day-mark, the upper part has been enlarged to obviate the possibility of confounding it with the steeples of the town of Royan, and it is also painted in wide bands of red and white. The sketches show the appearance of some of these light-houses.

31

STAMFORD HARBOR LIGHT.

See page 151

CHAPTER XV.

ISLE OF MAY LIGHT-HOUSE.

The light-house situated on the Isle of May, Scotland, at the mouth of the Firth of Forth, was originally lighted in 1636 by an open coal-fire; it was altered in 1816 to argand lamps, with

Light-house on the Isle of May.

silvered parabolic reflectors; in 1836 it was converted to the dioptric system, and on the 1st December, 1886, the electric-light was substituted: as this light is now one of the most powerful in the world, a general description may be of interest in this connection.

The Board of Trade suggested its introduction at the Isle of

May, on the ground that "there was no more important station on the Scottish shores, whether considered as a land-fall, as a light for the guidance of the extensive and important trade of the neighboring coast, or as a light to lead into the refuge harbor of the Forth."

Notwithstanding its isolated position and the difficulty of access, it was decided to accept the view of the Board of Trade. The

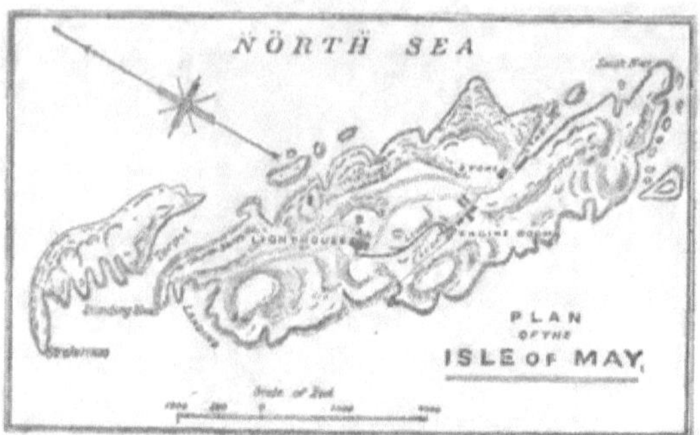

necessary plans were prepared by the Messrs. Stevenson, and the works commenced in June, 1885, were completed and the light established by the first of December, 1886. The existing establishment consisted of a light-house tower, with accommodation for three keepers — it was necessary to provide dwellings for three more keepers with their families, and buildings for the steam and electric plant, coal-houses, etc. All these were placed near the base of the island, in order to be near the small fresh-water loch, and to save the cost of transporting the coal and of pumping the water to the top of the island, while the saving of the cost of carriage of the materials and machinery to the top of the island, and of piping and pumping machinery would more than counterbalance the original cost of the conductors.

It was originally intended to use the Brush compound wound Victoria dynamo, giving a continuous current and supplying a single automatically-fed arc-lamp of 30,000 candle-power. The Brush Company at once set to work to make such a lamp, but after numerous trials they were unable to do so, consequently recourse was had to the more expensive alternate current magneto-electric machines of

HORIZONTAL SECTION THROUGH FOCAL PLANE.

De Meritens, which, though not so powerful, had given excellent results in several light-houses and at the experiments at South Foreland; they were of the L type and of the largest size hitherto constructed, weighing four-and-one-half tons each.

They are so arranged that one-fifth, two-fifths, three-fifths, four-fifths or the whole of the current of a machine can, at pleasure, be sent to the distributor for transmission to the lantern, the two machines can also be coupled and the full current from both be employed. The engines and boilers are in duplicate.

The conductors are copper-rods one inch in diameter, well insulated, the length is 880 feet, the loss of the total energy is twenty per cent.

The lamps are of the Serrin-Berjot type, and the carbons are of Siemens make, and have a soft central core of pure graphite which improves their steadiness in burning; they are 1.6 inches in diameter, but two-inch carbons can be used when both machines are running. With one machine the power of the arc is estimated at 12,000 to 16,000 candles.

The dioptric apparatus (see figure showing horizontal section through focal plane) is of a novel description, the condensing principle being carried farther than in any other apparatus previously constructed. Certain sectors are darkened by diverting the light from them, and the light is thrown into adjoining sectors so as to reinforce their light. Thus the power of the light is increased in proportion as the dark arc is increased. The light gives four flashes in quick succession every half minute; and during the bright periods the effect of this concentration of the rays is that the light radiating naturally from the focus is increased in power fifteen times in azimuth in addition to the vertical condensation, excepting, of course, the loss due to reflection and absorption.

The apparatus consists of a second-order fixed lens fifty-five inches in diameter, which operates on the rays so as to make them issue from the lens in horizontal planes.

Outside this lens there is a revolving cage of straight vertical prisms, extending the full height of the lens, or five-one-half feet, and composed of two panels on opposite sides of the centre, each operating in the horizontal plane on 180° of the light coming from the lens, in such a way as to condense the whole 180° into four flashes of 3° each—that is, 45° into 3°, with the proper intervals of darkness between them. This cage of glasswork makes one complete revolution every minute round the lens, thereby producing the characteristic of four flashes every half minute.

The resulting beam of light from this apparatus is about 3,000,000 candles when one magneto-electric machine is in use, and with both machines about 6,000,000 candles. The light has been picked-up and recognized by sailors at forty and fifty miles off, by the flashes illuminating the clouds overhead, though the geographical range, *i. e.*, the distance which the curvature of the earth would permit the light to be seen, is only twenty-two miles.

Surprise has frequently been expressed by masters of vessels and by residents on the neighboring shores who live in view of the Isle of May light, that this light, which is so exceedingly brilliant in clear weather as to cast shadows at a distance of ten or fifteen miles, is so cut down by the fog that some go the length of believing the old oil-light (9446 candles) was better in a fog. All who have had experience with the electric-light are quite prepared for the first part of this statement, while the last, it need hardly be said, is a mistake, inasmuch as the electric-light has been proved, by experiments in both natural and artificial fog and also by observation on existing light-houses lighted by electricity, to be in all circumstances of weather the most penetrating.

Every night at 12 o'clock the lightkeepers at St. Abb's Head, twenty-two miles distant, where there is a first-order flashing light, and one of the most powerful oil-lights in the English service, observe the Isle of May light, while the keepers at the latter also observe the St. Abb's Head light. The result of five months' observation is that the Isle of May light is seen one-third oftener from St. Abb's Head than the St. Abb's Head light is seen from the Isle of May. It is perfectly true, however, that the superiority which is so apparent in clear and in rainy weather is very much reduced in hazy weather, and practically disappears in very dense fog. Looking to this fact and to the large first cost and annual maintenance, there is no doubt, that the conclusion arrived at by the Trinity

House[1] is sound, that electricity should be used only for important landfall lights.

[1] The Trinity House of England and the Scotch Board of Northern Lights instituted an exhaustive series of experiments at South Foreland, England, in 1884-85 to determine the relative values of oil, gas and electricity as light-house illuminants; the following is a summary of their report so far as oil and electricity are concerned:

"The electric-light, as exhibited in the A experimental tower at South Foreland, has proved to be the most powerful light under all conditions of weather, and to have the greatest penetrative power in fog.

"For the ordinary necessities of light-house illumination mineral-oil is the most suitable and economical illuminant; for salient headlands, important landfalls and places where a very powerful light is required, electricity offers the greatest advantages."

A single oil-burner, placed on a focus of a proportionally sized lens, is sufficient for the generality of cases.

This is specially the case since the introduction, on Messrs. Stevenson's suggestion, of hyper-radiant apparatus suited for use with burners of large diameter. An experimental lens of 52⅜ inches focal distance was constructed by Messrs. Barbier & Fenestre, and was fully experimented upon at the South Foreland. It proved entirely satisfactory, and since then the Light-House Board of the United States has ordered and received one of these lenses which is now in store at the United States General Light-House Depot, Tompkinsville, Staten Island, New York.

This lens is composed entirely of brass and cut-glass, and when the sun shines on it, it sparkles with all the colors of the prism, reminding one of an immense soap-bubble. Its cost was nearly $16,000.

CHAPTER XVI.

MISCELLANEOUS LIGHTS.

PIER-HEAD LIGHTS.

On the great lakes most of the harbors are improved by build ing two parallel piers of cribwork filled with stone out into the lake

"Bug" Light, Boston Harbor.

until these piers reach a certain depth of water; the relief afforded by them is but temporary and they have to be extended from time to time.

The end of one pier is marked by a small light of the fourth or fifth order, supported on a frame structure either square or polygonal. In the tower there is room for the spare lamps, supply of oil, etc., and a place for the keeper to sleep. When the pier is extended these towers can be readily moved out to the end. The story that they are so light that a schooner ran her bowsprit through one and carried it from Grand Haven to Chicago is current but not trustworthy.

When the pier is entirely completed, the practice is to build a separate foundation and to place on it a conical cast-iron tower similar to the one at the entrance to Portsmouth Harbor, N. H.

Quite a pretty light of the kind, but modelled after a small Roman temple, is on the end of the Portland, Maine, Breakwater.[1]

RIVER-LIGHTS.

The total number of lighted aids to navigation in the United States on the 1st of July, 1887, including light-ships and lighted buoys was 2034, of these 1232 are what is known as river-lights.

Congress has specially authorized the following rivers to be lighted: Hudson and East Rivers, N. Y.; Delaware River between Philadelphia, Pa., and Bordentown, N. J.; Elk River, Md.; Cape Fear River, N. C.; Savannah River, Ga.; St. John's River, Fla.; Mouth of Red River, La.; Chicot Pass and navigable channel along Grand Lake, La.; Mississippi, Missouri, Ohio, Tennessee and Great Kanawha Rivers; Columbia and Willamette Rivers, Oregon; and Puget Sound, Washington Territory.

A river-light is an exceedingly simple affair, consisting of a pole or mast with an arm or a shelf at its top by which to support a lantern. These are generally placed on the shore, but sometimes the light is needed in mid-stream in which case a small crib filled with stone forms a base for the pole.[2] Or, sometimes, an iron spindle is inserted in the rock as is the case in several places on the East River, N. Y.

The lanterns in general use are known as tubular lens lanterns, they are not liable to be blown out and will burn all night.

[1] See sketch, page 100. [2] See sketch, page 186.

Whale Rock, R. I.
B/86

WHALE'S ROCK LIGHT.

See page 152

There are many places difficult and dangerous of access in stormy weather where small lights would be of great value could they be constantly maintained; this has been accomplished by a simple addition to the lens lantern of a reservoir containing a gallon of oil, which is automatically fed to the lamp on the principle of the German

The rear beacon Edenton Range N. C.

student-lamp. By this device the lamp will burn and give a good light for at least eight days and nights without attention and during this time there is almost sure to be weather calm enough for the keeper to attend to the light. This improvement was made at the Light-House Depot at Staten Island; it is of recent date and already promises to extend the use of the stake-lights to places where formerly it was thought necessary to establish regular light-houses.

One of the simplest towers in the Light-House service existed for many years at Edenton, N. C. As the sketch shows it was a tree, whose branches supported a box for the lantern and a platform reached by a ladder.

I regret to say that this picturesque structure perished through

old age and was replaced by a prosaic pole to the top of which the lantern was nightly hauled by a rope.

As soon as the energetic citizens of the neighborhood discovered that the light-keeper was no longer condemned to the exertion of climbing a ladder night and morning, the Light-House Board received a number of applications for his position.

FLOATING-LIGHTS.

Floating-lights are of two kinds, light-ships and lighted-buoys. The former are very strongly built schooners, which show during the day a colored disk from each mast to distinguish them from ordinary vessels, while at night powerful lights are hoisted to their tops: these lights consist of eight or nine lamps with reflectors hung on gimbals so that their rays will be projected horizontally. They are arranged in a circle and enclosed in a lantern; during the day the whole apparatus is lowered to the deck into a small house at the foot of each mast. Light-vessels are also provided with a fog-bell and sometimes with a fog-whistle operated by steam or hot air; they are stationed on outlying shoals where it is difficult if not impossible to erect light-houses. There are twenty-three of these light-vessels in

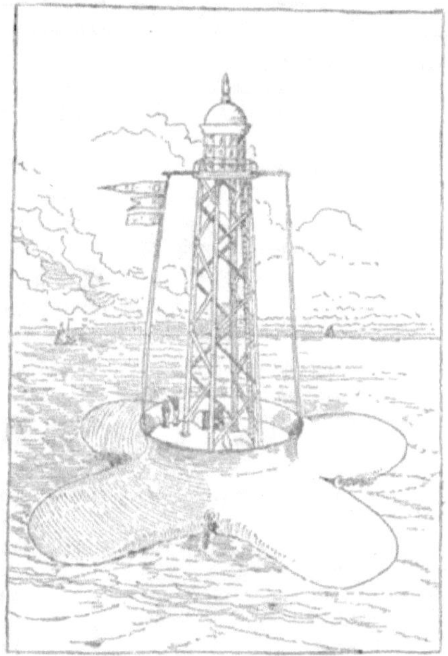

Captain Moody's Floating Light-house.

position on the Atlantic Coast and one on Lake St. Clair: there are none on the Pacific Coast.

As light-ships are occasionally driven from their moorings by severe storms or may in some way be disabled, relief light-ships are kept in readiness to replace them until they can be returned to their stations.

Lighted buoys are comparatively of recent invention; they consist of a buoy filled with compressed illuminating gas; on the top of the buoy is a gas-jet in a lens; the latter is so arranged that neither wind nor wave can extinguish the light, while an ingenious governor determines a constant flow of gas to the burner irrespective of the pressure in the buoy. When lighted they will burn for a long time without attention, generally about three months, though this length of time may be altered by changing the size of the buoy and the pressure to which the gas is subjected.

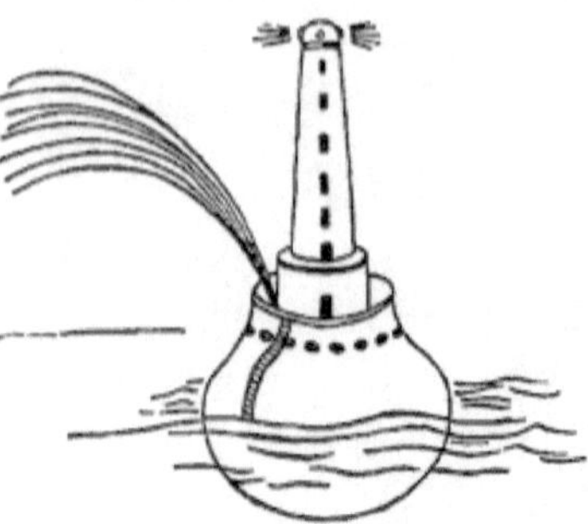

Capt. Harris's Floating Light-house.

This system of lighting by compressed gas is, of course, also applicable to stationary lights and is used in the beacons in Currituck Sound, N. C., and also on the Romer Shoal, New York Harbor. Another kind of lighted buoy has just passed successfully its experimental stage and is now being actively pushed to completion

Foster's Gas-lighted Buoy.

as a practical aid to mariners. It is the joint invention of Lieut. Comdr. M. R. S. Mackenzie, U. S. N., and Lieut. John Millis, Corps of Engineers, U. S. A., and in general terms consists of a spar-buoy supporting an incandescent electric-light connected to a dynamo machine on shore by an armored cable.

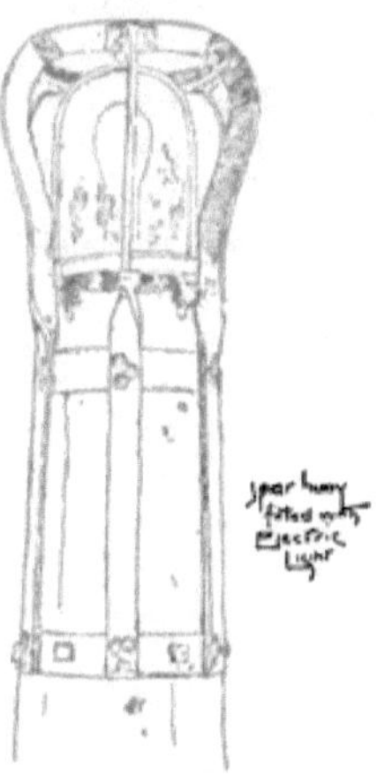

The incandescent lamp is enclosed in a cylinder of stout glass to protect it from the waves, and this cylinder is further protected against the shocks of ice or other floating bodies by a kind of cage of steel bars.

Six of these buoys, three on each side, will be set to mark Gedney's Channel, New York Bay: the house containing the engine, boiler and dynamos will be located at Sandy Hook; the whole work is now under contract and will probably be in operation by the fall. of 1888.

It has been frequently suggested that that portion of the Atlantic Ocean most frequented by vessels should be lighted by a series of floating light-houses. At our Centennial Exhibition at Philadelphia several drawings and paintings were shown exhibiting the methods by means of which it was proposed to accomplish this object.

The following are some of the advantages claimed

by the inventors: the light-houses could be anchored anywhere on the high seas and both guide and light vessels to their destination (one inventor showed his light-houses strung across the ocean like street lamps in a city); they could be used as post-offices, telegraph, signal and life-saving stations. Pilots would await on them the arrivals of vessels; in stormy weather ships could moor to them and outride the gale. Captain Harris's painting, quite a large one, showed three floating light-houses and several vessels in a violent storm, the latter are much tossed but the light-houses are steady and are assisting the vessels by firing rockets and throwing life-lines from mortars. The supports of the light-houses are apparently can-buoys of large size. Captain John Moody's float is also of wrought-iron and shows considerable originality. It has four immense rays or arms, these being intended primarily to steady it and could also be used for storage purposes; the Captain claims that its peculiar form allows it to be boarded at any time and in any weather and that in time of war it could be used as a fort.

It is needless to say that none of these projects have been put into effect, perhaps the reason may be found in a remark by one of the inventors: "The undertaking is certainly great, and to carry it out in a series of vessels across the Atlantic would cost a great sum of money."

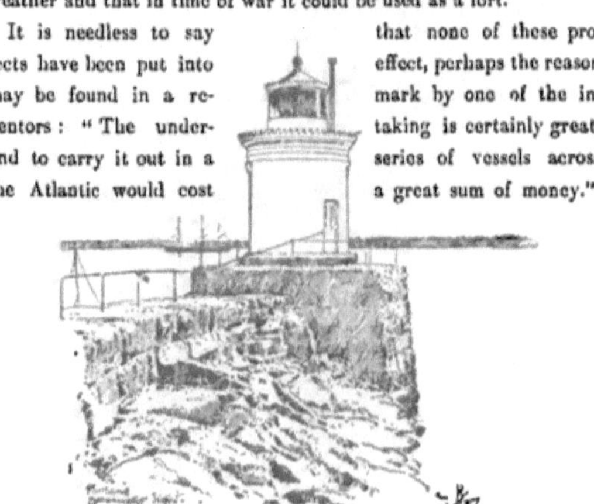

CHAPTER XVII.

LIGHT-HOUSE ADMINISTRATION.

To select the proper sites for light-houses, to plan and erect them on difficult sites, to devise suitable optical apparatus, illuminants and lamps, to appoint proper keepers, to furnish the

supplies, and to attend to all the minutiæ consequent upon a service whose stations are scattered along a coast and are frequently difficult and dangerous of access, requires a combination of qualities seldom found in one individual. Therefore, in the more important maritime nations the control of the light-house system is vested in Boards whose members are as a rule selected with a view to their ability in the various lines indicated above, and whose orders are carried into effect by district officers.

FRANCE.

The Light-House Board of France, known as the *Commission des Phares*, has its office in Paris, on the hill Trocadéro, overlooking the Seine and Champ de Mars. This board consists of four engineers, two naval officers, one Member of the Institute, one inspector-general of marine engineers, and one hydrographic engineer.

Longstone Light-house, Farne Islands.

The executive officers are the Inspector General of the Corps of Engineers *des Ponts et Chaussées*, who is Director of the French light-house administration, and another engineer of the same Corps, who is Engineer-in-Chief and Secretary to the Commission.

The entire administration on the seaboard is entrusted to the engineers who in addition are charged with the work of river and harbor improvements.

The buildings of the Commission are placed around a rectangular court-yard in which are models of light-houses, buoys and other

SHARP'S ISLAND LIGHT.

See page 152

apparatus pertaining to the establishment. The principal building, containing the offices is a handsome structure two-stories high, built of brick and limestone in alternate courses. It is surmounted by a tower and first-order lantern, for experimental purposes.

The grand entrance-hall also contains many models, the most striking being those of the rock light-houses of France.

The council-chamber is richly decorated and upon its walls are painted two large charts, each occupying an entire side: one shows all the light-houses of the world, the other the light-houses of France, showing the illuminated areas. A bust of Fresnel, the inventer of the dioptric system occupies a prominent position, not only here but at all French light-stations where it is placed over the entrance-door. The museum is well-stocked with every kind of illuminating apparatus, both dioptric and cata-dioptric, though the latter is no longer used in French light-houses. It includes many objects of historical interest, among them the first lens apparatus made from Fresnel's designs, and placed in the Tour de Cordouan, and also the various apparatus showing the successive steps by which he arrived at the lens now used in all parts of the world.

At this depot the lenses and lamps undergo a thorough trial, the oil, however, is sent directly to the various districts and is there tested by the district engineers.

The light-keepers are known as "masters" and "keepers," and are appointed by the prefect or chief civil officer of the department on the nomination of the district engineer; men who have served in the army or navy are given the preference. The following requisites are necessary: They must be Frenchmen, between twenty-one and forty years of age, free from all infirmities which would prevent an active daily life, they must present a certificate of good moral character, know how to read and write, and have an elementary knowledge of arithmetic.

In return for their services the following annual salaries are paid: master $200, principal or keepers of the first class $170, second class $155, third class $140, fourth class $125, fifth class $110, sixth class $95. There is also allowed to each master and keeper a certain amount of fuel, and those at isolated stations receive rations. These salaries are paid in monthly instalments subject to a deduction of five per cent, which is used for a fund for retiring pensions.

There are never less than three keepers at a first-order light, and two at lights of the second and third orders. Masters are charged with the supervision of the service of several lights, the title (*maître*

Bressay Light-house, Shetland Islands.

de phare) can also be granted to those of the principal keepers (*chefs gardiens*) who have merited it by exceptional service. The masters and principal keepers have general charge and attend to the correspondence, the other keepers owe obedience to them, but have the right of appeal to the engineer.

Every year on the recommendation of the Engineer-in-Chief, a bonus not exceeding a month's salary may be allowed by the prefect to the most meritorious keepers, the number receiving such bonus not to exceed one-fifth of the total number of keepers in the department. Masters and keepers may be punished or dismissed by the prefect on the report of the Engineer-in-Chief.

Each keeper is allowed one kitchen and two bedrooms for himself and family; the kitchen and one bedroom is supplied with furniture by the Government; there is no regulation prohibiting the acceptance of gratuities from visitors, on the contrary it is rather expected.

ENGLAND.

The Corporation of Trinity-House, or, according to the original charter, "The Master, Wardens, and Assistants of the Guild, Fraternity, or Brotherhood of the Most Glorious and Undivided Trinity, and of St. Clement, in the Parish of Deptford, Stroud, in the county of Kent," existed as early as the reign of Henry VII (1485 to 1509), and was incorporated by royal charter during the reign of Henry VIII (1509 to 1547). In 1565 during the reign of Queen Elizabeth, the corporation was empowered by act of Parliament "to preserve ancient sea-marks, and to erect beacons, marks, and signs of the sea," but it was more than a century, *i. e.*, not until 1680, before the corporation constructed or owned any light-houses. After that date it from time to time purchased the lights which were owned by private individuals, or by the Crown, and erected new ones. In 1836, an act of Parliament vested in the Trinity-House the entire control of the light-houses of England and Wales, and gave it certain power over the Irish and Scotch lights.

Prior to the act of 1836 the charge was from one-sixth of a penny to one penny per ton on all ships at each time of passing a light-house, but by this act uniform light-dues of a half-penny per ton were established. The charge of one penny per ton at Bell Rock light-house is the only exception to this uniform rate. National ships, fishing-vessels and vessels in ballast are exempt from dues.

The English lights are placed under the corporation of the Trinity-House; the Scottish lights are under the management of the Commissioners of Northern Lights, and the Irish lights are under the care of the Corporation for Preserving and Improving the Port of Dublin, commonly called the Ballast Board.

The principal provisions of the act of 1853 affecting light-houses are as follows:

(1.) The light-dues of the United Kingdom are to form one *imperial fund*, under control of the Board of Trade. (2.) From this fund all expenses of erecting and maintaining the lights of the United Kingdom are to be defrayed. (3.) The three Boards which manage the light-houses of England, Scotland and Ireland are to render account of their expenditure to the Board of Trade. (4.) The Trinity-

Howth Baily Light-house.

House, or English Board, is to exercise a certain control over the Boards in Scotland and Ireland, and is to judge of all their proposals to erect new lights, or to change existing ones; but in every case the sanction of the Board of Trade must precede the acts of each of the three Boards.

This subordination to the Board of Trade causes much trouble and embarrassment.

The Elder Brethren of the Trinity-House, twenty-nine in number, comprise sixteen active members, including two officers of the Navy, and thirteen honorary members, all of whom are elected by the body as vacancies occur.

The honorary members include H. R. H., the Prince of Wales, some of the ministers to the Crown, several members of the nobility and of Parliament.

The Duke of Edinburgh is the present Master, but the Deputy-Master, who is elected by the Elder Brethren from their active list, is the executive officer.

The Corporation of the Trinity-House also includes the Junior Brethren, who are elected by the Elder Brethren, and have no duties, simply forming a reserve from which the Elder Brethren add to their number when vacancies occur.

Out of the annual revenues $1,725 are paid to each of the active members; these members are organized into committees which meet twice a week except when absent on duty. The entire Board holds weekly sessions, at which the matters previously considered in committee are disposed of.

Trinity-House is an ancient structure on Tower Hill, opposite the old Tower of London, in the "City"; it has a handsome freestone front in Classic style. The main entrance is on the ground-floor through a capacious hall, where are exhibited models of many of the most famous light-houses in England, and also of beacons and buoys. There are ample accommodations for the officers, for the Board and Committees, for the Engineers' Department, and for photometric experiments, and in addition there is a grand banqueting-hall and *salon.*

The principal depot of the Trinity-House is at Blackwall, on the lower Thames; here are repaired the numerous light-ships employed on the coast above and below the mouth of the Thames. There is also a completely appointed lamp-shop. The grounds are limited in extent and some of the buildings are old and inconvenient. Here is also stored a supply of buoys of all kinds.

There are two experimental towers fitted with second-order lenses for testing lamps, oils, effects of fog, etc.

There are other depots at Yarmouth, Coquet Island and other places, but the one at Blackwall is the principal depot for manufacture, supply and repair.

The immediate agents through whom the authority of the Trinity-House is exercised are called Superintendents, and each has some special duties assigned him, either the sole care of the service in some specified part of the coast or the charge of some special branch, such as the supply and storehouses at Blackwall. The tenders are under their orders; they wear a uniform on all occasions when on duty.

Light-keepers are appointed by the Corporation. The requirements are that they should be between nineteen and twenty-eight years of age, be of good moral character, be physically sound, and be able to read, write and perform the simpler operations of arithmetic. As vacancies occur successful applicants are taken on probation, *i. e.*, are appointed *supernumerary* light-keepers. They are then sent to the depot at Blackwall and placed under the orders of the Superintendent there. They are carefully trained in the use and care of lamps and all light-house apparatus, including meteorological instruments, the keeping of the light-house journal and accounts, and the general management of affairs at a light-house. A certificate of the lowest grade is given for competency in their duties. A second course of instruction includes the use of tools and plumbing, that he may be able to make minor repairs, and also the management and general knowledge of the steam-engine. A third course teaches the management of the magneto-electric machine and lamp, and the fourth course the use and management of fog-horn apparatus. Separate certificates are given for each course.

There are always eight of these candidates for light-keepers positions at Blackwall and two at South Foreland, the latter for instruction in the management of electric-lights, and to the great care taken in their selection and to the thoroughness of their instruction is to be attributed the excellent condition and efficiency of English light-houses.

The keepers and supernumeraries are supplied with neat uniforms; the supernumeraries are paid $225 per annum, and on receiving four certificates and giving satisfactory proofs of steadiness and sobriety they become entitled to an assistant-keeper's pay.

The rates of pay differ, depending upon whether the keepers are insured or not, as will be seen from the following table:

RATES OF PAY.

Grade of Keeper.	Gross rate per annum.	Deduct insurance.
Principals who have served as such above 10 years, if insured	$360.00	$15.00
Same if uninsured	350.00	
Principals, above 5 and under 10 years, if insured	340.00	15.00
Same if uninsured	332.00	
Principals under 5 years, if insured	330.00	15.00
Same if uninsured	322.00	
Assistant-keepers who have served as such above 10 years, if insured	290.00	15.00
Same if uninsured	282.00	
Assistant-keepers, above 5 and under 10 years, if insured	280.00	15.00
Same if uninsured	272.00	
Assistant-keepers under 5 years, if insured	270.00	15.00
Same if uninsured	262.00	

When no longer able to do service, keepers are pensioned, the pension being computed on an estimated allowance of $90 in addition to the above scale.

Flag-staffs are provided at each station, placed either on the tower or in the grounds surrounding it; from which is displayed the Trinity-House flag on Sundays, holidays and whenever the light-house tenders are seen approaching the station. At stations where there are detached dwellings, each keeper is furnished with a living-room, three bedrooms, a scullery, wash-room, a place for coal, and if the site permits, with a garden. A certain amount of standing furniture is provided. Small libraries are provided at each station for the use of the keepers and their families; these libraries are interchanged between the stations on the annual visits of the supply-vessels, medicine-chests are also supplied.

SPAIN.

In Spain the system of administration is the same as that of France. They form a part of the especial branch of public works and depend on a general board of direction established at the Department of Public Works. To this board is attached a permanent commission, composed of engineers of high rank, of the Corps of Roads, Canals and Ports, and of officers of the Royal Navy of like rank, who are always consulted when it is intended to modify or vary the general plan of lighting, or to establish some new light in which the site of the light-house, its height above the sea and its distinctive characteristic is to be determined. In all else the construction, establishment and repair of light-houses appertain to the engineers who are distributed in the provinces; they and their works are usually visited at stated periods by their immediate superiors who are also engineers with the title of Inspectors, and who form a superior class of the corps. Their duties, powers and responsibility to each other and to the Government are entirely analogous to those which are established in France.

With regard to the lights and beacons, the captains of ports are required to watch their effects and to report to the engineer, and also, if they think necessary, to the chiefs of the Marine Department, so as to secure the adoption of such improvements as may prove desirable.

A special tax is collected, the product of which is applied to lighting the coasts; but the revenue thus derived enters at once into the public treasury, and the liabilities for each year, whether for new works or for the maintenance, lighting and service in general, are met by drafts on the credits opened by the budget of the State.

DENMARK.

The light and buoy service of Denmark is placed under the superintendence of the Ministry of Marine, who decides directly upon everything concerning the personnel, the establishment of new lights, the alteration of old ones, and upon all matters relating to the development of the light and buoy system.

The necessary funds are obtained by appropriation of the Legislature, "The Council of the Realm." There are two kinds of expenditures, the first for ordinary expenses for the maintenance of existing lights, the second for the erection of new lights and for works of considerable magnitude.

There are two kinds of lights, Governmental and Communal: all "sea-lights" are in the first class, and are maintained by the Government. In the second class are small lights placed at the entrance to roadsteads or harbors, and maintained by the respective communities. The light-house inspectors are naval officers, and receive pay and allowances as such.

A first-order light has three keepers, second, third, fourth and fifth order lights two keepers each, and sixth-order lights one keeper. The number of keepers is sometimes augmented when the light is situated on isolated points or uninhabited islands. At sixth-order lights, where the nature of the service does not prevent, the keeper is allowed to have other occupation in addition.

HOLLAND.

The management of the coast lights, buoys and beacons of Holland is solely in the hands of the Government, and rests with the Ministry for the Marine, under whom there is an inspector-general and seven inspectors for as many districts, who are charged with the direction and superintendence of their branch of the service. The cost of construction and maintenance is placed yearly on the list of Government expenses.

The harbor-lights being generally of only local importance are excluded from the care of the Government, being under the direction of the communities where they are situated. Plans and specifications for the construction of light-houses are furnished by the Government, and the work is let by contract to the highest bidder.

There are no general instructions for the district inspectors. The regulations conform to the local circumstances of each district.

In addition to the inspections by district inspectors, a general inspection is made by the inspector-general at times not stated.

Buoys and beacons are maintained by contract.

BELGIUM.

The construction of Belgian light-houses and harbor-lights is part of the general administration of roads and bridges (*Ponts et Chaussées*) under the superintendence of the Minister of Public Works. An annual sum is appropriated for repairs and maintenance.

The care of the light-houses is intrusted to the navy after they have been built by the engineers of the Ponts et Chaussées. The navy is under the control of the Minister for Foreign Affairs, and the "budget" includes each year the sum necessary for supplies and salaries.

The light-houses on the coast of the North Sea are under the authority of the Inspector of Pilotage at Ostend.

The inspectors of pilotage see that the lights are lit at the proper hours, and are kept in an efficient condition. The keepers, watchmen, etc., are under the orders of these inspectors who have the right to suspend them for five days; heavier punishments are inflicted by the General Director of the Navy, which can only be remitted by the Minister.

Light-house apparatus is purchased by the Department of Public Works from those makers who seem to offer the best guaranty.

The Departments of Foreign Affairs and of Public Works consult together concerning any proposed changes in the lighting of the coasts.

AUSTRIA.

The superintendence of all the Austrian light-houses, buoys and beacons belongs to the Imperial Royal Admiralty.

The deputies of the Exchange at Trieste attend to the management of light-houses and instruct their inferiors. The duties of these deputies include the erection of light-houses, repairs, salaries of keepers and their discipline; they also collect light-house taxes and appoint the keepers.

All taxes levied on commercial vessels belong to the Treasury of the Deputation of the Imperial Exchange Commission, in order to pay for the lights and all necessary expenses, repairs and renovations.

Every renovation or alteration of a light is first submitted for approval to the Admiralty by the Commission of Exchange, and the necessity for a new light is investigated by a commission.

THE UNITED STATES.

Prior to 1852 the Light-House Service of the United States was in the most inefficient condition; its shortcomings became so glaring that in 1851 Congress passed an act authorizing the Secretary of the Treasury to appoint a Board consisting of two officers of the navy of high rank, two officers of the engineers of the army, an officer of high scientific attainments, and a junior officer of the navy to act as secretary, whose duty should be to inquire into the condition of the light-house establishment of the United States and to make a detailed report to guide future legislation on the subject. With characteristic economy a further proviso was added to the act, providing that none of the above officers should receive any additional compensation for their services.

In obedience to the above act, the Hon. Thomas Corwin, then Secretary of the Treasury, appointed the following officers to form the above Board: Commodore William B. Shubrick, U. S. N.; Commander S. F. Dupont, U. S. N.; Brevet Brig.-Gen'l Jos. G. Totten, U. S. Corps of Engineers; Lieut.-Col. James Kearney, U. S. Top. Engineers; Prof. A. D. Bache, LL.D., Supt. Coast Survey; Lieut. Thornton A. Jenkins, U. S. N., Secretary. It would

have been difficult to have selected a Board of more ability or probity. They entered on their duties with a patience and zeal which the importance of the subject required, and found that the existing system demanded a thorough purification and reorganization; that it was inefficient and wasteful; that the light-houses were neither properly built, located, nor distributed in accordance with the needs of commerce; that there was no efficient system of inspection and superintendence; that changes were constantly taking place in the aids to navigation without any official notice being given to the public; that the light-keepers in many cases were not competent, and they were never instructed in reference to their duties nor examined as to their ability to perform them, and, in short, that there was no proper system in the management of the Light-House Establishment of the United States.

This Board made a detailed report and recommendations to Congress and in consequence the following act was passed and is still in force: "The President shall appoint two officers of the navy of high rank, two officers of the Corps of Engineers of the army, and two civilians of high scientific attainment, whose services may be at the disposal of the President, together with an officer of the navy and an officer of the engineers of the army, as secretaries, who shall constitute the Light-House Board. The Secretary of the Treasury shall be *ex-officio* president of the Light-House Board." *Act approved* 31 *August*, 1852.

Further acts provided that the Board should elect one of its members as chairman, who should preside at its meetings in the absence of the president; that the Board should meet on the first Mondays in March, June, September and December, and at such other times as the Secretary of the Treasury should require; that it should be attached to the office of the Secretary of the Treasury, and under his superintendence should discharge all administrative duties relating to the construction, illumination, inspection and superintendence of light-houses, light-vessels, beacons, buoys and sea-marks and their appendages, embracing the security of existing works, procuring illuminating and other apparatus, supplies and materials for building and for rebuilding when necessary and keeping in repair the light-houses, light-vessels, beacons and buoys of the United States; should furnish to the Secretary of the Treasury estimates of the expense which the several branches of the light-house service may require, and such other information as may be required to be laid before Congress at the commencement of each session; should make such regulations as they deem proper for securing an efficient, uniform and economical administration of the Light-House Establishment, and should arrange the Atlantic, Gulf, Pacific and Lake Coasts of the United States into light-house districts. An officer of the army or navy was required to be assigned to each district as light-house inspector, subject to the orders of the Board.

The President of the United States was required to cause to be detailed from the Engineer Corps of the army such officers as may be necessary to superintend the construction and renovation of light-houses. And all plans, drawings, specifications and estimates of cost of all illuminating and other apparatus and of the construction and repair of towers, buildings, etc., were to be prepared by the engineer secretary of the Board, or by such officer of engineers of the army as may be detailed for that service.

In conformity to the act of 1852, the President appointed, on October 9, 1852, the following gentlemen to form the first Light-House Board: William B. Shubrick, Commodore, U. S. N.; Samuel F. Dupont, Commander, U. S. N.; Joseph G. Totten, Colonel, Chief of Engineers, Brevet Brigadier-General, U. S. A.; James Kearney, Lieutenant-Colonel, Corps of Topographical Engineers, U. S. A.; Prof. Alexander D. Bache, LL.D., Superintendent U. S. Coast Survey; Prof. Joseph Henry, LL.D., Secretary Smithsonian Institution; Thornton A. Jenkins, Lieutenant, U. S. N., Naval Secretary; Edmund L. F. Hardcastle, Lieutenant, Corps of Topographical Engineers, Brevet Captain, U. S. A., Engineer Secretary. The Board elected Commodore Shubrick as its chairman.

The chairman and the two secretaries are the executive officers of the Board and are members of all standing committees. Under the direction of the chairman the naval secretary has charge of all matters pertaining to floating aids to navigation, to supplies, to nominations and salaries of light-keepers, to inspection of the returns and accounts of the inspectors and the appropriations, petitions, applications and correspondence connected therewith. The engineer secretary, under the direction of the chairman, has charge of all fixed aids to navigation, the preparation of plans, specifications and estimates relating to them, the purchase and repair of illuminating apparatus, the real estate of the Light-House Establishment, the manufacturing establishments of the Board at Staten Island and the general depot at that place, except that part of it relating to supplies, the nomination and salaries of employés of light-house engineers, the inspection of the returns and accounts of light-house engineers, and the appropriations, petitions, applications and correspondence in relation to the foregoing.

The United States is divided into sixteen light-house districts. The first to the sixth inclusive comprises the Atlantic Coast, the seventh and eighth the coast of Florida and the Gulf of Mexico, the

ninth, tenth and eleventh the Great Lakes, the twelfth and thirteenth the Pacific Coast and the fourteenth, fifteentl. and sixteenth the Ohio, Mississippi, Missouri and Red Rivers.

To each district is assigned a naval officer as inspector, who has charge of all the floating aids to navigation, the supplies of the light-stations, the salaries of keepers, and the disbursement of funds relating to the above objects. The inspectors are required to inspect the lights at least once every three months, at which time they ascertain the condition of the station and report it to the Beard. They also furnish to the engineer of the district notes of such repairs as may be needed.

Every district has also an engineer officer of the army as district engineer, though in some cases this officer may be in charge of two or three districts; his duty is to superintend the construction and renovation of the fixed aids to navigation; he visits the lights as occasion demands, furnishing the Board with a report of the condition and needs of the stations visited, and sending to the inspector a copy of his notes so far as they relate to the latter's duties.

Both the district inspectors and engineers submit to the Board monthly and annual reports of the work done under their charge.

When the Board receives petitions for the erection of new lights, the matter is referred to both the district officers for their views as to the necessity for the light and its proper location; the district engineer also submits plans and estimates of cost of the proposed structure; the Board then decides as to what should be done, and makes a report to Congress through the Secretary of the Treasury.

If Congress makes an appropriation, the district engineer is charged with the erection of the light, which must be done by contract, if possible, after due advertisement.

When the light-house is completed, the district engineer informs the Board, the keepers are appointed and the light-house is placed in charge of the district inspector.

Prior to completion, the Board issues a notice to mariners, giving a short description of the light and the probable date on which it will first be lighted.

The annual expense of maintaining the Light-house Establishment is approximately as follows, and is divided under the following heads:

Supplies.—$340,000. This is mainly for mineral-oil, but also includes cleansing materials, books, boats and furniture for stations.

Repairs.—$300,000. This includes the repairs of light-stations, the building of pier head-lights and the purchase of illuminating apparatus to replace that already in use.

Salaries.—$585,000. This includes salaries of light-keepers, fuel, rations and rent of quarters where necessary.

Light-vessels. — $215,000. This includes all expenses of maintaining, supplying and repairing light-vessels.

Buoyage. — $325,000. This includes all expenses relating to buoys, spindles and day-beacons

Fog-signals. — $60,000. This includes all expenses relating to the establishment and repairs of fog-signals and buildings connected therewith.

Inspecting Lights. — $3,000. This is to pay for the travelling expenses of the Board and for rewards for information as to collisions.

Lighting of Rivers. — $225,000. This pays for the establishment, maintenance and supply for the river-lights previously mentioned.

Surveys. — $2,500. This is to pay for the preliminary examinations of sites and for plans, for which estimates are to be made to Congress.

Total. — $1,415,500.

The total sum is never exceeded and frequently is not spent, in which case the balance on hand at the end of the fiscal year is returned to the Treasury.

Every new light-house is the subject of a special appropriation which is available until the light-house is completed, any balance remaining is turned into the Treasury and is not available for any other purpose.

The number of lights increases from year to year to keep pace with the needs of commerce. The following table shows the aids to navigation maintained by the United States Light-house Establishment on June 30, 1887.

The Board at present has its offices in the Treasury Department at Washington, and for a number of years past has complained of lack of room.

The Board has had to move four times since its organization in 1852, each time with damage and loss to its archives, and delay and inconvenience in the despatch of its business, which is yearly increasing in size and importance.

Aids.	First district.	Second district.	Third district.	Fourth district.	Fifth district.	Sixth district.	Seventh district.	Eighth district.	Ninth district.	Tenth district.	Eleventh district.	Twelfth district.	Thirteenth dist.	Fourteenth dist.	Fifteenth district.	Sixteenth district.	Atlantic and Gulf coasts.	Pacific coast.	Lake coast.	Rivers.	Total for entire coast, 1887.	Total for entire coast, 1886.	Increase.
Electric lights	..	..	1	..	..	..	..	..	..	..	..	..	..	..	..	..	b1	..	..	..	1	1	..
First-order lights	2	4	6	5	6	5	9	2	..	..	.	7	5	..	..	..	39	12	..	..	51	51	..
Second-order lights	7	3	1	..	..	1	..	4	1	6	2	1	..	..	..	..	16	1	3	..	20	20	..
Third-order lights	5	1	5	3	..	4	4	4	8		8	3	1	..	..	..	26	4	22	..	52	52	..
Three-and-a-half order lights	..	2	1	..	..	..	..	..	3	1 23	4	..	..	..	..	..	3	..	8	..	11	11	..
Fourth-order lights	19	22	a33	12	32	8	6	14	26	6	24	9	7	..	..	..	146	16	73	..	235	231	4
Fifth-order lights	20	16	17	9	22	6	..	12	13	20	14	2	2	..	..	..	102		33	..	139	137	2
Sixth-order lights	1	6	33	3	14	7	1	2	17	6	20	..	..	..	..	..	67	..	57	..	124	122	2
Lens-lanterns	..	..	..	1	14	7	..	13	2	..	5	..	30	..	..	..	35	30	13	..	78	57	21
Range-lenses	..	..	6	8	2	1	..	..	..	1	..	..	..	..	..	..	17	..	..	..	17	17	..
River-lights	..	1	52	..	2	64	..	1	..	7	..	..	..	441	371	295	124	..	1	1107	1232	1227	5
Reflectors	..	9	..	8	4	16	..	2	..	..	..	..	..	..	..	..	39	..	7	..	46	44	2
Light-ships in position	..	8	7	3	..	3	..	2	..	..	1	..	..	..	..	..	23	..	1	..	24	23	1
Lighted buoys	..	..	..	..	2	2	..	..	..	..	..	..	..	..	..	..	4	..	..	..	4	2	2
Total lighted aids	54	72	102	52	98	128	20	56	70	70	78	22	45	441	371	295	642	67	218	1107	2034	1995	39
Fog-signals operated by steam or hot-air	10	7	11	3	1	..	..	2	10	1	14	12	6	..	..	..	34	18	25	..	77	76	1
Fog-signals operated by clock-work	7	8	37	8	54	3	..	6	3	5	3	4	2	..	..	..	123	6	11	..	140	139	1
Day beacons	95	58	44	2	13	29	27	13	..	..	1	41	38	..	..	..	281	79	1	..	361	321	40
Whistling-buoys	9	8	5	4	1	4	1	2	..	..	..	7	3	..	..	..	34	10	..	..	44	40	4
Bell-buoys	12	9	8	4	2	11	2	1	..	..	1	..	1	..	..	..	49	1	1	..	51	44	7
Other buoys	510	471	510	100	1006	265	200	89	49	167	135	57	172	..	..	..	3211	229	351	..	3791	3758	33
Total unlighted aids	643	561	615	181	1077	312	230	113	62	173	154	121	222	..	..	..	3732	343	389	.	4464	4378	86
Total number of aids	697	633	777	233	1175	440	250	169	132	243	232	143	267	441	371	295	4374	410	607	1107	6498	6373	125

[1] a Including Blackwell's Island Light, not maintained by Light-house Board. b Statue of Liberty, **New** York Harbor.

It has petitioned to Congress for an appropriation to erect, on one of the Government reservations at Washington, a suitable building in which its office, its records, its library, its museum and its laboratory can find a permanent home.

Congress, so far, has not seen fit to grant this appropriation.

The Board has depots for supplies and buoys in various districts, but the most important one is on Staten Island, N. Y., in the Third District. It is the general depot for the whole United States; all the oil is sent there, tested and distributed, and from it are furnished nearly all the supplies for the other districts. The inspector of the Third District has charge of the above, while the engineer has charge of a well-appointed lamp-shop, blacksmith and carpenter shop, where lamps, lanterns and general metal-work are made and repaired, oil-cans and boxes for mineral-oil manufactured, illuminating apparatus set up and tested prior to shipment, buoys repaired, photometric tests made, and, in general, the multifarious work done which the light-house service requires.

A large tender, the "*Fern*," distributes the supplies from this depot to the Atlantic and Gulf coasts. She is soon to be replaced by a larger vessel, as the needs of the service are rapidly exceeding her carrying-capacity.

The supplies for the Pacific Coast, for the lakes and for the rivers are shipped by rail and distributed by the tenders of the districts.

Wherever it is possible light-keepers are furnished with commodious dwellings of five or six rooms; where vacancies occur they are filled by promotion from keepers in service of a lower grade, and the Collector of Customs of the district nominates for the ultimate vacancy; his nominee receives an appointment as acting-assistant keeper, and if he proves satisfactory after trial, he receives an appointment as assistant-keeper.

The salaries paid to light-keepers vary considerably, both on account of the importance of the lights and of the cost of living in different parts of the United States. The principal keepers at most of the first-order lights on the Pacific Coast receive $1,000 a year.

while on the Atlantic Coast there is but one who receives so much, and that is at Minot's Ledge; he has three assistants at $550 each.

As a general rule the keeper of a first-order light receives from $700 to $800, of a second-order light from $600 to $700, and of the lower orders from $500 to $600. Assistant-keepers receive various rates of pay ranging from $400 to $550.

Captains of light-vessels receive from $750 to $1,000.

Keepers are required to be in uniform.

At some stations difficult of access rations are furnished in addition to the salary, and most stations also receive an allowance of coal.

Neat libraries, of about thirty books each, are left at isolated stations and changed from time to time.

The Light-house Board issues the following publications for the use of the public, in addition to notices to mariners.

Annual Report of the Light-house Board. This gives an account of all the work done during the year, and includes recommendations for future work.

List of Light-houses, Lighted Beacons, and Floating Lights on the Atlantic, Gulf and Pacific Coasts, corrected to the first of January of each year.

List of Lights in the Waters and on the Shores and Banks of the Northern Lakes and Rivers of the United States, and also of the Canadian Lights in those Waters, corrected to the opening of navigation in each year.

List of Beacons, Buoys, Stakes, and other Day-marks in each Light-house District, corrected to the first of July of each year.

These lists are furnished free of charge to shipmasters on application to the Board.

The Light-house Board, at this date,[1] is constituted as follows:—

Hon. Charles S. Fairchild, Secretary of the Treasury, *ex-officio* President of the Board; Vice-Admiral Stephen C. Rowan, U. S. N.,

[1] December, 1888.

Chairman; Brigadier-General Thomas Lincoln Casey, Chief of Engineers, U. S. A.; Mr. Walter S. Franklin; Commodore David B. Harmony, U. S. N.; Colonel John M. Wilson, Corps of Engineers, U. S. A.; Commander Robley D. Evans, U. S. N., Naval Secretary; Major James F. Gregory, Corps of Engineers, U. S. A., Engineer Secretary.

There is a vacancy on the Board not yet filled.

D. P. HEAP.

APPENDIX.

APPENDIX A.

From Longfellow's Journal I make the following extracts, mentioning his visit with Sumner to Minot's Ledge Light-house: —

"Aug. 22, '71. The steam-tug comes for us, and Sumner, Mr. James Ernest, and myself go to meet the revenue-cutter in the harbor, find on board the Collector, with Agassiz and a young Japanese prince, and we steam away for Minot's Ledge. Dinner (on board) ended, we find ourselves at the base of the light-house, rising sheer out of the sea like a huge stone cannon, mouth upward. We are hoisted up forty feet in a chair, some of us; others go up by an iron ladder, — all but the young Japanese, who refuses to go up at all. Whether he was afraid, or thought it only a trick to imprison him, will remain a mystery till his travels are published."

In a letter to G. W. Greene, dated Nahant, Aug. 25, 1871, Longfellow says: —

"On Tuesday we made our expedition to Minot's Ledge, — it was every way pleasant and successful. We wished you could have been with us; but it was impossible to notify you in season. The light-house rises out of the sea like a beautiful stone cannon, mouth upward, belching forth only friendly fires. We went up into it, — even into the lantern itself, the glass of which (beautiful plate glass) cost ten thousand dollars. I can believe this, having seen it, and knowing what telescopic lenses cost. The lantern will hold six people easily."

By "lantern" Longfellow meant the lenticular apparatus.

APPENDIX B.

As another evidence of the great fury of the storms at this station, I append an official report of the light-keeper. When it is remembered that the light is one hundred and thirty-six feet above the sea level, or about as high as the Statue of Liberty to top of torch, excluding the pedestal, some idea may be formed of the tremendous force to which this station is subjected, when even at this height the waves have sufficient power to crash in heavy plate-glass panes.

TILLAMOOK ROCK LIGHT STATION, OR., Dec. 7, 1887.

U. S. L. H. Inspector, Portland, Oregon.

SIR, — I have to report, that about 9 P. M. of the 3d, a gale from the S. E. set in, and continued with varying force until the 7th. About 9 A. M. of the 4th the seas commenced breaking over the building, some of them going twenty or thirty feet over the tower. About 11 A. M. the sea broke in the window of the oil-room, flooding it and the hall. At 2 P. M. the lumber for the landing platform, which was piled against the fence on the eastern end of the house, got adrift, but was removed and piled against the house, with the loss of one plank. The seas in going over caused the water to come in the south and west windows of the tower, also caused the roof to leak very much, and the ceiling and walls of all the rooms to leak, — in some of them we had to place buckets to catch the drip; in the siren room it leaked so much, especially around the smoke-stack, that the boilers and machinery were covered with salt, and causing them to rust very much; it also came through the ventilator into the lantern. We covered the clock-work and revolving wheels as much as possible, but it did not do much good, and it will take some time to get them in condition again.

Shortly after 4 P. M. the sea broke in the upper pane in the W. by S. tier in the tower. As soon as possible we set a storm-pane, with a backing of sheet-iron, but the sea soon broke them out, leaving the clamps fast to the frame. It being impossible to light the lamp, started the siren and made a wooden shutter, in place of storm-pane. At 6 P. M. the northern tank at the west end of the siren soon broke adrift: we plugged the feed-tank and saved the water in it. About 7 o'clock the lower pane of the same tier was broken in; tried a storm-pane, but it was soon stove in, and we made a wooden shutter, and calked both with cotton waste, so that very little water or wind came in. The three upper and three middle panes next south of the broken ones are started and leak. The lens cover is badly cut, and about thirty of the lenses chipped by glass thrown against them. At midnight the three tanks at the west end were wedged together against the N. W. corner of the fence. The fence is bent, and broken in four places. Several large pieces of the rock on the south side were washed away, and one piece is lodged under the fence at the S. E. corner.

The wind varied from S. E. to S. W.; the seas were mostly from the S. W. At 12.30 on the morning of the 4th, I shut down the siren, and hung a large lantern in the tower on the W. side. The water in the feed-tank was low, and the moon up, and the Cape light in sight. It was unsafe to attempt to fill the tank from the cistern, on account of the sea breaking over so often and heavy. There are two upper and three middle panes on hand, but none for the lower, and no way of cutting one of the others to fit. As soon as the weather permits, the upper pane will be set.

On the night of the 5th a lantern was swung in the tower, as it was impossible to have the lamp in order. The siren was in operation from 2.15 to 8 A. M. of 6th; at 11 A. M. had the lamp in order, and lighted it to dry the lens; started the revolving machinery at sunset time. There should be two more sets of clamps for storm-panes furnished,—there is but one set here. All is being done that is possible to put the station in order. There is a great deal of work. I have made requisition on the engineer for material to repair damages.

27th. The following damage was caused by the gale of yesterday (26th). The ash shoot and rail of derrick platform were carried away, the guy boom of the derrick was broken off at the outer edge of the platform, two steps of the iron stairway broken, upper pane in the tier next south of those broken on the 4th, and the middle pane in the tier next to it were broken out by the sea, and replaced with wooden covers. It was impossible to light the lamp last night. Two lanterns were hung in the tower, one on the S. side and one on the N. side, and to-night the lamp will be lighted. The upper pane of glass broken on the 4th has been replaced, and there are now three broken panes. The frames on the S. and W. sides of the lantern are strained, and all joints in tower and lantern are full of salt and rust. The smoke-stack is started, also the north siren hood. We need the clamps for storm-panes very much.

Very respectfully,

(Signed) J. M. FLYNN,

Acting 1st Assistant Keeper.

APPENDIX C.

Researches as to the origin of words and names have great interest for the philologist, so I append a ballad giving an ingenious explanation how Barnegat Light-house came to be so named, *Si non e vero ben trovato.*

THE LIGHT-KEEPER'S DAUGHTER.

A NAUGHTYCAL BALLAD.

AIR — "*The Pretty Little Rat-Catcher's Daughter.*"

In the Bay of Barnegat sailed a jolly, jolly tar,
And he watched like a cat o'er the water,
Till he spied from the main-top-gallant-forward-mizzen spar
The pretty little light-keeper's daughter.

Then he landed on the land, did this jolly, jolly tar,
And he chased her o'er the sand till he caught her.
Says he, "My pretty miss, I've got to have a kiss
From the pretty little light-keeper's daughter."

But she squealed a little squeal at the jolly, jolly tar,
And said she didn't feel as if she'd ought to;
Then she scooted up the bar and hollered for her ma, —
Oh, the pretty little light-keeper's daughter!

"Sure my name is Barney Flynn," said the jolly, jolly tar,
"And at drinking Holland gin I'm a snorter."
Then a tub of washing-blue — soap suddenly she threw —
Did the mother of the light-keeper's daughter.

"Now, Barney, git!" she spat, at the jolly, jolly tar;
And you bet that Barney gat for the water.
Thus the place from near and far was named by the ma
Of the pretty little light-keeper's daughter.

— *Adam Clark.*

INDEX.

INDEX TO FULL-PAGE ILLUSTRATIONS.

NO. III. AMES MEMORIAL BUILDINGS

AT NORTH EASTON, MASS. H. H. RICHARDSON, Architect. 22 plates, 13 x 16, also two lithographs. In portfolio. $6.00.

General View of the Town Hall and Memorial Library, from the Southwest — General View, from the Northeast — Front View of Town Hall — Arcade of Town Hall — Detail of Arcade — Interior of Loggia — West End of Town Hall — View from Southeast — East End — Detail of East End of Town Hall — General View of Library — Entrance Archway — Details of Library Front (Two Plates) — East End — Chimney-piece in Reading-Room — Interior of Book-Room — The Gate-Lodge, from the Grounds of F. L. Ames, Esq. — The Gate-Lodge, from the Southwest — The Gate-Lodge, from the Street — The Railroad Station from the Track — Plans of Town Hall and Memorial Library — Plans of Gate Lodge and Railroad Station.

NO. IV. THE MEMORIAL HALL

AT HARVARD UNIVERSITY. WARE AND VAN BRUNT, Architects. 13 plates, 13 x 16, and one Photo-Lithograph. In portfolio. $5.00.

General View of Cambridge, from the West — Harvard Memorial Hall, from the Southeast — The Main Entrance — The Memorial Vestibule — Entrance of Dining Hall — Southwest Porch — Cloister and Memorial Tablet — Views of Memorial Hall, from the West, with Statue of John Harvard — Dining Hall, looking West — Dining Hall, looking East — East End — Sanders' Theatre — Plan.

NO. V. TRINITY CHURCH, BOSTON, MASS.

22 Gelatine Views and 1 Heliochrome, 13 x 16. $10.00.

Portrait of H. H. Richardson — West Front of Trinity — General View, from Southeast — Apse and Tower, from Southeast — General View, from Northwest — Main Entrance — Detail of West Front — Tower from South — Details of Tower — Cloister and Chapel — Cloister and Tracery Window — Cloister Garth — Chapel Stairway — Entrance to North Transept — Chancel — North Side of Nave — Font — Bust of Dean Stanley — Nave, from Gallery — Interior of Tower — Cartoon for Window — Plan of the Church.

Indispensable to Architects:

MODERN PERSPECTIVE.

A Treatise upon the Principles and Practice of Plane and Cylindrical Perspective, by WILLIAM R. WARE, Professor of Architecture in the School of Mines, Columbia College. 1 vol. 12mo. 321 pages, with 27 plates in a portfolio. $5.00.

This is by far the most exhaustive of modern works on the subjects relating to perspective, plane and panoramic, and will be of great value to all architects and artists, and others interested in the problems of art. The scientific and pictorial aspects of these investigations are carefully and thoroughly considered, both independently and in their connection with drawing; and the propositions of the author are illustrated by plates of architectural objects and perspective plans. An invaluable book for artists, architects, draughtsmen, and civil engineers.

"Much that Prof. Ware has to say is as pertinent to the work of the landscape or historical painter as to that of the architect. The needs of the practical draughtsman are provided for in a chapter at the end of the book, which shows just how one goes to work to lay out the main lines of a perspective drawing according to the system presented in the previous chapters." — *Boston Herald.*

"The book is written in clear English, free from unnecessary technicalities, and in a much more felicitous style than such text-books usually are. The plates required a prodigious quantity of careful work and are correspondingly valuable." — *New-York World.*

JAPANESE HOMES.

AND THEIR SURROUNDINGS. By EDWARD S. MORSE, Ph. D., late Professor at the Tokio University, Japan, etc. With 307 Illustrations. 8vo, richly bound, $5.00; in half-calf, $9.00.

"Professor Morse's book is well worthy of study by every architect and decorator, because of its fresh ideas in design of detail and construction, and because of its graphic presentation of an artistic spirit manifested in the work and manners of a whole nation."— HENRY VAN BRUNT.

"For cultivated people having tastes which lead them to take pleasure in beautifying their homes and surroundings, we know of no other publication so brimful of suggestion and valuable information as this handsome and profusely-illustrated volume."— *Scientific American.*

A Valuable Text-book:

BUILDING SUPERINTENDENCE.

A MANUAL: For young Architects, Students, and others interested in Building Operations as carried on at the present time. By T. M. Clark, Fellow of the American Institute of Architects. 1 vol. 8vo. 336 pages. Illustrated with 194 Plans, Diagrams, etc. Price, $3.00.

Introduction — The Construction of a Stone Church — Wooden Dwelling-Houses — A Model Specification — Contracts — The Construction of a Town Hall — Index.

"This is not a treatise on the architectural art, or the science of construction, but a simple exposition of the ordinary practice of building in this country, with suggestions for supervising such work efficiently. Architects of experience probably know already nearly everything that the book contains, but their younger brethren as well as those persons not of the profession who are occasionally called upon to direct building operations, will perhaps be glad of its help."

This volume is based on a series of thirty or more carefully prepared papers, originally contributed to *The American Architect*, and now revised and augmented, and published in handsome and permanent form.

There is hardly any practical problem in construction, from the building of a stone town-hall or church to that of a wooden cottage, that is not carefully considered and discussed here; and a very full index helps to make this treasury of facts accessible. Every person interested in building should possess this work, which is approved as authoritative by the best American architects.

This volume has been used for years as a text-book in the chief Architectural Schools of the United States.

HOMES AND ALL ABOUT THEM.

By E. C. Gardner. 716 pages. Illustrated. $2.50.

Invaluable instructions and suggestions as to interior decoration, exterior finish, and varied forms of architecture.

ARTISTIC HOMES

IN CITY AND COUNTRY. By A. W. FULLER, Architect. Oblong folio. Fourth Edition, enlarged and improved. 76 full-page illustrations of rural and urban homes, many of which are from gelatine. Also one colored plate. $4.50.

"It has in many cases proved a very valuable assistant, a faithful friend and reliable adviser, to persons of refined taste and artful feeling who contemplated building a home. . . . We heartily commend it to all who intend building a home. To the architectural student and draughtsman the book should prove a valuable aid in teaching him how to effectively draw perspectives or interior views." — *Building*.

DECENNIAL INDEX OF ILLUSTRATIONS

IN THE AMERICAN ARCHITECT AND BUILDING NEWS, 1876–85. 8vo. Price, $2.00.

A carefully-made topical index to the thousands of illustrations printed in "The American Architects" for the past ten years, with the architects and costs of the buildings illustrated. These include

Sketches — Etchings — General Views — Towers and Spires — Monuments — Statues and Tombs — Interiors and Furniture — Entrances and Gateways — Educational, Mercantile, and Public Buildings — Churches and Parish Buildings — Dwellings — Club-Houses — Theatres — Stables and Farm Buildings — Hotels — Museums — Libraries and Town Halls.

DISCOURSES ON ARCHITECTURE. By E. E. VIOLLET-LE-DUC. With many Steel Plates and Chromos, and hundreds of Wood-cuts. 2 vols. 8vo. $15.00.

ART FOLIAGE. By J. K. COLLING. Entirely new plates from the latest enlarged London edition. Folio. $10.00.

MURAL PAINTING. By FREDERIC CROWNINGSHIELD. 1 vol. Square 8vo. With numerous full-page illustrations. $3.00.

HOME SANITATION. A Manual for Housekeepers. 1 vol. 16mo. 50 cents.

HOUSEHOLD SANITATION. By WILLIAM E. HOYT. 16mo. 30 cents. Paper covers, 15 cents.

LECTURES ON THE PRINCIPLES OF HOUSE-DRAINAGE. By J. PICKERING PUTNAM. With Plates and Diagrams. 16mo. 75 cents.

SKETCHES ABROAD.

By J. A. SCHWEINFURTH, Architect. This contains 30 plates, reproduced in *fac simile* from the author's sketches in pen, pencil, and water colors, by the most approved processes, and printed on 15 x 20 heavy plate paper, in specially designed portfolio. The edition is limited to 250 copies for sale, each of which is numbered. Price, $15.00 per set.

A portfolio of sketches of interesting and useful examples of architecture, details, etc., never before published, and for the most part never photographed, of work of peculiar interest to architects at the present time. These sketches were made during a nine months' tour of study abroad in Italy, France, Spain, and in the South Kensington Museum, during the year 1886. The work is as interesting to the non-professional as it is useful to the architect in his daily work in design, not only in reference to detail, but as to mass and grouping; avoiding details which are tiresome, fragmentary, and useless, but giving those of peculiar interest and charm.

The author has found, away from beaten paths, interesting examples of the old *manoirs*, or French manor houses, and *chateaux*. Among the plates are presented several of these *manoirs* half-timbered houses, with details, from Normandy and Brittanny; work of the period of Francis I.; towers, *chateaux* details from the Italian and French Renaissance; Romanesque and Byzantine work of Venice and Ravenna, and the Romanesque of the Auvergnes; wrought iron from Venice and from Spain, and from the South Kensington Museum.

THE OPEN FIRE-PLACE IN ALL AGES.

By J. PICKERING PUTNAM, Architect. It has been carefully revised and greatly enlarged, with handsome and large type, pages and binding, fine and heavy paper, and with over three hundred illustrations, including numerous *chefs d' œuvres* of designs of Fire-Places and interior decoration, contributed for this edition by the ablest Architects of the country. 1 vol. 8vo. $4.00.

The First Section treats of the Fire-Place as it now is, explaining how incorrectly it is constructed, and gives many startling facts, based on careful experiment, to show how great a loss of heat (from 80 to 90 per cent.) it occasions.

The Second Section reviews in an attractive manner, the historical development of the subject from its remotest origin in the dim ages of the past to the present day. This chapter contains over 179 charming illustrations.

The Third and last chapter treats of the improvement of the Open Fire-Place, and teaches us how it is possible to combine, in one construction, the healthfulness, beauty, and charm of the Open Fire-Place, with the efficiency and economy of the closed stove or hot-air furnace.

The designs, even of the most unimportant accessories, are made with the same careful study and refined taste as of the more important features.